Sociology of Sanitation

"SOCIOLOGY OF SANITATION
TEXT BOOK SERIES"

under the aegis of

Sulabh International Centre for Action Sociology

in close collaboration with

Sulabh International Social Service Organisation

Sociology of Sanitation

Richard Pais

ISBN: 9789351281573

Price : ₹ 890

First Published, 2015

Published by

Kalpaz Publications
C-30, Satyawati Nagar,
Delhi – 110052
E-mail: kalpaz@hotmail.com
Ph.: 9212142040

Laser Typesetting: Gyan Print (AB-I)
Printed at: G. Print Process, Delhi

Cataloging in Publication Data—DK
Courtesy: D.K. Agencies (P) Ltd. <docinfo@dkagencies.com>

Pais, Richard, 1951- author.
Sociology of sanitation / by Richard Pais.
pages cm
Includes bibliographical references.
ISBN

1. Sanitation—Social aspects—India. I. Title.

DDC 363.720954 23

Dedicated to

Shri Narendra Damodardas Modi
Hon'ble Prime Minister of India
For igniting the mind and spirit of
Indians towards Swachh Bharat.

Dr Bindeshwar Pathak
Sociologist & Social Reformer
Who worked tirelessly to reinstate the human rights
and dignity of 'Untouchables' and to eliminate
the evil of untouchability.

Contents

Foreword

I feel extremely privileged to write this foreword to Dr Richard Pais's book, Sociology of Sanitation. Dr Richard Pais hails from Mangalore, Karnataka state. He has Masters Degrees in Sociology and Psychology from the University of Poona and Ph.D. from the Mangalore University. He was Professor and Head, Department of Sociology, St Aloysius (Autonomous) College, Mangalore, Karnataka. He has written/edited 17 books and equal number of research papers/articles. This is his 18th book, and I am happy to write the foreword to this book.

Besides teaching, he has actively involved himself in the organization of the academic events at the national, state and regional levels. He was the organizing secretary of XX All India Sociological Conference and XXIII All India Conference of Indian Social Science Association held at St Aloysius College, Mangalore. He has contributed significantly by being the President of Mangalore Sociology Association, Secretary of Karnataka Association, Member of Managing Committee of Indian Sociological Society, New Delhi and being the Convener of Research Committee on Dalits and Backward Classes of Indian Sociological Society. At present, he is the Managing Editor of *Social Science Gazetteer,* the Journal of Indian Social Science Association and Chief Editor of *Samaja Shodhana*, the Journal of Mangalore Sociology Association. He is the recipient of L.P. Vidhyarthi Award conferred by Indian Social Science Association, Agra.

Sanitation is of critical importance in the modern world nay India. Dr Pais in his book has given a comprehensive picture of sanitation. The study of sociology of sanitation has greater value in the modern complex society. It studies sanitation conditions, the human behaviour and culture regarding sanitation in a scientific way. It identifies the problems and suggests solutions and generates new knowledge about sanitation. Sociology of sanitation studies the human society from bottom to the top level what the human being applies for a better sanitation world. It also explores the relationship of the individual and the institution in the field of sanitation. Sociology of sanitation improves the understanding and increases the power of social action for better sanitation. Finally, sociology of sanitation plays an important role in the solution of sanitation as social problem by applying different scientific measures.

The book highlights the meaning, origin, nature, subject matter and importance of sociology of sanitation. Sociology of sanitation is also related to other social sciences as history, economics, sociology, psychology and anthropology. Dr Pais also includes the scientific methods used in the study of sociology of sanitation. In this process he has highlighted the methods of data collection as historical method, observation, interview, questionnaire and case study.

Studying the relationship between sanitation and other social institutions such as caste, religion, education, village community, slums and health institutions is an important aspect of Dr Pais's study. He has clearly shown how caste and religion in Indian society have perpetuated inequalities among people nay given a low status to people engaged in sanitation. As India is becoming urbanized the need for sanitation is greatest in the slums of developing towns and cities. He has also stressed the social responsibility of the corporate sector. Their initiatives can include environmental protection, protection of human rights, health promotion, education and disaster relief.

Dr Pais being a sociologist and psychologist has ably dealt with the social psychological aspects of sanitation. In this connection, he has not only examined the beliefs and values associated with dirt but also the dirt attitudes, both caste and religious. In the very interesting topic of culture and sanitation he has examined the concepts of purity and impurity which is essential aspect of Hindu social life. In the problems of manual scavenging he has studied health, socio-economic and psychological problems.

The topic, Reinvention of Sanitation in the Modern World, makes an interesting reading where Dr Pais has given the changes that have taken place from ancient times to modern. He has not only elaborately explained the modern technology in sanitation but also highlighted how modern sanitation can be a business for many. Whether it is paid toilets, biogas plants or sanitary arts or designs can generate employment for many.

The book also includes environmental sanitation which is the important aspect of sanitation. Besides stressing the importance of sanitation Dr Pais has also dealt with the levels of sanitation i.e. the individual, household and community level. He has also highlighted the important causes of lack of environmental sanitation in India as lack of social responsibility, lack of social awareness about sanitation, lack of education and over-crowded population. The organization and functioning of public toilets is presented with successful case studies.

The role of the state has been discussed in the topic, State and Sanitation in India. It starts with the sanitation policies, planning and programmes of government at the Central level starting with the Central Rural Sanitation Programme launched in 1986 to *Swachh Bharat Abhiyan* started by present Prime Minister, Mr Narendra Modi on Gandhi Jayanthi day, 2nd October 2014. The National Scheme of Liberation and Rehabilitation of Scavengers and their Dependents of 1992 is also discussed in detail. Dr Richard Pais has done justice to his own state of Karnataka by including a topic on Sanitation in Karnataka and to his own city, Mangalore by including a successful case study of solid waste management in Mangalore City Corporation.

Though the book is mostly related to sanitation in India, a chapter has been devoted to Globalization and Sanitation where the role played by WHO and UNICEF are discussed in detail. A brief picture of World Toilet Organisation (WTO) with its Wold Toilet Summits and World Toilet College (WTC) is also presented. The roles played by NGOs are also highlighted.

Dr Pais in his book, Sociology of Sanitation, has given due importance to Sulabh Sanitation Movement in India starting with the life history of its founder, Dr Bindeshwar Pathak and the origin, objectives and growth of the movement. The areas of major initiative of the movement as Sulabh technologies, Sulabh public toilet complex, Bio-gas plants, Waste water treatment, Sulabh International Institute of Technical Research and Training, Sulabh International Institute of Health and Hygiene, and Sulabh International Museum of Toilets are discussed. He considers that Dr Pathak as the forerunner in the study of Action Sociology, and has started Sulabh International Centre for Action Sociology with a public school, vocational training centre, social up-gradation programme and slum children welfare programme. He sees Dr Pathak as the Founder of Sociology of Sanitation.

I thank profusely Dr Richard Pais for writing this excellent book giving in-depth knowledge of sanitation. The book will be useful to students, educators, social workers, social scientists, social planners and policy makers. I wish Dr Pais all the best in his future endeavours.

Dr Bindeshwar Pathak

Sociologist & Social reformer

Preface

The need for sanitation has arisen 10,000 years ago, when mankind adopted an agrarian way of life and started living in permanent settlements. Sedentary agricultural life made it possible to construct villages, towns and cities, all of which were highly dependent on water and sanitation. We find well-planned sanitation systems in Egypt, Mesopotamia, Mohenjo-Daro and Rome. However, the importance of proper sanitation was not understood until the nineteenth century. The social scientists thought that developing sanitation was a major social aspect of life. Now, sanitation has developed as a major subject of study.

Dr Bindeshwar Pathak has played a pioneering role in sanitation by establishing Sulabh International Social Service Organisation. It is a movement to continue the work of Mahatma Gandhi who worked tirelessly to restore the human rights and dignity of scavengers and to eliminate the evil of untouchability. Sulabh is envisioned as an agent of social and cultural change. It seeks to develop an egalitarian society, based on equal opportunity for every human being irrespective of caste, creed and natural endowments.

I thank Dr Bindeshwar Pathak for inviting me to attend and present a paper in the National Conference on Sociology of Sanitation: Environmental Sanitation, Public Health and Social Deprivation at New Delhi on January 28 and 29, 2013. I also thank him for inviting me again to New Delhi in July, 2013 to participate in a workshop on Sociology of Sanitation and giving me an opportunity to write this book on Sociology of Sanitation. I am really inspired by his life and activities.

I thank my wife, Dr Diana Pais Prabhu and Mr Hazrath Saheb, Research Assistant, Mangala Publications, Mangalore for assisting me to collect data for this book.

I also thank Dr Basil Hans, Associate Professor and Head, Department of Economics, St Aloysius Evening College, Mangalore for making available his paper, Solid Waste Management in an Urban Agglomeration: A Case Study of Mangalore City and Professor Shaukath Azim, Professor of Sociology, Karnataka University, Dharwad, Karnataka for making available his paper, Sanitation and Hygiene Deficit in Karnataka.

Finally, I thank the Sulabh International Social Service Organisation, New Delhi for publishing this book.

Dr Richard Pais

CHAPTER 1

Introduction to Sociology of Sanitation

Introduction

Though sanitation was a part of human life since the ancient times, it gained importance with the development of human civilisation. As human civilisations started to expand with its diversity, sanitation became one of the necessities of human society. The social scientists thought that developing sanitation was a major social aspect of life. Now, sanitation has developed as a major subject of study. Thus, socio-cultural aspects of human life forced the social thinkers to develop sanitation as a subject of study rather than just as a health science. Sanitation is not only the need of an individual; it's the requirement of the society.

According to Bindeshwar Pathak, Founder of Sulabh International Social Service Organisation, in the ancient civilisation, there was no problem of sanitation, because humans were not provided with latrines or particular places, inside or outside the houses, for defecation. The people used open spaces, riverbanks and outskirts of habitats for defecation. With the development of human civilisation, there cropped up the problem of the disposal of human excreta. Further, with the development of latrine system in civilised societies people started facing the problem of disposal of human excreta. With the advancement of human knowledge they implemented different kinds of technologies as a solution on the basis of different conditions prevailing in their habitats. In this way, different kinds of technologies developed throughout the world in protecting their surroundings to maintain better health hygienic conditions. Thus, sanitation gained an importance in the human society.

Sanitation gained public policy importance only recently in India. The Seventh Five-Year Plan (1985-1990) launched a rural sanitation programme in India that aimed to provide 25 per cent of rural households with individual household sanitary latrines by 1995. Consequently, households with individual sanitary latrines increased from one per cent in 1981 to nine per cent in 1991. In 1999, the Central Rural Sanitation Programme was restructured into a demand-responsive, community-led Total Sanitation Campaign (TSC). The Zila Parishads and other district-level project implementation agencies currently implement TSC as a district-level project model.

The United Nations declared 2008 as the International Year of Sanitation. The Ministry of Urban Development launched the National Urban Sanitation Policy in 2008. November 19th is celebrated as the World Toilet Day to raise awareness on the use of toilet, sanitation and clean water.

1.1 Meaning and Definition

Sanitation refers to formulation and application of measures designed to protect public health. It also refers to the safe conditions which includes; clean and safe water supply, clean and safe ambient air, efficient and safe animal, human, and industrial waste disposal, protection of food from biological and chemical contaminants, and adequate housing in clean and safe surroundings.

In the words of WHO, sanitation generally refers to the provision of facilities and services for the safe disposal of human urine and faeces. Inadequate sanitation is a major cause of disease world-wide and improving sanitation is known to have a significant beneficial impact on health both in households and across communities. The word 'sanitation' also refers to the maintenance of hygienic conditions, through services such as garbage collection and wastewater disposal.

According to UNICEF, sanitation literally means measures necessary for improving and protecting health and well-being of the people. Sanitation is any system that promotes proper disposal of human and animal wastes, proper use of toilet and avoiding open space defecation.

Sanitation is not to be restricted to one particular act of human civilisation; it's the cluster of acts which human being does for the clean and safe healthy environment. Adequate sanitation, together with good hygiene and safe water, are fundamental to good health and to social and economic development. It's very important to remember the words of Mahatma Gandhi who said that "sanitation is more important than independence".

In other words, sanitation refers to conditions relating to public health, especially the provision of clean drinking water and adequate sewage disposal.

1.2 Sociology and Sanitation

Sociology is the study of man and society in general. Sociology studies the behaviour of man with his fellow beings in a social surrounding. It studies the collective behaviour of man and its origin, developments, organisation and its institutions. Sociology is a social science which conducts various investigations, researches to find out the facts from general understanding. Sociology enables to understand the relationship between man and his action in the society. It enhances the knowledge of social action.

Society is considered as the laboratory of sociology, because society is a group of individuals who have organised themselves and follow a given way of life. Sociology is the study of individual as well as groups in society. Sociology studies the relationship of human beings and examines how they change in different parts of the world and at different times. It goes with the behavioural pattern of human society. Human behaviour is not only determined by the physical environmental or biological patterns, it is also determined by the social factors.

It has been said that every human behaviour has a social component. We cannot separate man from society nor society from man. It's the relationship which cannot be separated. Sociologists are interested to study the social determinants of human behaviour. Sociology is to search the pattern of relationships between people in order to pave the way for the betterment of individuals in relation to society.

Growth of Specialisation in Sociology

Sociology is a vast subject which includes almost everything of society which human beings deal with. We can mention some of the major social institutions like family, caste, religion, education, health, politics, industries etc., which human behaviour encompasses as a part of society. Sociology has developed rapidly since World War II, resulting in an increase in the specialisations within the general field of sociology. We can observe some of the major fields of specialisation as: tribal sociology, medical sociology, urban sociology, rural sociology, sociology of health, sociology of religion, sociology of education, criminology, sociology of health and demography.

Recently, the importance of sanitation in the human society forced social scientists to improve sociology of sanitation as a specialised study in sociology. Thus, the relationship of man and human society enabled further development in sociology of sanitation.

Sociology and Sanitation

It is true that one need not search for instances of the failure of people, in general, to recognise the close relationships which exist between sanitary conditions and social progress. The ignorance or lack of understanding of the relationship between the sanitation and sociology may be considerable. The earlier society did so little to diffuse general information concerning the facts and the theories, or the actual and ideal achievements of either sanitation or sociology. Because now importance is given to this problem of life, people find interdependence of sanitation and sociology. The extension of the study of sanitation was a requirement to improve the physical life of human beings in the society.

It's understood that the sanitation process should begin from the individual itself and the work of sanitarian is, therefore, acknowledged to be of greater scope. Further, the sanitary reforms should not be restricted to the physical life of man, but to all the activities that affect human beings. When the physical condition and the moral attitude of human beings are identified, the study of sanitation becomes important. So, a more rational and practical view of sanitation is gaining ground.

The relationship of sociology and sanitation can be considered as: the individual is the essential element of society, his social values depends largely upon his health, whilc in turn his health is partly determined by the conditions of society where he lives and which are imposed by the society. The disheartening status of mankind today is undoubtedly the result of the sanitary and social condition of past ages, but the influences under which men of the present generation place themselves are more or less within their control and may be made to work for both present and the future good of society.

According to Marion Talbot, sanitation will show what steps should be taken by society, individually and collectively, to secure good health of the race. Sanitation and sociology must go hand in hand in their effort to improve the human kind. The value of relation which exists between them will be great on proportion as its importance is consciously and openly recognised.

1.3 Origin of Sociology of Sanitation

Sociology of sanitation is the necessity of present world. Day after day human population is suffering from the problems of sanitation which is the result of their own life style. It is very difficult to survive in the modern world without proper sanitation measures. From home to the large social life everywhere man is facing the problem of sanitation. It's been very difficult to find out a toilet in very developed cities like Delhi, Bangalore and Chennai. We are developing in almost everything by forgetting the basic requirement of human life. Lack of sanitation is turning as the enemy of human health and good social life.

As referred by Mohammad Akram, sanitation in public life is the responsibility of an individual, community and the state. Some of the important persons say that sanitation can only be brought by changing the attitude or personal habits of individual or public itself. When the habits won't change, the people are blamed for their own poor surroundings. It is waste of constructing public toilets, where we hardly get water. Public policies go as a waste if the state is not interested to maintain it. Technical solutions are often suggested without understanding the habits or the social life of the people; sometimes they go unnoticed and often they create more problems than they solve. Hence, sanitation needs to be seen as an integral component of the public health programmes, individuals and communities.

Sanitation is all about:

- Safe collection, storage, treatment and disposal of human excreta (faeces and urine)
- Management of solid wastes (trash or rubbish)
- Drainage and disposal of household wastewater (often referred to as sullage or grey water)

- Drainage of storm water
- Treatment and disposal of sewage effluents
- Collection and management of industrial waste products and management of hazardous wastes (including hospital wastes, and chemical/radioactive and other dangerous substances).

The first challenge for countries seeking to solve the problem of access to sanitation is to understand what "sanitation" really means. The question of understanding sanitation led a foundation for the study of sanitation. The requirement of sanitation in public life developed the concept sanitation as a subject. The key issue here is that each community, region or country needs to work out what is the most sensible and cost-effective way of thinking about sanitation in the short and long-term and then act accordingly. Since it's the part of both human and society, we understand that human habits, life style, cultural and social behaviour is the major reason for the problem of sanitation. Thus, it's been found that, the understanding of sanitation should be taken in the views of sociological method. Sociological study enables the depth analysis of the subject for better result. Scientific study of sanitation was one of the requirement for its development as a subject.

Sociology of sanitation emerged as branch of medical sociology in the early 1940s. The discipline that investigates the social causes and consequences of health and illness was inspired by the health and sanitary reforms that took place in Western society. It was well recognised that the relations between sociology and sanitation are extremely intimate. The individual is the essential element of the society, his social values depends largely upon his health, and his environment depends on his habits. The disheartening status of mankind today is undoubtedly the result of the sanitary and social conditions of past ages and former generations. We can understand that clean food, adequate clean supply of water, sanitary schools, public baths, adequate housing are sanitary measures which are most effective in both sanitary and social aspects. Hence, sanitation and sociology must go hand in hand in their effort to improve the society and now, their relations are consciously and openly recognised.

1.4 Nature of Sociology of Sanitation

Sanitation is crucial but mostly a hidden aspect of everyday life and consumption. Sociology of sanitation includes human beings and their social life, interaction and behaviour with reference to sanitary conditions. Sociology of sanitation is a social science. Sociology of sanitation is the study of society and human social action for sanitation activity. It generally concerns itself with the social rules and processes that bind and separate people from sanitary conditions as individuals, but as members of associations, groups, and institutions, and includes the examination of the organisation and development of human social life for better world. The sociology of sanitation ranges from the analysis of individuals on the street to the study of global social processes. Sociology of sanitation is a science which is the implementation of scientific measures for better understanding of sanitation conditions in the society. It helps to understand the sanitation conditions in society. So, it has its own nature or characteristics.

Sociology of sanitation is the branch of knowledge and it differs from other subjects.

The following are the main characteristics of sociology of sanitation:

- *Sociology of sanitation is not an independent subject:* It is treated and studied as a branch of sociology with the implementation of sociological knowledge and methodology.
- *Sociology of sanitation is a social science and not a physical science:* As a social science it concentrates its attention on man, his social behaviour, social activities and social life and cultural life regarding sanitation. It studies human habits of cleanliness.
- *Sociology of sanitation is a positive discipline:* It confines itself to statements about what is, what can be. As a social science, we can study about sanitation in groups and societies and suggest remedies.
- *Sociology of sanitation is a pure and applied science:* The main aim of pure science is the acquisition of knowledge and this knowledge is applied to groups and communities to solve their sanitary problems.
- *Sociology of sanitation is abstract in nature:* Sociology of sanitation does not confine itself to the study of toilet or disposal wastage. It deals with complete sanitation activity of human society without the restriction of any group or community.
- *Sociology of sanitation is general and not a particular in nature:* Sociology of sanitation tries to find out the general laws

or principles about human attitude towards sanitation. Sociology of sanitation tries to find out the relationship of human groups and societies in sanitation. It tries to make generalisations on the basis of the study of some selected events.

- *Sociology of sanitation is general and not special in nature:* The area of inquiry of sociology of sanitation is general not specialised. It is concerned with human interaction and human life with or without sanitation in general. It only studies human activities in a general way.
- *Sociology of sanitation is both rational and an empirical study in nature as sociology:* There are two broad ways of approach to scientific knowledge. Empiricism is the approach that emphasises experience and the facts that result from observation and experimentation. Rationalism stresses reason and the theories that result from logical inference. Sociology of sanitation uses both ways to collect knowledge.

We discussed the nature of sociology of sanitation which helps to know about the character of sanitation on its field. It is clear from the above that sociology of sanitation is not an independent subject, rather a positive discipline, pure, abstract, general not particular, not specialised, empirical and a general science in nature.

1.5 Subject Matter of Sociology of Sanitation

Sociology of sanitation is the study of human action which includes the individual, community, and the public policies, for the betterment of sanitary measures in the environment. It studies the present infrastructure of sanitation and the required development of sanitation, from the individual household to community living.

Sociology of sanitation is a field of study that seeks to analyse and explain important matters that affect our everyday sanitation problems in our society, and the world in which we live. At a personal level, sociology of sanitation investigates the causes and consequences of such things as lack of toilets in the houses and in public places, lack of drainage facilities, lack of proper drinking water facilities, gender and sanitation issues, behavioural approach towards sanitation, disposal of waste, and cultural practices of various ethnic groups and management of sanitation.

At societal level, sociology of sanitation examines and explains such matters as existence of night soil carriers, prejudice and discrimination of night soil carriers in the society, toilet as business, sanitation at schools and education, and social movement's regarding sanitation. At the global level, sociology of sanitation studies such things as contribution of WHO, UNICEF etc. It studies economic contribution towards sanitation development policies.

One of the most important things that sociology of sanitation can offer to its students is the ability to grasp clearly a connection between broad behavioural pattern of individual and community towards sanitation. This provides personal experience regarding the unknown faces of sanitation problems. This is an extremely important preparation for living effective personal lives in a changing and complex world. It is also equally important for the future development of our society.

Sociology of sanitation includes:

- The sanitary measures at household
- The sanitary conditions at public places
- Sanitation at work place
- Relation of sanitation with the caste
- Gender and sanitation
- Social status of manual scavengers
- Culture of sanitation
- Sanitation at school or educational sector
- Disposal of waste
- Public policies of sanitation
- Non-governmental organisations

1. The Sanitary Measures at Household

It is very important to understand the relationship between house and the sanitation issues. Sanitary measures at household refers to the disposal of liquid or solid waste. It refers to the disposal of urine and faeces of human and animal at household. One should understand the importance of management of waste; other than human or animal excreta, and maintenance of proper drainage system for sullage water at household. Getting sanitation to people's houses is also the best way to deliver the health and environmental benefits we strive for. In the reference of resource organisation, public or community toilets are often dirty or broken down. They may have long lines, or be closed at night. Even if they're open at night, it's usually unsafe to walk there at night, especially for women. That means that people don't always use public toilets, and that means lots of waste still ends up where it shouldn't- in the alley, on the roof, in the drains and rivers – where it can cause disease and contamination. Thus, people need effective sanitation at home, so they can use it whenever they want or need to.

2. The Sanitary Conditions at Public Places

It refers to the sanitary measures at public places like, bus stops, hotels, malls, railway stations, cinema theaters, stadiums, hospitals etc. In the past decades, many public places (markets, bus parks, recreation parks, town centres, etc) have not been having sanitation facilities. The few that were in use under the management of the local authorities were totally run down to a state where they were unsuitable for human use. They were filthy and overflowing with human waste. No management system had been put in place for the daily operation of these facilities which were mainly toilet blocks for gents and ladies. These are the places where public suffers a lot because of lack of sanitary measures. Public places are the places from where the disease spreads to individuals. Thus, it is very important to take measures to develop sanitation in public places.

3. Sanitation at Work Place

Living without safe drinking water and adequate sanitation is an unacceptable situation for human, social and economic development, which violates basic requirements of human dignity and safety and has enormous impact on people's health, education, and capacity to lead fully productive lives and sometimes it is hard to find out a separate toilet for male and female in the work place. It is just because of lack of importance given to sanitation. Considerably working place will grow day by day, just leaving the importance of sanitation behind. It's been found that, lack of proper sanitation measures at work place leads to social problems like harassment etc. Toilets, proper drinking water facility, disposal of wastage etc., are important things in the work place.

4. Relation of Sanitation with Caste System

Caste-based discrimination leading to human rights violation regarding carrying of nights soil makes it an important social issue. The social status of lower caste people and the ethnic group people in the matter of sanitation is a matter of discussion. It is the discrimination of social status in the matter of human scavengers. Promotion and development of public policies for these people is a necessity.

5. Gender and Sanitation

Problems are faced by women in the society because of lack of sanitary measures. 66 per cent of the women in Delhi slums are verbally abused, 46 per cent are stalked and more than 30 per cent are physically assaulted while accessing toilets. Effective sanitation and hygiene promotion pays attention to gender differences and the effects of such differences early on in the process to ensure that different groups are treated equitably. No one should be excluded from hygiene and sanitation services on the basis of their sex, age, disability, socio-economic, or cultural/ethnic group. We can see that most of the sanitation labourers are women and they won't get what they deserve.

6. Social Status of Manual Scavengers

In the traditional Indian society people of particular section were ordained to carry the night soil. It was a worst kind of exploitation done against any kind of community in the traditional Indian society. These people are hated and shunned for this dirty job. It is clearly denial of social justice. Manual scavenger means a person engaged or employed on regular or frequent basis by an individual or a local authority or a public or private agency, for manually cleaning, carrying, disposing of, or otherwise handling in any manner, human excreta in an insanitary latrine or in an open drain or pit into which human excreta from insanitary latrines is disposed of, or on a railway track, before the excreta fully decomposes. There is a need for depth analysis of manual scavengers to understand their social problems. Development of these community people is necessary in the modern world. Sociology of sanitation is goal oriented towards the development of social status of manual scavengers.

7. Culture of Sanitation

India's enduring shame is clearly rooted in cultural attitudes. More than half a century after Independence, many Indians continue to relieve themselves in the open and litter unhesitatingly, but keep their homes spotlessly clean. The state has failed to extend sanitation facilities, but people must also take the blame. In some of the tribal communities we have observed that even though government provided the toilets to the family, people are less interested to use them. To understand the cultural consequences has become one of the important works of sociology of sanitation. It is the lack of toilets and preference for open defecation a cultural issue in a society where the habit actually perpetuates social oppression. Cultural attitude differs from place to place even though government provides the toilets; people don't want to use them. It's not only lack of knowledge; it is also cultural attitude lead to sanitation problems.

8. Sanitation at School or Educational Sector

It's very important to generate the knowledge of sanitation and impart it by education at school level. Even the requirement of sanitary measures in school and educational institutions are the most important thing. The requirement of proper toilet facility is most essential things, in the rural places even today the children or the students go outside in the nature for their urinals. It's not only about toilet it's the requirement of good and healthy environment in the school compound. There should be a proper place for disposal of waste. School is the public place from where diseases can spread easily. In the co-education institution girls face lot of problems because of lack of sanitation measures. Even some of the schools don't have proper drinking water facilities. In the words of World Bank, schools may be better locations in which to enforce certain behaviours in children than the home. Schools can also provide an arena where sanitation can be shown at its best, and certain positive hygienic behaviours (hand washing with soap before eating and after going to the toilet) can become an engrained habit at a young age. Sociology of sanitation does find out the problem of sanitation in the educational institution and it suggests the remedies for the development of sanitation infrastructure.

9. Disposal of Waste

As cities are growing in size with a rise in the population, the amount of waste generated is increasing becoming unmanageable. The local corporations have adapted different methods for the disposal of waste – open dumps, landfills, sanitary landfills, and incineration plants. Disposal of solid waste depends on the geography of the habitat. In the rural places the animal wastage is used for bio-gas and bio-compost for agricultural purpose. In the urban places it's been considered as a major problem of disposal of solid waste of humans and animals. Urban places lack disposal places, even the municipal or city corporation is struggling with the disposal of waste. Understanding of measures which are to be followed in the disposal of waste is necessary. Urban society generates different kinds of waste which cannot be disposed together. It's been observed that nowadays the bigger cities like Mumbai, Delhi, and Bangalore are following their own kinds of waste disposal. They are trying to collect the waste from door to door by charging some fees.

10. Public Policies of Sanitation

The Ministry of Drinking Water and Sanitation was created and notified by the Government of India as a separate Ministry, keeping in view of the extreme importance of the sector. The Ministry of Drinking Water and Sanitation is the nodal Ministry for the overall policy, planning, funding and coordination of the flagship programmes of the Government for rural drinking water viz., the National Rural Drinking Water Programme and for rural sanitation, the Total Sanitation Campaign in the country. There are three programme divisions namely, Water, Water Quality and Sanitation to carry out the functions of the Ministry. It makes policies for the development of sanitarian measures in the nation.

11. Non-Governmental Organisations (NGOs)

As for NGOs, they've been involved in informing objectively the actors (communities, local authorities, media, technical and financial partners), by setting up coalitions to establish stable reference situations and to carry out issue-based advocacy on the basis of rigorously constituted reference documents. In this framework, NGOs' work as the pressure group to the government for the implementation of sanitary measures is important. NGOs spread initiatives related to public health. They specifically focus on sanitation, which remains poor in public action.

Sociology of sanitation, conceptualise how people perceive and experience sanitation within informal settlements. Sociology of sanitation contextualise existing sanitary practice and explore it in relation to potential sanitation interventions by state, and civil society and it relates urban sanitation experience, perception and coping strategies to debates in urban theory and development studies.

1.6 Importance of Sociology of Sanitation

A look at sanitation provides a number of unique benefits and perspectives. Sociology of sanitation provides an understanding of social issues and patterns of sanitation. It helps us to identify the social rules that govern our lives with sanitation or without sanitation. Social scientists study, how these rules are created for human society, maintained, changed, passed between generations, and shared between people living in various parts of the world.

Sociology of sanitation helps us to understand the working of the social systems of sanitary conditions. Social scientist brings sanitation into a social context. This means social scientist looks not only at sanitary equipments or measures, but behaviours and relationships, and also how the larger world we live in, influences these things. A sanitation structure that is the way society is organised around sanitation and social sanitation processes that is the way society operates sanitary system are at work shaping our lives in ways that often go unrecognised.

Sociologists strive to bring these things out of the fog, to reveal and study them, and to examine and explain their interrelationships and their impacts on individuals and groups. By describing and explaining these social arrangements and how they shape our lives, social scientists help us to make sense of the world around us and better understand ourselves. Sociology of sanitation helps us understand why we are in need of proper sanitation. Sociology helps us examine the behavioural pattern, cultural attitudes, and geographical influence towards sanitation.

Sociology of sanitation helps us to identify what we have in common within, and between, cultures and societies. Social scientists know that, although people in different parts of the city, country, or world dress differently, speak differently, and have many different beliefs and customs, but the requirement of sanitation is same among all people by considering that we are humans. Social scientist looks for what sanitation and hygiene means to various groups. They look at how various groups follow sanitary measures.

Sociology of sanitation helps us understand changing pattern of sanitation and also helps us to understand why and how these changes takes place in the society. Obviously, the social world is constantly changing. However, it's very important for us to know the importance of sanitation. With a sociological perspective, we can more effectively take action. We can better participate in shaping the future for ourselves and for others.

Sociology of sanitation provides us theoretical perspectives within which to frame these understandings and research methods that allow us to study sanitation scientifically. Sociology of sanitation is a social science.

That means social scientist works to understand sanitation in very structured, disciplined ways. In the case of sociology of sanitation, theories focus on how social institutions operate sanitation. They provide a way of explaining these institutions. Scientific methods provide ways of generating accurate research results.

Sanitation is so important to the health and well being of all people on earth. Without good, clean sanitation systems disease can break out very quickly and be easily spread. Sanitation is an important way of promoting good health and preventing diseases. It is the hygienic means of promoting good health through prevention of contact of hazards such as wastes.

According to World Bank, globally 2.5 billion people live without access to improved sanitation: one billion of these people practice open defecation. Despite significant gains – almost 1.9 billion people gained access to toilets or latrines since 1990 – sanitation remains one of the most off-track Millennium Development Goals (MDG) globally. Only 64 per cent of the world's population has access to improved sanitation, but 70 per cent of the Sub-Saharan Africa population and 59 per cent of South Asia still lack access to sanitation. At current rates of progress, the world will miss the MDG for sanitation by over half a billion people.

Sociology of sanitation is needed for the depth study of sanitation problems faced by the society. Sanitation lies at the root of many other development challenges, as poor sanitation impacts public health, education, and the environment. Without sanitation girls are more likely to drop out of school or are vulnerable to attacks while seeking privacy. Globally, poor sanitation leads to about 700,000 premature deaths annually. Recent analysis shows that ending open defecation can save children's lives by reducing disease transmission, stunting, and under-nutrition, which are important for childhood cognitive development and future economic productivity.

World Bank says, lack of sanitation also holds back economic growth. Poor sanitation costs billions to some countries, amounting to the equivalent of 6.3 per cent of GDP in Bangladesh, 6.4 per cent of GDP in India, 7.2 per cent of GDP in Cambodia, 2.4 per cent of GDP in Niger, and 3.9 per cent of GDP in Pakistan annually. The economic losses are mainly driven by premature deaths, the cost of healthcare treatment, lost time and productivity seeking treatment, and finding access to sanitation facilities. Pollution resulting from improper disposal and treatment of wastewater and domestic fecal sludge also affects both water resources and ecosystems. At the same time, fecal sludge and wastewater and can provide valuable resources (water, nutrients, and energy) and economic opportunities, especially in urban areas and in water-scarce environments.

One who had visited the public places in India would instantly understand the need for clean toilet facilities. The lack of clean sanitation facilities has been a common cause for many diseases in India. Most of the places where large number of people assemble, such as at schools, railway stations, bus stations, hospitals, parks, beaches, markets and places of worship, lack adequate toilet and urinal facilities for public use.

The importance of sociology of sanitation can be explained as follows:

Sociology of sanitation makes a scientific study of sanitation: Sociology of sanitation allows the researcher for a scientific study of sanitation issues in the society. It enables to collect the data in given prescribed format. It suggests remedies for the identified problems of sanitation. Scientific study of sanitation highlights sanitation as a greater importance in the social aspects.

Sociology of sanitation studies role of the institutions in the sanitary conditions: It is through sociology of sanitation that scientific study of social institutions and the relation of the individual is being made. The home and family, the school and education, the church and religion, the state and government, industry and work, the community and association, are institutions through which society functions. Sociology of sanitation studies these institutions and their role in the development of sanitation. Sociology of sanitation explains them with a view to enable them to serve the individual and the society with better sanitation.

Study of sanitation is important for understanding and planning of healthy society: Society is a complex phenomenon with a multitude of intricacies. It is impossible to understand and solve its numerous problems without support of sociology and it is rightly said that we cannot understand and mend society without any knowledge of its mechanism and construction. Without the investigation carried out by sociology no real effective social planning would be possible. It helps us to determine the most efficient means for reaching the goals agreed upon. Thus, certain amount of knowledge about society is necessary before any social policies can be carried out.

Sociology of sanitation is of great importance in the solution of social problems: The present world is suffering from many problems which cannot be solved without scientific study of the sanitation problems. It is the task of sociology of sanitation to study the sanitation problems through the methods of scientific research and to find out solution to them. The scientific study of human affairs will ultimately provide the body of knowledge and principles that will enable us to control the conditions of sanitation and improve them. It's very important to bring the problem of sanitation into mainstream.

Sociology of sanitation has drawn our attention to the effects of lack of sanitation: Sociology of sanitation has been instrumental in understanding the need for sanitation. In a specialised society we are all limited as to the amount of the whole organisation and culture that we can experience directly. Problem of sanitation conditions in the society also affecting our social life directly or indirectly in the form of harassment, school drop outs and social injustice etc. In order to have insight into the problem of sanitation the existence of knowledge of sociology of sanitation is essential.

Sociology of sanitation has changed our outlook with regard to the problems of manual scavengers: It is through the study of sociology of sanitation that our whole outlook on various aspects of manual scavengers changed. The manual scavengers are now treated as equally in the matter of social relationships.

Sociology of sanitation has made great contribution to culture of sanitation: Sanitation culture has been made richer by the contribution of sociology of sanitation. Sociology of sanitation has given us training to have rational approach to questions regarding sanitation concerning oneself, one's religion, customs, morals and institutions regarding sanitation. It enables man to have better understanding of sanitation. By comparative study of societies and groups other than his existence, his life becomes healthy.

Sociology of sanitation is of great importance in the global understanding of sanitation: The progress made by physical sciences has brought the nations of the world nearer to each other. Sociology of sanitation gives knowledge about the policies for sanitation at global level. But in the social field the world has been left behind by the revolutionary progress of the science. Now, it's an important need for sanitation globally. Every nation has to think better for the future world.

The value of sociology of sanitation lies in the fact that it keeps upgrading sanitation condition. It contributes to making good environment and finding solutions to the community problems. It adds to the knowledge of sanitation. It helps the individual find his relation to sanitation. Sociology of sanitation pulls the people from the older sanitation measures.

Conclusion

Sociology of sanitation gives knowledge about the history of sanitation in the ancient civil society. It compares the sanitation of different geographical places for better understanding. The study of sociology of sanitation has greater value in the modern complex society. It studies sanitation conditions, the human behaviour and culture regarding sanitation in the scientific way. It identifies the problem and suggests solutions and generates new knowledge about sanitation. Sociology of sanitation studies the human society from bottom to the top level that what the human applies for a better sanitised world. It also explores the relationship of the individual and the institution in the field of sanitation. Sociology of sanitation improves the understanding and increases the power of social action for better sanitation. Finally, it plays an important role in the solution of sanitation as a social problem by applying different scientific measures.

CHAPTER 2

Sociology of Sanitation and Other Social Sciences

Introduction

Sociology of sanitation as a branch of sociology deals with the sanitation conditions of human life. Sociology of sanitation cannot be separated from any other discipline. It can be studied in detail in relationship with other disciplines. The comparative study of sociology of sanitation enables better understanding to the persons concerned with sanitation. In this connection, we can understand how other disciplines are important in the study of sanitation. Scientific study of sanitation highlights the importance of other disciplines of social sciences like history, economics, anthropology, political science, psychology, sociology etc. Social scientists are of the view that comparison with other disciplines enhances the knowledge and the area of sociology of sanitation.

2.1 Sociology of Sanitation and History

Sociology of sanitation and history are closely and intimately related to each other. Sociology of sanitation as a branch of sociology cannot be separated from history and history cannot be isolated from sociological study. That is why Professor G.E. Howard remarked, "History is the past sociology and sociology is the present history". John Seely says that "history without sociology has no fruit, sociology without history has no root". In fact, present society bears symbols of the past.

History is mainly concerned with past events. In general, history refers to the study of the past in a systematic order. It is systematic record of the story of mankind. History presents a chronological account of past events of the human society and examines in detail. It is the social science which deals with past events and studies the past social, political and economic aspects of the country. According to Gettle, "History is the record of the past events and movements, their causes and inter-relations". It includes a survey of conditions, or developments in economic, religious and social affairs as well as the study of states, their growth and organisation and their relation with one another.

If human society wants to study today, and plan tomorrow it has to look into its past. Lack of understanding of the past events of life may lead to the blind way of future. The picture of the past can frame the future of tomorrow. Sociology of sanitation is the subject which is related to the social, cultural and religious life of the society. It is not possible for the social scientist to come to a conclusion without the reference of the past. We can only understand what we can do, by only understanding what we did. Sociology of sanitation is a related subject with history and we cannot move further in sociology of sanitation by separating history from sociology of sanitation.

Both sociology of sanitation and history depend upon each other and can influence one another. Sociology of sanitation depends upon history in order to study past events and situations. History of cultures and institutions is helpful in the understanding of sanitation and on the collections of materials regarding sanitation. In order to understand the past society and activities, we have to take the help of history. Sociology of sanitation is concerned with the study of the historical development of sanitation in human society. It studies ancient customs, modes of living, and various stages of sanitation and past social institutions which contributed to sanitation through the historical analysis. This information about the past is of great importance to sociologists. For instance, if a sociologist has to study health and hygiene as of social importance he has to study their historical developments also.

It not only studies the past but also establishes relations with present and future. That is why it is said that "History is the microscope of the past, the horoscope of the present and telescope of the future". However, both the sciences are closely inter-related and inter-dependent on each other.

Though history and sociology of sanitation are different subjects we can still observe some similarities between them and the similarities are highlighted below:

- Sociology of sanitation is the study of sanitation as a branch of sociology; history studies the sanitation as a part of history.
- Requirement of the study of the past is very important in both the subjects.
- History and sociology of sanitation both use scientific techniques.
- In both, history and sociology of sanitation the data is recorded.
- History supplies the material for sociology of sanitation as well as sociology of sanitation gives the social background of sanitation for the study in history.
- History would be meaningless without explaining socially significant events. Sociology of sanitation will also be meaningless without the reference of history.
- Sociologists are most interested in the contemporary events and recent past which is also related with history.

History helps and enriches sociology of sanitation. History is the store house of knowledge from which sociology of sanitation gained a lot. History provides materials for social scientists to use. History is a record of past events, social customs and information about different stages of life. Sociology of sanitation uses this information.

Though there are differences between sociology of sanitation and history, there are also differences between them. The differences between them are given below.

Sociology of Sanitation	*History*
Sociology of sanitation is a science of sanitation and is concerned with the human habits regarding sanitation in the past, present and the future.	But history deals with the past events and studies the past society.
Sociology of sanitation is a modern or new subject.	Whereas history is an older social science.
Sociology of sanitation is abstract in nature.	Whereas history is concrete in nature.
The scope of sociology of sanitation is very wide. Sociology of sanitation includes history within its scope.	Whereas the scope of history is limited.

(*contd.*)

(*contd.*)

Sociology of sanitation is an analytical subject.	Whereas history is a descriptive subject.
Sociology of sanitation covers small part of human life.	Whereas history studies human activity as a whole.
Sociology of sanitation is a generalising discipline. Sociology of sanitation seeks to establish generalisations after a careful study of the human habits.	But history is an individualising discipline.
Sociology of sanitation uses sociological approach. It studies human events from the sociological point of view, i.e., from the viewpoint of social relationship involved.	History rarely makes generalisations. It seeks to establish the sequence in which events occurred. But history studies with historical approach; history studies human events in accordance with time and order.

2.1 Sociology of Sanitation and Economics

Sociology and economics as social sciences have close relations. Relationship between the two is so close that one is often treated as the branch of the other, because society is greatly influenced by economic factors, and economic processes are largely determined by the environment of the society. Sociology of sanitation as the branch of sociology tries to understand the interrelationship between economics and the sanitational behaviour of the community.

Economics deals with the economic activities of man. It deals with production, consumption and distribution of wealth. The economic factors play vital role in the very aspect of our social life. Total development of individual depends very much on economic factors. Without economic conditions, the study of society is quite impossible. All the social problems are directly connected with the economic conditions of the people. That is why Marshall defines economics as "on one side the study of wealth and on the other and more important side a part of the study of man".

In the same way, the study of sanitation is influenced by economics in society. The economic conditions of community determine the standard of sanitation which they adopt for their goodness. Without the economic understanding the study of sanitation in the society is quite impossible. Economists have contributed to the study of different aspects of social institutions. On the other hand, property system, division of labour, occupations etc., are provided by a sociologist to an economist.

The area of co-operation between sociology and economics is widening. Economists are more and more making use of the sociological concepts in the study of social problems.

Economists are working with sociologists in their study of the problems of economic development in underdeveloped countries and vice versa sociologists are working with economists. Combined efforts of both the experts may be of great practical help in meeting the challenges.

Nowadays, understanding of economic issues has become quite indispensable for all sections in the society. Everyone wants to get rich; wants to increase their wealth; wants to have hold over productive resources; wants to expand their business activities. People want to earn more and more profits, and exercise control over the market and other economic system; people want to raise their living standard and enjoy more and more consumption; people want to make their future secure; everyone wants to grow from the current position; given these, people want to update their knowledge of economic issues and take advantage of that. Besides, these expectations it is the fact that social problems of society affects the economic development of a nation as well as individual. Sanitation as a social problem in society will lead to economic loss to the nation as well as to the individual. The better conditions of improved sanitation can contribute to the economical development of the nation as well as individual.

This shows that people want to become economically stronger and viable so that they can lead a better life style. This requires proper understanding of the economic issues and contributing social issues. Such understanding might be developed through formal and informal methods of learning. Most of the people learn informally in the society through their experiences as they get exposed to certain real life situations. Economical understanding of sanitation as issue cannot be separable in the social aspects of civilised life. Economical understanding of sanitation begins from the cost of sanitation measures and ends with the cost of expenditure on medical treatment which is done for the treatment caused by lack of sanitation in the environment. The relationship of material value with sanitation speaks of the 'Economics of Sanitation'.

Sociology of sanitation and economics are inseparable, because it affects one another directly or indirectly in the socio-economic aspects of society. One has to understand the importance of two subjects relatively to overcome the doubt regarding the relationship of sociology of sanitation with economics. The contribution of economics in sanitation makes us understand the need for economical study of the sanitation issues in the society. On the other hand, it will also makes us to understand the contribution of sanitation in the field of economy or in other words economical development of the individual or nation.

What is Economics?

It is very difficult to define economics because economics is a dynamic subject. Its scope keeps on changing rather expanding. Still for proper understanding of any subject, it becomes necessary to define it as close as possible.

Economics is the social science that is concerned with the production, distribution and consumption of goods and services. "Economics aims to explain how economies work and how economic agents interact. Economic analysis is not only applied throughout society, business, finance and government, but also in crime, education, the family, health, law, politics, religion, social institutions, war, and science. The expanding domain of economics in the social science has been described as economic imperialism".

The above description of economics shows the nature of economics in modern context. It tells that economics can be used for raising the living standard of people and their welfare. However, it also wants that economic issues or economic objectives might become a tool in the hands of people, who want to exploit it for ulterior motive like separation from others.

Relationship between Sociology of Sanitation and Economics

Sociology of sanitation as branch of sociology deals with the social issues with sociological methods. Sociology and economics are the branches of the social science. They have very close relationship. Economics deals with the economic activities of man which is also called science of bread and butter. Economics is the study of production, distribution and consumption of goods and services. Economics is concerned with material welfare of the human beings. Economics welfare is only a part of human welfare and it can be only sought only with the proper knowledge of social laws. It cannot go far ahead without the help of sociology and other sciences.

Sociology and economics are helpful to each other. Economic relationships are closely related with social activities as same as social relationships are also affected by economic activities.

Thus, due to such relations, Thomas regarded economics as the branch of sociology which is known as economic sociology and is useful to study economic processes of the society. Some economists like Sam Bart, Max Weber, and Pareto have explained economic changes as aspects of social change. According to them, the study of economics would be incomplete without understanding of human society. The society, its structure, organisation, its institution, its strength and weakness etc., are bound to affect economic activities of its people. On the other hand, according to Karl Marx, the social phenomena are determined by economic forces. And social reality or social change can be explained in terms of economic forces.

According to Karl Marx, the infrastructure of society is nothing but the economic relations among it's people. Now the area of co-operation between sociology and economics is becoming wider. Economists are now analysing the social factors influencing economic growth. Economists are now more and more making use of the sociological concepts and generalisations in the study of economic problems. Moreover, there are certain social and economic problems of greater importance to be studied by both economists and sociologists. The problems like poverty, unemployment, overpopulation, sanitational issues, manual scavengers etc., have both social and economic implications.

Further, the relationship of sociology of sanitation and economics can be understood better with the explanation of the WHO. According to WHO improved sanitation has positive impacts on economic growth and poverty reduction. According to a recent WHO study, every dollar spent on improving sanitation generates an average economic benefit of $7. The economic cost of inaction is astronomical. Without improving sanitation, none of the other Millennium Development Goals, to which the world has committed itself, will be achieved. It is clearly noted that, inadequate sanitation can cause economic loss and better sanitation can lead economic development. Improved sanitation generally involves better access and safer disposal of excreta via septic tank, pour-flush or simple pit latrine, small bore sewer or ventilated improved pit-latrine. On the benefit side, time savings are valued at the country's minimum wage, which assumes that people can make economically productive use of the additional time.

Poor sanitation causes economic losses associated with the direct costs of treating sanitation-related illnesses and lost income through reduced or lost productivity. In addition, poor sanitation also leads to losses of time and effort in due to distant or inadequate sanitation facilities, lower product quality resulting from poor water quality, reduced income from tourism (due to a high risk of contamination and disease), and clean up costs. Thus, it leads to economic loss, and hence, social problems become economical issues.

Though economics and sociology of sanitation are intimately connected and help each other there are a few differences between them and they are given below:

Economics	*Sociology of Sanitation*
Economics deals with only those social relationships which are economic in character.	Sociology of sanitation studies issues related to sanitation only.
Economics is concrete in nature and its variable can be measured and quantified more easily and accurately.	Sociology of sanitation is abstract in nature and sanitation variables are very difficult to measure and to quantify, because it is related with culture of the people.
The scope of economics is wider.	The scope of sociology of sanitation is narrow compared to economics.
Economics is a special social science.	Sociology of sanitation is a branch of social science.
In economics the individual is the target of study.	In sociology of sanitation community or society is regarded as the unit of study.
Economics uses its own methods in research.	Research methods in sociology of sanitation are from sociology.
Economics studies man as an economic being.	Sociology of sanitation studies man as a social animal, cultural being.
Economics is older than sociology.	Sociology of sanitation is branch of sociology and younger to economics.

2.2 Sociology of Sanitation and Sociology

A question may be asked about the necessity of studying sociology of sanitation as a branch of sociology. Sociology of sanitation studies the concept of sanitation in detail while sociology studies the sanitation as a part. Sociology of sanitation is not only considered as a branch of sociology but also as an area of study in sociology. Sociology of sanitation is the subject which we deal in the sociological view point. We can say that sociology of sanitation is the child of sociology which is growing because of the requirement of the present society.

Sociology of sanitation and sociology go together to identify and generalise the hypotheses. They also go hand in hand in the study of the human behaviour. Sociology studies general group behaviour whereas sociology of sanitation studies behaviour related to sanitation. We cannot separate sociology of sanitation from sociology. Sociology can survive as a major subject without the help of sociology of sanitation. But sociology of sanitation requires sociology. It has to take the techniques from sociology. The relationship of sociology and sociology of sanitation is inseparable.

As it is highlighted in chapter one, sociology is the study of man and society in general. Sociology studies the behaviour of man with his fellow beings in a social surrounding. It studies the collective behaviour of man and its origin, developments, organisation and its institutions. Sociology is a social science which conducts various investigations, researches to find out the facts from general understanding. Sociology enables to understand the relationship between man and his action in the society. It enhances the knowledge of social action.

The study of sociology of sanitation and sociology are interrelated. Sanitation can be defined as hygienic measures taken to maintain public health, which includes safe disposal of human wastes, waste water and solid wastes, control of vectors of diseases, domestic, personal and food hygiene. The study of sanitation with the help of sociology and the sociological techniques enables better understanding of the issue. As sociology is older science, it will be the guide for sociology of sanitation.

The subject matter of sociology of sanitation cannot be separated from the daily life of human beings. The area of study of sociology of sanitation lies within the grounds of sociology itself. So the necessity of sociology is very important for sociology of sanitation as an emerging subject. Without the reference of sociology it is hard to understand actually what sociology of sanitation is.

With reference to the explanation given above we can understand some of the differences between sociology and sociology of sanitation as given below:

Sociology	*Sociology of Sanitation*
Sociology is an independent science.	Sociology of sanitation is the branch of sociology, it depends on sociology.
Sociology follows its own techniques of research.	It depends on sociological techniques.
Area of study of sociology is wider in nature.	Sociology of sanitation is specific in nature.
Sociology studies human relationships and institutions or all aspects of man in general.	It studies human habits and attitude regarding sanitational issues only.
Sociology is older than sociology of sanitation.	Sociology of sanitation is the child of sociology; it's too young and growing.
Sociology studies sanitation as a part.	Sociology of sanitation studies sanitation and its issues in detail.

2.3 Sociology of Sanitation and Psychology

Sociology of sanitation as a branch of sociology and its nature is not much different from sociology. Sociology of sanitation is mainly concerned with the sanitational conditions in the society. But it has been understood that the behaviour of people from place to place is different and it directly affects the sanitation conditions of society. For the better infrastructure in sanitation we have to understand the mentality of people. So, sociology of sanitation can get help of psychology. Psychology provides details about the individual behaviour. Sociology of sanitation and psychology are closely related to each other. Both are interrelated and inter-dependent. To understand the relationship between two subjects we have to go through the subjects individually.

Psychology is concerned with the exploration of the depth of man's mind and behaviour in society. It is said that psychology shows the significance of the relationship between the organism (individual) and environment and the response of the former to the latter. It is defined as "the study of man's mental life and behaviour". It is the science of mind of mental processes. The aim of psychology is to arrive at the laws of mental life and behaviour of human beings. Sociology of sanitation, on the other hand is the study of sanitation in society. It studies man's social behaviour towards sanitation in society.

Psychology is the science of mental process or mind. It is the study of the individual. Sociology studies groups. It studies the human experiences and the behaviour in groups. Social psychology is the branch of sociology, which is the combination of psychology and sociology. Sociology and psychology are both involved in solving the existing social problems. Sociology helps psychology and psychology helps sociology. Thus, they are interrelated in many respects. Besides, social psychology studies individual social behaviour. Social psychology serves the bridge between psychology and sociology. It deals with mental process of man considering him as a social being. Social psychology enables better understanding of sanitation issues in the society in sociological view point.

Sociology of sanitation studies society in general whereas psychology is concerned with human behaviour as individual. So, there are resemblances between psychology and sociology of sanitation. Both are regarded as positive subjects. These two disciplines have a great deal in common and are inter-related. It is difficult to understand the inter-relations and the activities of human beings; without an adequate knowledge of human psychology. In the same way, many truths of psychology would remain unintelligible without a comprehensive idea about social relationships, behaviour and activities.

Treads in psychology support sociology of sanitation and the help sociology of sanitation is extended to psychology regarding sanitation. In other words, they depend on each other for their existence. The psychological approach and the sociological approach in the study of sanitation may be different but the objectives of these will be the same. Thus, we can say that sociology of sanitation can be successful in its approach towards sanitation with the help of other discipline like psychology.

Social scientists can only identify the problems in society which are the results of group or community. But, there is also a requirement to study the individual as a part of community. Psychology can help social scientist in this point of view. The assistance of psychology can bring a clear change in the study of sanitation in society. With the help of psychology the sociological framework of sanitation will be meaningful.

In psychological studies, it is understood that the individual is responsible for all his activities, whereas in sociology of sanitation it studies not only individual but also group activity. Sociology of sanitation assumes that an individual's act is influenced by his surroundings or pertains to the group he belongs to.

Although the psychology and sociology of sanitation are interdependent, they differ from each other as shown below:

Psychology	*Sociology of Sanitation*
Psychology is concerned with the human mind.	Whereas sociology of sanitation is concerned with human habits.
Psychology uses psychological method which is experimental in nature.	Sociology of sanitation uses sociological method.
Psychology studies the personality.	Sociology of sanitation studies the social behaviour.
Psychology deals with human emotions.	Sociology of sanitation deals with the human attitude.
Psychology deals with individuals or small groups.	Sociology of sanitation deals with a larger group or the society itself.
Psychology can be termed as an experimental process.	Whereas sociology of sanitation is an observational process.
In psychological studies, it is perceived that the individual is singly responsible for all the activities.	Whereas in sociology of sanitation, it is not an individual act. Sociology assumes that an individual's act is influenced by his surroundings or pertains to the group he belongs to.
Psychology is often defined as the subject of mental process.	Whereas sociology of sanitation is the subject for society.
Psychology is an individual science.	Sociology of sanitation is branch of sociology.

2.4 Sociology of Sanitation and Anthropology

Sociology of sanitation and anthropology are closely related. Some people are of the opinion that sociology and anthropology are the same. In fact, sociology and anthropology are different in nature and methodology. Similarly, the sociological study of sanitation is different from the anthropological study of sanitation. For better understanding of these two subjects first we have to understand what is anthropology.

Anthropology as a discipline is closely related to sociology. Anthropology is the study of man. Anthropology has been divided into three divisions: (i) Physical Anthropology which deals with bodily characteristics of early man and our primitive contemporaries, (ii) Cultural Anthropology which investigates the cultural remains of early man and of the living cultures of some of the primitive contemporaries and (iii) Social Anthropology which deals with the institutions and human relationships of primitive, of the past and present. Social anthropology and sociology are very close. Both of these disciplines are fast growing. Sociology of sanitation uses the knowledge given by both disciplines, sociology and anthropology, to frame the area of sociology of sanitation.

Anthropology is the study of humanity and human behaviour. It is the only discipline that offers a conceptual scheme for the whole context of human experiences. It provides a broad framework into which many other subjects can be fitted. The knowledge of anthropology, physical as well as socio-cultural, is necessary for a social scientist to understand, explain and explore sanitation in the society. An understanding of society can be gained by comparing various cultures, particularly, the modern with the primitive.

Anthropology is the comprehensive study of the human condition, the origin of our species in evolutionary biology, and the development of culture and society in its many variations among ancient and contemporary peoples. Its subject matter encompasses an immense time depth and a vast spatial range, including the simplest human societies and the most complex modern industrial civilisation. Anthropology brings together many areas of scientific and humanistic inquiry, unifying and integrating knowledge about people and their perceptions of the world.

The conclusions drawn by sociologists have also helped anthropologists in their study. Sociology and anthropology both study human society, how societies are organised and how humans interact and behave within them. Sociology of sanitation, thus, uses the knowledge of society which is gained by anthropological study for the better understanding of the sanitation in the past, primitive societies and helps to understand the sanitation condition in the modern or present society. The difference is in how all of this is studied. Anthropology and forensic anthropology can be seen as more oriented to the biological, historical, and holistic nature of human society and interaction, while sociology of sanitation uses sociological techniques and looks at the entire spectrum of human interaction regarding sanitation, social structure for better sanitation environment and social organisation of sanitation with interest in quantitative analysis of the causes and effects of individual and group activity. Sociology of sanitation looks at groups, from small to global in scope, while anthropologists work closely or even live with groups and societies in order to study the human action and interaction regarding sanitation.

Sociology of sanitation as a branch of sociology shares common interest as anthropology to study the conditions of sanitation and its relative issues. Sociology of sanitation share some detailed interests in the same theory, methods, historical backgrounds, and scientific approaches. Sociology of sanitation and anthropology are also highly understanding of the fact that some aspects of human life and society cannot be studied in the same ways that are dictated by the "hard" scientific approaches. In most cases, there is no testing under strictly controlled conditions, where results can be replicated.

Anthropology relates to sociology of sanitation in the sense that anthropology provides cultural understanding for the study of sanitation in the society. The difference between the two is proximity. Anthropology is the study of other cultures abroad and in the past, whereas sociology of sanitation is the study of one's surroundings and relatively local way of life.

Anthropology is the study of human beings and their ancestors through time in terms of physical characteristics, environmental and social relations, and culture. On the other hand, sociology of sanitation is the study of human action regarding sanitation at a given period in time. Anthropology covers all characteristics of humanity, including physiology and evolutionary origins while sociology of sanitation focuses on social issues of sanitation.

Anthropology and sociology of sanitation make study of man, his behaviour, culture and interactions with the society. But sociology of sanitation has keen interest in sanitation issues only. Anthropologists focus upon tribes and cultures of colonised people, sociologists work with present societies. Sociology of sanitation uses the anthropological studies for the better reference of sanitation. Anthropology helps social scientists to understand the sanitation condition at the bottom to top level of the social structure. Sanitation can be studied well at urban and rural society with the help of anthropology.

Anthropology and sociology of sanitation attempt to answer questions pertaining to man and his behaviour in society. While anthropology studies man in his entirety, sanitation in society is at the focus of study in sociology of sanitation. Sociology of sanitation is the scientific study of sanitation issues in societies and the participation in social institutions. In sociology of sanitation the main purpose of sociologists is to gain an insight into human behaviour for sanitation.

Though some people are of the opinion that sociology and anthropology are the same, we can still observe some differences regarding the sociology of sanitation as a branch of sociology. Notwithstanding their inter-dependence the two sciences differ from each other in many respects. The points of differences are as follows:

Differences between Sociology of Sanitation and Anthropology

- There are many differences right from the subject matter to approach and methodology of sociology of sanitation and anthropology.
- The fundamental difference between sociology and anthropology is that while sociology of sanitation studies social habits, anthropologists study cultures.
- Anthropology has for its subject matter the small and static culture of people who belong to the pre-literate period. In sharp contrast to this, sociology of sanitation investigates the culture of sanitation in society.
- Often, sociology of sanitation can easily manage with secondary data, while anthropologists depend upon primary data.
- Anthropology is concerned with the past whereas sociology of sanitation is concerned with the present.
- Sociology of sanitation and anthropology has dissimilar methods since their subject matter differs.

The subject matter of anthropology is the primitive, pre-literate people and their culture. The complete human society is the basis of its investigation. It not only studies, the physical characteristics of the human race but also studies the influence itself. On the other hand, sociology takes note of the influence of the human race exerts on social institutions and it deals with people and their culture of sanitation in the present context. It focuses the attention of sociologists on some of the particular aspects of society. Thus, it is quite obvious that the subject-matter of sociology of sanitation is not the concern of anthropology. In respect of subject matter, both anthropology and sociology of sanitation differ from each other.

Sociology of Sanitation	***Anthropology***
Scope of sociology of sanitation is limited.	Scope of anthropology is universal.
Initially it studied societies and cultures for only sanitation issues.	Initially it studied societies and cultures in depth.
It studied hygiene, sanitation, water facilities, manual scavenging and disposal of waste of societies.	Anthropology studied marriage, family and kinship, political and religious life of the primitive societies.
It studies several aspects of sanitation it has limited focus on culture.	It studies every aspect of biology, culture and social life of preliterate, peasant and urban societies.
Sociology of sanitation studies evolution of human society in sanitation condition.	Anthropology studies the biological, social and cultural evolution of humankind in relation to each other.
Sociology of sanitation treats humans as objects subject to many forces.	Anthropology treats humans as endowed with consciousness. Does not treat humans as objects.
Sociology of sanitation focuses its attention on extensive study.	Anthropology focuses its attention on intensive study.

Through the references of co-disciplines we can understand that sociology of sanitation cannot be studied as an individual subject. There is inter-relationship between all the disciplines with sociology of sanitation. The study of other disciplines helps a reader to understand sanitation in a better way. Sociology of sanitation will be successful in giving sanitation a sociological touch with the help of other disciplines. As an emerging subject it is very important for sociology of sanitation to understand the relationship of other disciplines with sanitation. We have observed relationship as well as the difference of other discipline with sociology of sanitation.

CHAPTER 3

Sanitation and Other Social Institutions

Introduction

Society consists of people who live in groups, such as family and friendship groups. It is very important for us to understand how the social institutions are contributing to the problem of sanitation. Study of social institutions in relation to sanitation enables the researcher to understand the base of the problem of sanitation. Various institutions as family, caste, religion, education and village community have their own problems of sanitation. In this connection, an attempt is made here to study the relationship of sanitation with various social institutions.

Now more and more people come to live in towns and cities. Recent migrant faces the problem of accommodation. As a result some of them will end up living in slums. Slums generally face the problem of disposal of waste, problem of toilets and drinking water. Since sanitation is a serious problem in slums, study is taken up to consider the relationship between slums and sanitation. These days the corporate sector is showing a keen interest to improve the sanitation conditions in the society. So, the present study also includes the contribution of the corporate sector in sanitation.

3.1 Caste and Religion

Introduction

The institutions of caste and religion are essentially related to sanitation. It is in the caste system a person is born, brought up and dies. Caste also determines one's occupation and choice in marriage. Caste largely determines the differences in modes of domestic and social life. The contribution of caste system in the problem of sanitation is valuable in the present society. Studies have shown that there are differences among castes regarding sanitation. For example, Scheduled Castes (SCs) and Scheduled Tribes (STs), most disadvantaged groups in India, suffer from poor household sanitation and drainage. In 2005, 18 per cent and 23 per cent of ST households had toilets and drainage facilities respectively. SC households fared slightly better with 32 per cent having toilets and 46 having drainage.

Religion is a major concern of man. It is concerned with religious rituals, beliefs and practices. Religion guides and influences people's behaviour. In the above study, religion-based differences were found regarding sanitation. Hindu households had the lowest percentage of households with a toilet (41 per cent), followed by Muslim (60 per cent), Christian (70 per cent) and Sikh (74 per cent) households.

Religion

A religion is an organised collection of beliefs, cultural systems, and world views that relate humanity to an order of existence. Religion in India is characterised by a diversity of religious beliefs and practices. India is the home of important world religions as Hinduism, Buddhism, Jainism and Sikhism. Throughout India's history, religion has been an important part of the country's culture. Since majority (80 per cent) of Indians are Hindus, Hinduism not only influences the lives of Hindus but also people of other religions.

Hinduism consists of many diverse traditions as Shaivism, Vaishnavism and Shaktism. Hindu practices include daily rituals such as puja (worship) and recitations, annual festivals, and occasional pilgrimages. Hinduism is a categorisation of distinct intellectual or philosophical points of view, rather than a rigid, common set of beliefs. It is based on the concepts of *karma* and *dharma*, which influence the daily life of Hindus. Dharma is a concept of central importance in Indian philosophy and religion. It is a broad concept and it includes one's duties, rights, laws, conduct, virtues and right way of living. Though Karma literally refers to action, it is the volitional action that is undertaken deliberately or knowingly. It refers to the actions of the individual performed in this world. It is essentially related to the concept of rebirth. According to Hinduism man passes through a series of births and deaths and ultimately gets united with Brahma. The actions of present life will determine the future life. These concepts of Karma and Dharma are essentially connected with the caste system. The birth in a particular caste is determined by the actions of man in the past life.

The Caste System

The caste system is a unique system of stratification found in India. It is not only the oldest system of social stratification in India; it is also complex, hierarchical and inter-related system. It is also understood as the basis of division of labour in society. The social, religious, political and economic and cultural life of the Indians is influenced by the caste system. Any person desirous of knowing the Indian society should know the caste system.

Though in modern society, class system is the type of stratification found all over the world, in Indian society caste system exists with the class system. In spite of the efforts of social reformers and the governments to remove inequalities and the operation of forces of change such as industrialisation, urbanisation, modernisation, education etc., the caste system still persists. However, the structure and functions of caste have changed.

E.A.H. Blunt defines caste as *"an endogamous group or collection of endogamous groups, bearing a common name, membership of which is hereditary; imposing on its members certain restrictions in the matter of social intercourse; either following a common traditional occupation or claiming a common origin and generally regarded as forming a single homogenous community"*.

According to Prof M.N. Srinivas, caste is "a hereditary, endogamous, usually localised group having a traditional association with an occupation and a particular position in the local hierarchy of castes; relations between castes are governed among other things, by the concepts of purity and pollution, and generally, maximum commensality occurs within the caste".

According to Prof G.S. Ghurye, when Hindu society was governed by the social philosophy of caste, which was free from the influence of the modern concepts of rights and duties, caste exhibited following outstanding characteristics. They are: segmental division of society, hierarchy, restrictions on feeding and social intercourse, civil and religious disabilities and privileges of the different sections, restrictions on the choice of occupation and restrictions on marriage. Dumont gave three characteristics of caste. They are: separation in the matters of marriage and contact; division of labour and hierarchy. According to M.N. Srinivas, hierarchy, endogamy and hypergamy; occupational association; restriction on food, drink and smoking; distinction in custom, dress and speech; pollution; ritual and other privileges and disabilities; caste organisation and caste mobility are the important characteristics of caste system.

The origin of caste is associated with the *varna* system. Varna literally means colour and it refers to the fourfold division of Indian society into Brahmana, Kshatriya,Vaishya and Shudra. Acquiring and disseminating knowledge and performing sacrifices were the functions of the Brahmans and they enjoyed highest status. Next in rank were Kshatriyas and their duties were defence, administration and government. Third in rank were the Vaishyas whose functions included trade, commerce and agriculture. Finally, there were the Shudras who ranked the lowest and whose work was serving others through crafts and labour. The untouchables were outside the *varna* system and were known as Panchmas i.e., persons belonging to the fifth varna. Inter-mixture of these *varnas* gave rise to caste groups also known as '*jatis*'. Today in India we find around 200 caste groups in any linguistic area and these are subdivided into as many as 3000 caste groups which are endogamous and constitute the area of effective social life for the individual. Though the caste system is an aspect of Hindu society it is also found among members of other religions.

Much has been said about the security afforded by the caste system to each of the castes in it. According to Hutton an individual's membership in a caste canalises his choice in marriage, acts his trade union, his friendly or benefit society, his status club and his orphanage; it takes the place for him of health insurance and if need be provides for his funeral. Mencher is of the view that the security afforded by caste is only to the man at the top or perhaps in the middle ranges. From the point of view of people at the bottom the caste has functioned and continues to function as a very effective system of economic exploitation.

Caste and Occupation

Not only each *varna* had its own occupation, each caste had its own occupation. These occupations were hereditary. With the hereditary occupations of caste it became obligatory monopolies of families belonging to a particular caste. It is not merely a right to perform such occupations but it is the duty imposed by birth. Wiser analysed the *jajmani* system to explain the mutual services rendered by different castes. Dumont conceded that this system was based on religious values rather than economic logic.

Jajmani system was an economic system where lower castes performed various functions for upper castes and received grain and other materials in return. It was also a social system since different castes were included in the exchange of economic goods and services. According to Jajmani system there is exchange of goods and services between landowning higher castes and landless service castes. The service castes are traditionally weavers, leather workers, blacksmiths, goldsmiths, barbers, washermen and so far constituting a group of artisans serving the community. The landed higher castes the Jajman or the patron and the service castes are the *kameen* (workers). The Jajmani system is based on agricultural system of production and distribution of goods and services. It is the link between the landowning high caste groups and occupational castes.

Concepts of Purity and Pollution

The concepts of purity and pollution are closely related to caste hierarchy. The higher the rank of a Hindu, the higher the level of purity and lower the rank, the more impure he is. Dumont holds the notion of purity and pollution interlinked with the caste system and untouchability. Purity restrictions are prevalent regarding marriage, drink, food, touch and occupation. Purity is associated with ritual cleanliness such as daily bathing in flowing water, dressing in properly laundered clothes of approved materials, eating only the foods appropriate for one's caste, refraining from physical contact with people of lower rank, and avoiding involvement with ritually impure substances. The latter include body wastes and excretions, most especially those of another adult person. Contact with the products of death or violence are typically polluting and threatening to ritual purity.

As people are graded on the basis of purity and pollution, occupations are also graded. The occupations of the Brahmins, highest in the caste hierarchy, are pure whereas the occupations of the Untouchables, lowest in the hierarchy, are impure. Occupations like handling of leather or a dead cow, the removal of human waste, and work on the cremation ground, sweeping the streets etc., are considered as lowest and impure. The prohibition against touching a dead cow seems to have extended to the playing of a cowhide drum, hence the Pariah caste. In the North, leather workers are known as Chamars (now many call themselves Ravidasis, the name of an untouchable Chamar saint of medieval times). Traditionally, the scavenging caste was known as Bhangi but now they prefer to be called Valmikis, after the legendary author of the epic Ramayana. Other occupations such as washerman, fishing and toddy tapper connote untouchability in some areas and not in others.

Untouchability and Sanitation

Though the caste system is more than 2000 years old, untouchability is of later origin. Till about the second century A.D. certain castes like the Ayogava, Paulkasas and the Nishads were despised, but not were considered to Untouchables. The notion of purity and pollution as Dumont observed, is integrally linked with the practice of untouchability. Gradually this notion of purity and pollution freed itself from its specific and original task of separating Untouchables from others but began to be operative at different planes of the caste system. Imputed with maximum degree of ritual and social impurity, the occupations of these castes were held to be the lowest in the hierarchy. With the emergence of castes there also arose many castes among the Untouchables.

The Untouchables were involved in occupations which were usually considered to be polluting or defiling. Swine herding is defiling because swine defiles. Leather defiles and consequently the making and repairing of shoes became an occupation of the Untouchables. Occupations like scavenging, removing carcasses from the village etc., became the occupations of the Untouchables. Though they were related to other castes through the *jajmani* relations, they themselves were not eligible to receive several services by the other upper caste service specialists.

Traditionally, the Untouchables were assigned occupations which were ritually polluting as fishing, killing or disposing of dead cattle or working with their hides for living, pursuing activities that brought the participant into contact with emissions of the human body, such as faeces, urine, sweat, and spittle, a category that included such occupational groups as sweepers and washermen. They also conveyed death messages, collected wood for the funeral and did work as agricultural labourers. Later, the occupations of the Untouchables where stigmatised that these jobs done by the Untouchables only. With the passage of time the Untouchables and lower caste people were not allowed to do any other kind of jobs where they can get the social status as other caste people. So, their social mobility was restrained.

With the development of towns and cities, there arose the need for scavenging. As other people were not ready to do these jobs, municipalities had to bring Untouchables from the rural areas. In many towns and cities they are housed in colonies and work as sweepers, cleaners of sewage lines and sweepers of railways.

Untouchables and Access to Water and Sanitation

The Untouchables, traditionally, had the lowest social status in society. They lived on the periphery of society, and handled what were seen as unpleasant or polluting jobs. They suffered from social segregation and restrictions, in addition to being poor. They were not allowed to worship in temples with others, nor draw water from the same wells as others. Persons of other castes would not interact with them. If somehow a member of another caste came into physical or social contact with an untouchable, he was defiled and had to bathe thoroughly to purge himself of the contagion.

In the words of Hannah Johns caste-based discriminations leading to human rights violation regarding drinking water makes it an important social issue. Water is synonymous with life and, therefore, it's the most integral and inevitable part of each individual. These disabilities are most pronounced with regard to access to water and sanitation. The Dalits or SCs still face multiple deprivation and discrimination with regard to access to natural resources specially water. In rural India, access to water shows differential pattern across regions, where coupled with poverty, physical separation of hamlets, ideas of purity and pollution, poor access to government welfare programmes, play a critical role in determining the possibilities for a humane existence.

In India, more than 20 per cent of Dalits do not have access to safe drinking water. 48.4 per cent of Dalit villages are denied access to water source. Only 10 per cent of Dalit households have access to sanitation as compared to 27 per cent for non-Dalit households, and the vast majority of Dalits depend on the goodwill of upper-caste community members for access to water from public wells. Dalit women stand in separate queues near the bore well to fetch water till the non-Dalits finish fetching water. Dalits are not allowed to use taps and wells located in non-Dalit area. The following figures illustrate the differences between Dalits and non-Dalits household in respect of drinking water and sanitation. 27 per cent Dalit households have water sources within premises as compared to 45 per cent for the general population. Further, 23.7 per cent of Dalit households have access to latrine facility as compared to 42.3 per cent for general households.

Dalits and Manual Scavenging

Though we have progressed still there are towns and cities where scavenging is done manually. It is estimated that every day 13 lakh people in India of which more than 80 per cent are Dalit women are forced to clean human excrement with their bare hands, a practice called manual scavenging, for little to no wages. Of the 7,70,338 manual scavengers and their dependents across India, so far only 4,27,870 persons have been assisted under the National Scheme of Liberation and Rehabilitation of Scavengers (NSLRS) and the remaining number yet to be rehabilitated is 3,42,468. The biggest violator of the Employment of Manual Scavengers and Construction of Dry Latrines (Prohibition) Act of 1993 is the Indian Railways which has toilets dropping all the excreta from trains on the tracks and they employ scavengers to clean it manually. Access to sanitation is in a complete denial for these people as they have to do these menial jobs with their bare hands and they have higher risk of occupational illness and health hazards.

Dalit Women's Access to Water and Sanitation

Dalit women are the worst affected with the lack of access to water and sanitation. Their connection with water resources is very intricate. A Dalit woman will have all the burden of household work in the family and she will be the one who is responsible to bring water to the family and, therefore, she is the one who will be facing discrimination at the place. Even young girls from the family are assigned to do this job and they also face similar conditions. They even drop out from the school as collecting water from faraway distances become their primary responsibility and thereby losing any chance of being educated and earning money to the family. They will be the one who face verbal and physical abuse from the dominant castes and they will be under constant threat while collecting water from public wells and taps. Sometimes, dominant caste women don't allow Dalit women to touch the public source of water and they pour water to the pots of dalit women. As a result, how much water should they take back home also depends on the whims and fancies of dominant caste women. The concept of purity and pollution still dominate the thinking of people even after untouchability is abolished legally. Availability and distribution of water too has a strong relationship with the social structure. The control of water and other natural resources by dominant caste women stigmatise Dalit women and further make them feel helpless.

Lack of access to water directly affects the health of Dalit women and children. Lack of access to drinking water and good sanitation facilities leads to poor health thereby children drop out from school. Dalit women and girls spend half their calorie intake in fetching water. Poor quality water and sanitation facilities are also the main source of communicable and other waterborne diseases. Dalits further face discrimination and marginalisation while accessing health facilities and this vicious circle goes on.

3.2 Family and Kinship

Sociologists have regarded the family as the cornerstone of society. It forms the basic unit of social organisation and it is difficult to imagine how human society can function without it. The family has been seen as a universal social institution, an inevitable part of human society. Regarding the usefulness of the family, there are sharp differences of opinion among sociologists. Some regard it as an extremely beneficial institution while others have pointed out many undesirable consequences of the family.

Murdock defines family as *"a social group characterized by common residence, economic co-operation and reproduction. It includes adults of both sexes at least two of whom maintain socially approved sexual relationships, and one or more children, own or adopted, of the sexually co-habiting adults"*.

According to Ogburn and Nimkoff, *"family is more or less durable association of husband and wife with or without children or of a man or woman alone with children"*.

With the definition family we can understand the intimate social relationship of family with society. The society begins from home where family lives. Family is the base for all social relationships and all social actions. Family can be the reason for social problems and also it can be a solution. If a home is in good condition, it will result in good condition of society. The sanitational measures which are adopted in a family can bring clean and healthy environment in the family and also in the society. Cleanliness and hygiene should begin from the family. Most of the families in the present India lack proper sanitation facilities.

The family performs certain universal functions as sexual, reproductive, economic, educational and social. The sociology of sanitation mainly deals with the educational and social function of the family. The family has to take care of sanitation of the individual right from the childhood. Education begins from home and the family can be the one of the solutions for sanitation which is faced by the modern world. By providing education regarding sanitation the family can develop awareness in the child.

Kinship

Man is surrounded by a number of people in course of his social life. Of these people, some are very close and others are not so close. He is related to these people either on the basis of blood or marriage. The relations based on blood or marriage may be close or distant. The bond of blood or marriage which binds people together in group is called 'kinship'.

In the words of Robin Fox, *"kinship is simply the relations between kin that is persons related by real, putative or fictive consanguinity"*.

To A.R. Radcliffe Brown, kinship is a *"system of dynamic relations between person or persons in a community, the behaviour of any two persons in any of these relations being regulated in some way and to a greater or less extent by social usage"*.

Kinship patterns may be considered to include people related by both descent and by marriage. Human kinship relations through marriage are commonly called 'affinity' in contrast to the relationships that arise in one's group of origin, which may be called one's descent group. Kinship is the system where the responsibilities of family are distributed among the family members. In the field of sociology of sanitation kinship gives an explanation of family responsibilities regarding the sanitation of family. Generally, responsibility of the household activities lies in the hands of female members of the family.

Dimensions of Family Sanitation

In the dimension of family sanitation we can understand the area of sanitation in the family. It explains how a family can take care of sanitation issue. The family is the group of people who do their respective activities, but question of family sanitation arise when all the people are doing their personal jobs. The sanitation of family begins from the kitchen and goes on washing of cloths, cleaning of house and disposal of household wastage, disposal of human and animal wastage and safe storage of water storage etc.

Kitchen is the place where family cooks food for the members of the family. The members of the family should take care of the kitchen sanitation in the household activities for the better health of the family members. Disposal of kitchen waste and the kitchen water should be maintained properly. Similarly, the water after washing clothes should be properly disposed. In the same way, the wastage of the house after cleaning should be disposed in a hygienic way.

Human waste should be properly disposed. The toilets should be connected to the sewage provided by the municipality. Where there is no such arrangement toilet waste can be connected to the septic tank. In the villages also toilets should be built and the waste should be directed to septic tank. In such cases the septic tank should be constructed 150 ft away from the drinking water source. In the rural families the animal or human waste should not be exposed to the environment and it can be used for other purposes like bio-gas, fertilizers etc. While digging wells and building water tanks precautions should be taken that they are away from the drains.

Sanitation in Urban Families

In India, the urban families are not much worried about sanitation as the government agencies are taking care of sanitation. The urban agencies collect the waste from the houses or from the public wastage dump tanks and dispose it off. The human waste or animal waste is removed by connecting the toilets to the drains. The urban families have to dispose the waste through the way prescribed by the Corporations or Nagar Panchayats. Sometimes the drain pipes get blocked by people disposing of unwanted things through the drains which cause a serious damage to public health. Sanitation is a serious problem in slum areas. In the slum areas families should ensure that their areas are clean and both human and animal waste is properly disposed off.

Sanitation in Rural Families

The families in the rural places have to make themselves responsible for the purpose of better sanitation. Often, since the rural people have to earn for survival they forget the importance of sanitation. So, they get exposed to different kinds of deceases.

In rural areas since there are no toilet facilities people defecate in the open. They also may not dispose of the kitchen and other waste water properly. It is a common scene in rural areas that people bathe, wash cloths and wash domestic animals in the ponds from where they will bring water for household use. In such instances there is need to educate rural families in sanitation.

3.3 Education and Sanitation

Education is one of the important institutions in modern society. It is one of the basic activities of people in all human societies. Like religion, education is also an important agent of socialisation and social control. Education is also an important factor for improving one's status or position. Education performs various functions which are necessary for the continued existence of the society. The function of transmission of culture to the younger generation is performed by education. In recent years, education has become the major interests of sociologists. Hence, a new branch of sociology called 'Sociology of Education' has been established.

According to Emile Durkheim, *"education is the socialisation of younger generation"*. He further states that it is a continuous effort to impose on the child, the ways of seeing, feeling and acting which he could not have arrived at spontaneously.

Samuel Koenig defined education as *"the process whereby the social heritage of a group is passed on from one generation to another as well as the process whereby the child becomes socialised"*.

Education is the essential part of human life. It is the process which starts at birth and ends at death. People learn so many things every day for the betterment of their future. Education, in its general sense, is a form of learning in which the knowledge, skills, and habits of a group of people are transferred from one generation to the next. Education frequently takes place under the guidance of others, but may also be autodiadictic. Any experience that has a formative effect on the way one thinks, feels, or acts may be considered educative.

The processes of education and sanitation are closely related. The educational institutions are the primary level contributors to the awareness of sanitation in the human life and the society. The education acquired right from pre-primary level to graduate level is supposed to bring about awareness about sanitation. But it is the duty of the teachers in the pre-primary and primary levels to teach the children about health and hygiene. In the school level, it will be the responsibility of school management to take care of the issues regarding sanitation. At college level the students and the institution can provide knowledge for the youth about the importance of sanitation and also the students or the youth can create awareness about sanitation by conducting camps. The medical colleges are the most responsible kind of institutions in the matter of sanitation.

The relationship of education and sociology of sanitation is quite interesting. Sociology of sanitation studies the dimension of education in the field of sanitation. Sociology of education deals with education in depth also in reference to the sanitation conditions. Education as a social institution studies the contribution of educational institutions to the development of sanitation, health and hygiene. Sociology of sanitation can lead educational institutions to the better future where there will not be any sanitational issue. Sociology of sanitation finds out the problems of sanitation in the education sector, raises questions and generates answers to the existing problems.

The primary education system in India is one of the largest in the world with over seven lakh primary and upper primary schools, over 30 lakh teachers, and student strength exceeding 10 crores children. Though, India has made rapid progress in school enrolment, the dropout rates are a cause of concern. It is estimated that over 40 per cent of India's children drop out of school before finishing eighth grade. Most students who quit school are from the lowest rungs of Indian society. The widespread problems of child labour and early marriage for girls are clearly the factors. A good number of girls also dropout from school when they start menstruating. In some places, nearly 66 per cent of girls skip school during menstruation and one-third of them eventually drop out.

Sanitation in Educational Institutions

School authorities should ensure healthy environment. If the environment of school is good the children will get good education. The classrooms should be well built with black boards and other requirements. The cleanliness should be maintained both inside the class rooms and also outside. The walls should be painted frequently. It is a healthy practice to write sayings of great people on the walls. The waste of the school should be taken out of the school at least 100 meters away. The children should be provided with safe and adequate drinking water.

There should be adequate latrine or toilet facilities for the children in educational institutions. There should be separate toilets for boys and girls. School authorities should also ensure that these toilets are regularly cleaned. Government records show that two-third of the schools lack adequate sanitation facilities. The few that existed have mostly been rendered non-functional with no water supply dilapidated soak pits, no soap and other materials, even there is lack of awareness about sanitation in the schools. Construction of child friendly toilets where the basins are not high and also the water taps should be at approachable level is desirable.

School Sanitation and Hygiene Education (SSHE) is an essential component of the school education, which includes provision of toilet infrastructure and hand washing facilities in schools and hygiene education, to promote behavioural change amongst children. SSHE recognises the role of children as the best change agents in absorbing and popularising new ideas and concepts of sanitation not only in their schools but also in their families and neighbourhood. Schools are learning laboratories where habits of good sanitation practices, personal health and hygiene by children can go a long way in inculcating these habits when they become adults. Besides, presence of school toilets, safe drinking water, clean surroundings and basic information on hygiene improves the learning abilities of children, improves health, and improves attendance, especially of the girl child, with far reaching consequence on the health of the community.

School development committee is in existence in every school, private or government. This school development committee should be aware of the sanitation facilities at school. Firstly, the members should understand the importance of the sanitation condition of the school. It is important to motivate the school committee members, students and the public to improve the school environment; with fencing, planting of trees and to maintain the sanitary block properly. School development committee should organise campaigns in the village or in the area of the school for better sanitation facilities. School health clubs could be formed to discuss, take responsibility and participate in making provision of water and sanitation facilities in the schools as well as to maintain these facilities.

Sociology of sanitation gives detailed structure of school and sanitation for the better understanding of the sanitation at school. It is based on the belief that children are far more receptive to new ideas and are at an age when they can be influenced to cultivate the habits of good personal hygiene. School sanitation programme aims to make a visible impact on the health and hygiene of children through improvement in health and hygiene practices of children, their families and the communities. The promotion of personal hygiene and environmental sanitation within schools can help the children to adopt good habits during the formative years of their childhood.

3.4 Village Community and Ethnic Group

Village is one of the important social institutions of Indian society. Since around 70 per cent of Indian population lives in villages, India can be called a land of villages. Villages play an important role in the Indian social life. After independence there have been concerted efforts to bring the advantages of development to the villages. Though hard work, simplicity and plain thinking are the characteristics of village life, they evoke an image of people living in problems and difficulties. The life depicts a state of deprivation, dependence and low physical health.

Scattered throughout India are approximately five lakh villages. Generally distinction between rural and urban society is based on absolute population. According to Census of India any settlement with less than 5000 population is called rural. So, village communities are those communities which have less than 5000 population with less than 40 persons per square km, who are engaged predominately in agricultural or any other occupations related to nature. These settlements range from tiny hamlets of thatched huts to larger settlements tile-roofed stone and brick houses.

For Sanderson, *"a rural community is relatively small, sparsely populated settlement of socially homogeneous individuals, majority of who are engaged in agricultural pursuits"*.

According to Metcalfe, *"the village communities are little republics having nearly everything that they want within themselves and almost independent of any foreign relations"*.

Indian villages are characterised by smallness in size, primary relations, social homogeneity and informal social control. They are based on agriculture though there may be few non-agricultural pursuits. Village people are close to nature and their socio-economic activities are influenced by natural elements like rain, heat, frost and drought.

Institutions like the joint family, caste system, religion and the Panchayat system have a lasting impact on their lives. There is strong bond of unity and solidarity among them and neighbourhood plays an important role among them. Finally, the status of rural women is low.

We can observe that sanitation is a problem in all sections of Indian society. But, it has been more in the village and in the ethnic groups of India. The general health of the rural masses is poor and as result their death rate is higher. Due to rural setup their birth rate is also high. Lack of facilities such as pure drinking water, latrines, drainage, health centres, clinics, medicines, and hospitals etc., affect the general health of rural people. The villagers depend on few sources of drinking water such as wells, rivulets and ponds. In summer, most of the villages suffer from acute shortage of drinking water. Though 70 per cent of the people live in villages only 30 per cent of the doctors are available to them. Due to lack of nutritious food and the ill-food habits the village people are becoming victims of various diseases. They are not aware of preventive medicines through which they can prevent diseases. Generally, rural people neglect cleanliness and live in unhygienic environment. For example, village ponds are used for washing animals, washing cloths and bathing. This results in the spread of contagious diseases. Only five per cent of the rural people have latrines.

Causes for Lack of Sanitation

There are some important reasons for the sanitation problems faced by the people of village community. They are:

1. Poverty: Poverty is the major reason for lack of sanitation in rural societies. The families or households may not be able to bear the expenses to establish sanitation conditions. For example, it will be too difficult for a villager to construct a toilet for the use of the family. Thus, the families are forced to defecate in open spaces.

2. Lack of Education: The village people are comparatively less educated than urban people. They will not know the importance of the sanitation or good health conditions. Lack of knowledge about sanitation makes them the victims of unhygienic environment.

3. Lack of Water Resources: As it is observed that village people have less water resources for their life. They use the water from ponds or wells for their domestic purposes and they wash their cloths and animals with the same water. Thus, it leads to health problems.

4. Lack of Awareness about Health Related Diseases: It so happens that the village people will not worry until they get some diseases due to lack of sanitation. They are not worried about healthy environment rather than they prefer to go to hospital once they get health problems.

Only 19 per cent of villages have safe water supply while 51 per cent depend on wells, tanks and other sources. 32 per cent of the villages do not have any water supply. According to a recent UNICEF report, 69 crores (54%) people still defecate in the open and only about 50 per cent of Indians regularly wash their hands with soap after contact with excreta. The practice of manual scavenging still exists very much in our country which is the worst violation of an individual's right to life with dignity. However, the progress to end this practice is slow. A UN report in 2010 revealed that more Indians have access to mobile phones than to toilets.

Solutions for the Problems of Sanitation

For successful implementation of sanitation in India it is essential to understand the local conditions. Water is an important element and shortage of water leads to sanitation problems. In India, many of the villages suffer from shortage of water in summer. People have to carry water from long distances. For this, rain water harvesting is one of the methods suggested. Rain water harvesting captures rainwater before it can be washed away, to be used once the rains have passed and soil is dehydrated.

In areas of less rain the existing wells and lakes can be recharged. For this, usually pits are built around wells and lakes and the water is allowed to be percolated slowly. With this water level in wells and lakes rises, as a result people are able to get water in summer from the charged wells and lakes. Similarly, sand or earth can be used to build dams across rivulets in the areas where precious rainwater does not come often enough. Simple irrigation techniques should be used to irrigate farms and provide water for drinking. Solar powered water pumps can be used to pump water where there is electricity

It is essential that villagers should be helped to have low cost latrines. Researchers have developed various types of toilets. Bucket latrines are elevated temporary structure over large container or tank that can be lined with large, replaceable plastic bag. Secondly, there are chemical toilets which include portable prefabricated sanitation units with water-tight excreta-holding tank, containing a chemical solution to aid digestion and reduce odour. Thirdly, there are trench latrines. They are narrow trenches with temporary privacy structure where waste is covered daily with soil. Finally, there are Sulabh latrines with two leach pits. Each pit is connected to the toilets alternately after a period of one and half years. Dried excreta are used as manure. Cooking gas can also be produced through these leach pits.

People living in villages have poor hygiene behaviour and lack of sanitation due to ignorance. People should be educated in simple habits of sanitation. The children should be taught basic lessons in sanitation in schools. The people should be advised to drink water after boiling and to wash hands after going to the toilet, have a handkerchief to clean themselves etc.

Sanitation in Ethnic/Tribal Groups

Ethnic group or tribal group is a socially defined category of people who identify with each other based on shared social experience or ancestry. Membership of an ethnic group tends to be associated with shared cultural heritage, ancestry, history, homeland, language (dialect) or ideology, and with symbolic systems such as religion, mythology and ritual, cuisine, dressing style, physical appearance, etc. Ethnicity is an important means by which people may identify with a larger group. They regard ethnicity as a product of specific kinds of inter-group interactions, rather than an essential quality inherent to human groups. Processes that result in the emergence of such identification are called ethno-genesis. Members of an ethnic group, on the whole, claim cultural continuities over time, although historians and cultural anthropologists have documented that many of the values, practices, and norms that imply continuity with the past are of relatively recent invention.

India has second largest tribal population in the world, next only to Africa. Over 84 million of India's people belong to Scheduled Tribes. Tribal population makes up eight per cent of India's population and they are the poorest in the country. Tribals are said to be original inhabitants of India. So they are called 'Adivasis'. Verrier Elwin called them 'Aboriginals'. They are also called as hill tribes or primitive tribes. Other names used for tribals are Girijans, Vanvasis, Aranyavasis etc. Though most of the tribes are living in their traditional life, some of them are in transition. It is estimated that there are more than 400 tribal groups in India.

Problem of Health and Sanitation

Sanitation in ethnic groups is considered to be a serious problem. The problem of ill-health is one of the serious problems among tribals. The tribals suffer from various diseases like forest fever, yellow fever, typhoid, malaria, small pox, venereal diseases, skin diseases etc. The intensity of these diseases is serious due to the absence of proper treatment and medical assistance. Like teachers, doctors are also not showing any interest to work in tribal areas.

Since the tribals do not get nutritious food and their life is hard their life expectancy is short. They live in huts, with small opening which prevents the sunlight and free flow of fresh air. They use wood as fuel for cooking which gives lot of smoke. As a result, they suffer from TB, eye problems and other diseases. Some tribals keep the cattle very close to their houses. They also do not get pure drinking water. In summer, they face acute water shortage. As a whole, they do not live in hygienic conditions which results in various sicknesses.

Causes of Sanitation

Sanitation among the ethnic groups is really in a deplorable condition. One of the important causes is that of inadequate water facilities. The tribal people hardly have water sources for their survival. Secondly, the tribal or ethnic people are poor. They may not be able to construct a toilet for their sanitation, when it is hard for them to earn money for the daily survival. They also lack education as a result they are not aware of the principles of sanitation. The cultural attitudes of the tribal people sometimes becomes problem in establishing sanitation facilities. Even though government provides sanitation facilities they do not wish to use the sanitation facilities like toilets inside their living area. Psychologically also they feel ashamed to use the toilets.

Tribal Welfare

The government has been initiating various welfare and development schemes for the tribals. In addition to the Constitutional and welfare measures the government should take basic steps towards sanitation in tribal areas. These should include providing water for drinking, sanitation and agricultural purposes. People should be helped in building toilets and also people should be educated properly in sanitation. General education will go a long way in developing sanitation in tribal areas.

3.5 Slums and Sanitation

Introduction

Slums are a common feature of urban landscape. Rapid urbanisation, in wake of huge economic growth, coupled with shrinking job opportunities in rural areas has led to urbanisation. In the absence of affordable housing for the urban poor, slums have proliferated in all urban centres of India and the most visible impact can be seen in metropolitan areas. Municipal bodies and utility service providers are constrained by capacities and resources to tackle this challenge and the poorest of the poor, living in slum clusters, end up receiving extremely low levels of service delivery for water supply, sanitation and solid waste management. There is a huge disparity between the level of service prevailing in planned settlements and unorganised slum clusters, this leads to both social discontent and frustration among the poor.

According to UN Habitat, *"a slum is a heavily populated urban informal settlement characterised by substandard housing and squalor"*.

According to National Sample Survey Organisation (NSSO) slum is *"a compact settlement with a collection of poorly built tenements, mostly of temporary nature, crowded together usually with inadequate sanitary and drinking water facilities in unhygienic condition"*.

A Slum, for the purpose of Census, has been defined *"as a compact residential area of at least 300 population or about 60-70 households of poorly built congested tenements, in unhygienic environment usually with inadequate infrastructure and lacking in proper sanitary and drinking water facilities"*.

Slums are characterised by a cluster of houses therefore, an individual house is not considered as a slum. Slum areas are generally found in the periphery of old inner city, which is a marginalised area from the point of view of old settlements. A slum generally lacks access to public services such as sewerage, water supply, roads, street lamps etc., or even if they have them, they provide poor service facilities. It, generally, has high density of people within the dwelling unit on the basis of space occupancy. Residents of the slum belong to low income or economically deprived group such as poor tenants. Further, the residents of slums belong to lower classes and lower castes. Houses in the slum areas generally use low-cost building construction materials with poor hygiene and sanitation.

Slums are caused due to many reasons. In India, more and more people are migrating from rural areas to towns and cities because neither urban areas are expanding enough, nor the rural areas are developing. These migrants mostly flock to urban areas in search of jobs because development of industries and services are mainly concentrated in cities. Slums develop because there is shortage of land for housing and whatever land is available is beyond the reach of the urban poor. Further, lack of proper management and implementation of law on the part of urban authorities leads to slums.

Sanitation is a serious concern in slum areas. In slums there is no access to basic facilities such as toilets, water facilities, disposal of waste etc. Not being able to have proper sanitation leads them to harmful diseases. Some of the diseases that sanitation has brought to Indian slums are: diarrhoea, water diseases, parasitic worms/infestation and faecal orals diseases. Children are the most affected ones and because of these epidemics, there is a high infant mortality.

Causes for Poor Sanitation in slums: Social scientists have observed different reasons for poor sanitation in slums.

1. *Lack of Education and Awareness:* Lack of education is considered as one of the reason as education is the way through which people are supposed to get knowledge about the importance of sanitation in their daily lives. Because of lack of education and awareness people defecate in the open places which will harm the social life of slum dwellers. Further, people are not responsible for proper maintenance of sanitation facilities.
2. *Poverty among Slum Dwellers:* People living in slums are economically poor. When people hardly afford a house they cannot afford a toilet. So, they use the public toilet which is always stuck with the drainage problems and is unclean, or defecate in the open.
3. *Inadequate Water Supply:* Water is the requirement of people in all the communities. In the slums, getting adequate supply of water is a serious problem. Inadequate water supply in slums will lead to unclean toilets and also create problems of water for drinking, bathing, washing clothes etc.
4. *Unplanned Slums:* The government and the city planners are very busy in the planning of towns and cities where they ignore the poor people. This will force poor people to settle themselves

in very congested areas, where they will not get sufficient sanitation facilities.

Effects of Inadequate Sanitation

Lack of sanitation has far-reaching effects. It imposes significant public health and environmental costs on urban areas that contribute more than 60 per cent of the country's GDP. A 2006 report by the Water and Sanitation Programme (WSP) estimated that the total annual impact of inadequate sanitation in India amounted to a loss of Rs 2.4 trillion.

Sanitation problems have become more and more problematic in India because the governments have not invested enough in sanitation and water facilities. Poor sanitation gives many infections the ideal opportunity to spread, plenty of waste and excreta for the flies to breed on, and unsafe water to drink, wash with or swim in. Human excreta and other wastes lead to the transmission of many infectious diseases including cholera, typhoid, hepatitis, polio, cryptosporidiosis, and ascariasis. WHO (2004) estimates that about 1.8 million people die annually from diarrhoeal diseases where 90 per cent are children under five, mostly in developing countries.

Ascariasis is another disease associated with inadequate sanitation. Ascariasis is one of the most common human parasitic infections. Upto 10 per cent of the population in slums is infected with intestinal worms – a large percentage of which is caused by ascariasis. Trachoma, a disease causing blindness, is closely linked to poor sanitation and is one of the best examples of an infection readily preventable through basic hygiene.

Infectious agents are not the only health concerns associated with wastewater and excreta. Heavy metals, toxic, organic and inorganic substances also can pose serious threats to human health and the environment - particularly when industrial wastes are added to the waste stream. Nitrates from waste water can build up to high concentrations in water sources underground. This is associated with methaemoglobinaemia (blue baby syndrome) when contaminated water is used to prepare infant feeds.

Solutions to Sanitational Problems

The provision of safe and affordable sanitation in poor urban areas is one of the formidable challenges for rapidly growing cities in India. Even where urban sanitation improvements have occurred, these have largely been in more formal housing areas. It is in the poorest urban areas where millions of people live in densely-packed slums that the least progress is being made. One of the important solutions is to build sewerage systems. In India, due to the complexity and high cost of centralised sewer systems, most cities must intensify efforts to improve their on-site sanitation systems.

Secondly, India must concentrate on building toilets for the slum dwellers. According to the NSSO survey, only 19 per cent of urban Indian slums have owned and shared toilets available to a majority of their residents. In 50 per cent of slums, the prevalent form of sanitation for residents is public or community toilet blocks. The physical infrastructure of existing community toilets and public toilets should be updated to ensure that all have an adequate number of gender-separated toilets and washbasins; sufficient lighting and ventilation; and enough water for all services. Number of both the community and public toilets should be enhanced. These toilets should be maintained by the community.

Subsidised individual facilities are usually facilities built through government subsidies or NGOs for individual families who then have the responsibility of maintaining them. Often they end up being shared by more families than intended. Dry latrines can also be planned. More than anything else, awareness should be created among the slum dwellers to end open defecation.

Conclusion

The life in the slums is not a life anybody would like to live in. It is full of diseases and lack of essential things such as water and sanitation. The difficulties and obstacles they have to face are so hard. Their prize at the end is death or if they are lucky enough they can escape and get education; but that only happens to certain people who are not a lot. The majority of them live their lives in the slum areas until they take their last breath.

3.6 Health Institutions and Sanitation

Health institutions are the institutions which are carrying the responsibility of social health. Health institutions are the only solutions for the result of lack of sanitation. Health institutions include small clinics, hospitals, laboratories and the medical dispensaries which are working for the betterment of the society. So, sanitation is one of the important aspects of health institutions. Health institutions have requirements for sanitation as they have to deal with patients who are infected with diseases such as cholera, typhoid and hephatitis. Staff caring for these patients is exposed to higher risk of infection than the general public, as are other patients are exposed to higher risk of infection than the general public, as are other patients who may be weak and unable to fight infection. So, sanitation has become the important need in the health institutions.

Important Problems of Hospital Sanitation

There are many problems associated with sanitation in hospitals and clinics.

Proper Infrastructure: Health institutions like hospitals, clinical laboratories and others should maintain a proper infrastructure for the maintenance of better sanitation. The building should be properly maintained. They should have better facilities of toilet, waste disposal room, rest room for the workers and for the people, proper drinking water facilities and wash basins.

Disposal of Hospital Waste: The health institutions should take care of the disposal of waste. It may be biological or chemical waste but it should be disposed with proper care. This waste should be disposed in particular condition in which the environment or people will not get affected. Hospital wastes are very dangerous for the society. There are various types of wastage generated in healthcare units such as general waste or non-infectious waste, bio-medical waste, contaminated waste, pathological waste, human waste, infectious waste, chemical waste, liquid waste, hazardous waste, blood and its waste products, radioactive waste etc.

Proper Labour Force: The health institutions should keep proper and sufficient labour force. In some of the hospitals the work is more than the labour force.

Awareness of Hospital Sanitation: It is very important to create awareness among the hospital staff and the people who come to use hospital for their requirement. Some of the people don't know about the importance of sanitation in health institutions.

Solutions for Hospital Sanitation

There are number of points which must be addressed to while planning for hospitals and health centres.

1. Toilets for patients with infectious diseases should be separated from toilets for the staff and other patients. If possible, staff treating infected patients must not work with other patients who may be vulnerable to infection.
2. Toilet facilities should be thoroughly cleaned several times during the day.
3. Excreta and sullage from hospitals and health centres should be correctly treated where they cannot contaminate water supplies or areas of human activity such as fields.
4. Facilities for washing and sterilising bed pans hygienically should also be available.
5. Chlorination of water supplies and storage tanks may be practiced if water does not meet quality standards.
6. Refuse must be disposed of safely. Bins with well fitted lids or sacks should be used. Refuse must be disposed of regularly and safely.
7. Any contaminated materials such as syringes, needles, drips and bedding should be collected separately from other waste and incinerated on the hospital site, well away from patients, to kill germs present.

General Hygiene

Building up immunity is vital to prevention of communicable diseases. It includes having a well balanced diet, adequate rest and sleep, regular exercise and being a non-smoker. Hygiene aims not only at preserving health but also at improving it. The purpose of hygiene is to allow man to live in healthy relationship with his environment. Air, weather, soil, waste, bodily cleanliness, disinfection and nutrition are the widely differing concerns of the hygienist.

Good personal, food and environmental hygiene should be observed. Since many germs are transmitted through contact or droplet, performing hand hygiene properly and maintaining respiratory hygiene are two prerequisites for the prevention of infections. Besides observing their own personal hygiene practices, staff should also supervise and provide support to residents and visitors to enhance their good personal hygiene practices.

Hygiene is a set of practices performed for the preservation of health. While in modern medical sciences there is a set of standards of hygiene recommended for different situations, what is considered hygienic or not can vary between different cultures, genders and sectarian groups. Some regular hygienic practices may be considered good habits by a society while the neglect of hygiene can be considered disgusting, disrespectful or even threatening.

The hygienic conditions in some of the public hospitals in India are deplorable. Nobody takes any interest in maintaining cleanliness in hospitals. Though officials visit the hospitals very often, things have not turned any better. Usually the hospital authorities give the excuse, namely, that the patients were brought in a critical condition and there was little that could be done. Infections spread very fast from patient to patient and the hospital authorities are unable to prevent it.

The public hospitals have to be provided with medicines that are required to treat patients and diseases. Those familiar with the conditions in government hospitals know that the infrastructure is hopelessly inadequate to deal with emergencies when a large number of patients come in at a time. Often two or three children are kept cramped in the same bed which helps spread infection. And the hospitals are often not able to treat the different types of infections the children are suffering.

The problem from not being careful and extra clean along with sterilising equipments has caused healthy people to become infected with these deadly diseases.

Those who don't agree with this problem of sanitation might oppose it on the thought that hospitals are better off today than it was back in the old days. We have to use the technology that we have now for better sanitation. It's important to prevent the spread of germs and infectious diseases. Washing your hands with soap and wearing gloves along with using hand sanitiser are modern ways of keeping clean. Though we have these, doctors and nurses tend to be too busy and forget to use or practice the use of these, thus, inhibits the full potential of it.

A major problem in hospitals and other healthcare establishments is hospital infections, i.e., infections contracted within the hospital. Hospital hygiene is aimed at protecting patients in healthcare institutions against additional diseases, but it also aims to protect healthcare workers.

Personal Hygiene of the Workers

The following rules can be applied for personal hygiene and sanitation in the workplace of hospitals:

- *Uniform* should be worn only in the workplace. The uniform should be changed daily and immediately if visibly soiled. Workers of the hospital should not mix uniform and private clothing. Uniform should not be laundered at home due to the prevention of disease.
- *Shoes* should be sturdy (non-slip, good grip, no high heels) and easy to clean (shoes made of suede, felt or textiles are not suitable for hygiene reasons) should clean regularly (around once weekly) and if visibly soiled.
- *Hair* should be worn such that there is no need to keep touching it with one's hands (pushing it back) and if necessary, protective headgear should be used to fully cover the hair.
- *Hand* gloves should be used, finger nails should be taken care of and cut short. Workers should not keep long nails.
- *Jewellery* should not wear around hand but other jewellery may be worn provided that it is not excluded by the following: interfere with working activities, hazardous, difficult to clean and/or disinfect.
- *Eating, drinking, smoking* should be avoided in the workplace and food and drinks must not be stored in the workplace.
- *Personal protective equipment* in workplaces with a high risk of contamination or splashing of possibly infectious materials, personal protective equipment must be worn (gown or apron, disposal shoes, goggles, or facial masks).

Understanding the relationship of social institutions with sanitation has been considered as one of the important task in the field of sociology of sanitation. With the relationship of social institutions with sanitation we can understand the past and the present of the sanitation issues in the societies. The role of social institutions helps us to find out the solution for the existing problems of sanitation.

3.7 Corporate Sector and Sanitation

The corporate sector consists of companies, financial institutions, producer boards, State Owned Enterprises (SOEs) and government organisations. It excludes households and individual persons. Basically it includes companies, industries and business houses. The corporate sector is associated with certain responsibility towards the community or society and it is known as Corporate Social Responsibility.

The concept of corporate social responsibility became prominent in the U.S. in 1960s. Corporate social responsibility is a process with the aim to embrace responsibility for the company's actions and encourage a positive impact through its activities on the environment, consumers, employees, communities, stakeholders and all other members of the public sphere who may also be considered stakeholders. Proponents argue that corporations make more long-term profits by operating with a perspective and they have the responsibility of sharing directly the profits with the community or society.

Corporate social responsibility is a management concept whereby companies integrate social and environmental concerns in their business operations and interactions with their stakeholders. Secondly, companies have a lot of power in the community and in the national economy. They control a lot of assets, and may have billions in cash at their disposal for socially conscious investments and programmes.

The corporate sectors of the society have understood the importance of social responsibility and as a result are involved in developmental works right from the village till large urban centres. In fact, the corporate sector is well suited to the service the poor because of their knowledge and understanding of the needs of the communities. At the rural level, the corporates are involved in rural development projects as education, construction of roads, health and sanitation projects. In the cities, they are involved in the development of slums and other poor areas.

Improving water and sanitation service delivery to the poor is a key factor in reducing poverty. So, in this way they can involve both in rural and urban areas, in solving the problem of sanitation.

Such initiatives can contain the following components:

1. ***Environmental Protection:*** The focus in this component is on finding sustainable solutions for the use of natural resources in order to reduce corporate's impact on the environment. Over the past several years, environmental responsibility has expanded to involve substantially more than compliance with all applicable government regulations or even a few initiatives such as recycling or energy efficiency. Regarding water and sanitation, a company can show its corporate social responsibility, for example, by constructing improved and innovative wastewater treatment plants or sustainable sanitation as well as applying rainwater harvesting.

2. ***Human Rights:*** Business practices can profoundly affect the rights and dignity of employees and communities. The main focus is on developing workplaces free from discrimination where creativity and learning can flourish decent codes of professional conduct and where a proper balance can be maintained between work and other aspects of our lives. Regarding water and sanitation, a company can show its corporate social responsibility by providing clean and safe sanitation facilities and adequate water supply to its employees and in their adopted areas in order to ensure their human rights.
3. ***Health Promotion:*** The workplace is now recognised as an important setting for health promotion. A company can promote adequate health standard by providing a healthy and safe work place for its employees and invest in health promotion in other projects implemented with development agencies. Regarding water and sanitation, a company can show its social corporate responsibility by contributing to health promotion projects in partnership with development actors such as NGOs. These projects may raise awareness about the correlation of sanitation, hygiene and public health.
4. ***Education:*** As education is one of the key elements of sustainable development and pro-poor growth, businesses, working together with the public sector or civil society can make an important contribution to providing an access to quality education of all. In this connection, a company can show its social corporate responsibility by supporting development organisations in education campaigns and projects related to safe sanitation behaviours.
5. ***Human Disaster Relief:*** Companies, in cooperation with public sector, civil society and international organisations have played an important role in supporting humanitarian relief operations. It can show its social corporate responsibility by supporting people in disaster areas with clean drinking water or sanitation facilities.

Apart from the government, coordinated efforts from all sections of society are needed to achieve the development of the society. The corporate sector is well suited to service the poor because of their knowledge and understanding of the needs of their communities. Moreover, since 'health' is one of the top priority activities under the wider umbrella of corporate social responsibility, sanitation demands a greater focus. With this background, sociology of sanitation brings a series of case studies, each describing how corporate sector has contributed in providing sanitation services and improving health of people.

Corporate sector's involvement in sanitation is to provide sanitation to Below Poverty Line (BPL) households by construction of individual household latrines. Assistance was also extended for construction of school toilet units, Anganwadi toilets and Community Sanitary Complexes (CSC) apart from undertaking activities under Solid and Liquid Waste Management (SLWM). To give a fillip to the CSC, Government of India also launched the *Nirmal Gram Puraskar* (NGP) that sought to recognise the achievements and efforts made in ensuring full sanitation coverage. The award gained immense popularity and contributed effectively in bringing about a movement in the community for attaining the cleanliness status thereby significantly adding to the achievements made for increasing the sanitation coverage in the rural areas. Encouraged by the success of NGP, the CSC is being renamed as "*Nirmal Bharat Abhiyan*" (NBA). The objective is to accelerate the sanitation coverage in the rural areas so as to comprehensively cover the rural community through renewed strategies and saturation approach. NBA envisages covering the entire community for saturated outcomes with a view to create Nirmal Gram Panchayats.

Total Sanitation Campaign

The Foundation works to complement the community led Total Sanitation Campaign, which is now known as *Rashtriya Swatchata Abhiyan* initiated by the Government of India. To make the programme people centric, the Foundation helps in increasing hygiene-related awareness amongst the communities, encourages people to prevent open defecation and mobilises the villagers towards achieving '*Nirmal Gram*', the total sanitation campaign was launched in the villages.

The programme recognises the diverse needs and capacities of the community and strives to seek peoples' participation in making the village an ideal place to inhabit. The aim is to help people achieve 100 per cent sanitation in their villages. Total sanitation programme introduced so many corporate sectors in the field of sanitation. The contributions of some of the important corporate sectors in the development of sanitation are given below.

Adani Foundation

The Adani Group is a business conglomerate headquartered in Ahmedabad doing business in the resources, logistics, agri-business and energy sectors. The Group is the largest port developer and operator in India with Mundra being the country's largest commercial port. It owns Fortune, India's largest edible oil brand through a joint venture with Willmar in Singapore. The Flagship Company of the Adani group is Adani Enterprises Limited. In April 2014, it added the fourth unit of 660 MW at its Tiroda Power plant, making Adani powers the largest private power producer of the country. Now it is trying to acquire Udupi Power Corporation Limited (UPCL).

Adani Foundation, the conglomerate of the Adani Group, was established in May, 1996. It is situated in Ahmedabad. It looks after the Corporate Social Responsibility related activities of the Group, which has now become synonymous with creating wealth and providing better living for the people. It began in a small way by working with a few rural communities around its Port at Mundra.

The Foundation runs projects in four key areas:

1. *Education* – Quality education and promoting girl child education.
2. *Community Health* – Innovation projects to meet the local needs and facilities basic healthcare to all by bridging gaps.
3. *Sustainable Livelihood Development* – Holding hands of all marginalised groups to improve livelihood opportunities and thus the quality of life at the local community level.
4. *Rural Infrastructure Developments* – Needs based quality infrastructure for better inclusive growth.

Rural sanitation is perhaps one of their most integral fields of their operation. As the root cause of health problems lies in poor sanitation practices, a movement to create awareness, motivates communities to accept the general concept of household sanitation unit and encourage people to get the same facilities has been the mission. The Foundation has aided six villages in getting 100 per cent household toilet coverage status by supporting the construction of more than 700 toilets during 2008-2009. The target for the year 2009-2010 was to cover 19 more villages with the same sanitary set up which required the construction of more than 1500 individual toilets in these areas with proper sewage.

Biocon

Biocon Limited, founded in 1978, is a biopharmaceutical company based in Bangalore. Within biopharmaceuticals, the Company manufactures generic active pharmaceutical ingredients that are sold in the developed markets of the United States and Europe. It also manufactures biosimilar Insulins, which are sold in India as branded formulations and in both bulk and formulation forms. While Biocon was involved in community programmes from inception, it started a corporate social responsibility wing, the Biocon Foundation, in 2004 through which it works in the areas of health, education and infrastructure, especially in rural areas.

Biocon Foundation's sanitation initiative began in 2007 with an aim to offer poor rural communities access to safe and sustainable sanitation facilities. Through their programmes, they endeavour to improve the health status of underprivileged village communities, decrease the environmental impact of inadequate sanitation practices and ultimately, generate economic benefits by increasing the number of workdays.

With technical help from the Karnataka Rural Water Supply and Sanitation Agency, the Bangalore Urban Zilla Panchayat, the Huskur Gram Panchayat and building contractors chosen from the community itself, Biocon Foundation is implementing a comprehensive sanitation and hygiene programme in Huskur. The aim is to ensure every household in the villages has its own private toilet and to encourage the use of household toilets by making community members understand the link between illness and unsanitary behaviour. A survey undertaken with the help of the Gram Panchayat committee revealed that out of a total of 1123 households, only 249 (22%) had toilets at home. Biocon Foundation and the Embassy of Ireland, New Delhi will bear the cost of construction however, to create a sense of ownership of the project and the programme, each beneficiary household is to contribute Rs 1000 towards the construction and also be responsible for digging the pit. They believed that pilot project will make Huskur Gram Panchayat a model of household and environmental cleanliness thus motivating other Gram Panchayats in Anekal (near Bangalore) to emulate it. To relieve villages surrounding the temple, Biocon Foundation has built a community toilet block with the help from the Bangalore Urban Zilla Panchayat and the Huskur Gram Panchayat.

Aditya Birla Group

The Aditya Birla Group is an Indian multinational conglomerate named after Aditya Vikram Birla, headquartered in Mumbai. It operates in 33 countries with more than 1,36,000 employees worldwide. The group was founded by Seth Shiv Narayan Birla in 1857. The group interests are in sectors as viscose staple fibre, metals, cement, viscose filament yarn, branded apparel, carbon black, chemicals, fertilisers, insulators, financial services, telecom, BPO and IT services.

For over 50 years now, the Aditya Birla Group has been and continues to be involved in meaningful, welfare driven initiatives that distinctively impact the quality of life of the rural poor. The vision is to actively contribute to the social and economic development of the communities in which they operate, in so doing build better sustainable way of life for the weaker sections of the society and raise the country's human development index.

Aditya Birla Group is engaged in 300 villages with the hope to develop model villages. Making of a model village entails ensuring self-reliance in all aspects viz., education, healthcare and family welfare, infrastructure, agriculture and watershed management, and working towards sustainable livelihood patterns. Fundamentally, ensuring that their development reaches a stage wherein village committees take over the complete responsibility and the teams become dispensable. It is against this backdrop that one will dwell on the Group's experience in sanitation.

The Foundation has been providing water on a continual basis to the villages that are in proximity to their plants. But, this is for their basic needs. With water scarcity, open spaces seemed perhaps the only option to the villagers. Hence, to tackle the issues related to sanitation, they had to first grapple with the challenge of tapping new avenues of water. For this, the Foundation evolved a multi-pronged strategy based on an integral development plan. Various schemes of the government viz., Swajaldhara Yojana, Jalnidhi, Rajiv Gandhi National Drinking Water Scheme, and many more were used and these schemes enabled them to extend their reach as catalysts benefitting thousands of villagers.

The second plank of their strategy entailed a massive awareness drive on cleanliness linking it with hygiene and sanitation. District Authorities and NGOs were roped in this endeavour to sensitise and persuade the villagers. The Foundation recoursed to 'Nukkad Nataks' (street plays) and puppet shows to drive messages linking hygiene and good health to sanitation. It was highlighted how they could prevent water borne and sanitation diseases from occurring and spreading, if we were able to have toilet blocks in the villages.

The third plank was to get this movement going amongst the villagers. In the village of Devari (Renukoot, Uttar Pradesh), the campaign was started in a creative way. Using the platform, of the Panchayat General Meeting, the Foundation began energising the villagers by highlighting how Devari can be positioned on the map of UP, if it received the President's Award under the *Nirmal Gram Yojana*. The thought of acquiring this fame was a great booster. This did help, and a year down the line, the Devari Pradhan did receive this Award.

Of the 300 model villages that the Foundation is engaged in, 60 have already reached the level of model villages and most of these have reasonable sanitation facilities. Of these, some have attained 100 per cent sanitation. In the last five years the Foundation has set up over 10,000 toilets in villages in proximity to the company's plants across India. These include community complexes and at several schools as well. In doing so, they have helped to provide sanitation facilities to nearly a million people in the villages that we work in, through collaborations and in an inclusive manner.

Ambuja Cement Foundation

Ambuja Cements Limited, formerly known as Gujarat Ambuja Cement Limited, is a major cement producing company in India. It was founded in 1986 and has its headquarters at Mumbai. The Group's principal activity is to manufacture and market cement and clinker for both domestic and export markets.

The Ambuja Cement Foundation is the Corporate Social Responsibility wing of Ambuja Cements Ltd. that works with the rural communities surrounding Ambuja's manufacturing sites. The Foundation is engaged in a variety of people-centric, integrated rural development projects. Since inception, the Foundation has expanded its reach and diversified its programmes to include as many members of its stakeholder group as possible.

Access to water has been one of the priority issues facing many villages. Hence, since inception, the Foundation has undertaken water resource management as one of our key focus programmes to be implemented across states in India to create an impact on the environment, groundwater resources, agriculture and allied livelihood activities. The programme lays emphasis on sustainability through community action, and involves water harvesting, conservation and bringing about an attitudinal change among communities. The focus has been on creating necessary infrastructure for water conservation, like check dams and roof rain water harvesting structures. The Foundation also works on reviving traditional water management resources like ponds, and have also converted mined out pits to serve as water reservoirs. These efforts have helped increase water storage capacities and recharged the groundwater in many villages. The Foundation also collaborates with various state governments, local NGOs and academic institutions to implement various state specific water conservation programmes. It also provides information and education on government policies on sanitation, hygiene and safe drinking water.

Tata Group and Sanitation

Tata Group is an Indian multinational conglomerate company headquartered in Mumbai. It encompasses seven business sectors: communications and information technology, engineering, materials, services, energy, consumer products and chemicals. Tata Group was founded in 1868 by Jamsetji Tata as a trading company. It has operations in more than 80 countries across six continents. Tata Group has over 100 operating companies with each of them operating independently. Out of them 32 are publicly listed. The major Tata companies are Tata Steel, Tata Motors, Tata Consultancy Services (TCS), Tata Power, Tata Chemicals, Tata Global Beverages, Tata Teleservices, Titan Industries, Tata Communications and Taj Hotels.

The Tata trusts are the unsung heroes of an extraordinary saga of philanthropy that has enriched India and its citizens in myriad ways. There are two principal trusts operating under the Tata umbrella. Sir Dorabji Tata Trust was established in 1932 by Sir Dorabji Tata, the elder son of group founder Jamsetji Tata. The Sir Dorabji Tata Trust and the Allied Trusts are India's oldest and largest philanthropic foundations. The trusts offer monetary assistance to students and economically disadvantaged patients, make financial contributions to institutions and provide financial support to more than 600 non-governmental organisations in the country.

The second is Sir Ratan Tata Trust and Navajbai Ratan Tata Trust. The Sir Ratan Tata Trust (SRTT) is a philanthropic institution established in 1919 in accordance with the will of Sir Ratan Tata, the younger son of group founder Jamsetji Tata. The Navajbai Ratan Tata Trust, formed in 1974, works together with SRTT to bestow grants. The trusts seek to be a catalyst in development through giving grants to institutions in various areas. They also provide grants for endowments, have a separate programme for small grants and give grants to individuals for education and medical relief. The bulk of the trusts' institutional grants are in the areas of rural livelihoods and communities, and education.

The trusts focus on the broad areas of agriculture, drinking water and sanitation, and microfinance. One of the important programmes is Mission Swach Jal. The initiative creates awareness among communities across India about safe drinking water and its impact on health, while providing alternative sustainable water supply systems.

Infosys and Sanitation

Infosys is an Indian multinational corporation that provides business consulting, information technology, software engineering and outsourcing services. It is headquartered in Bengaluru, Karnataka. Infosys is the third-largest India-based IT services company by 2014 revenues. On 31 March, 2014, its market capitalisation was Rs 1,88,510 crores ($31.11 billion), making it India's fifth largest publicly traded company. Infosys was co-founded in 1981 by N. R. Narayana Murthy, Nandan Nilekani, N. S. Raghavan, S. Gopalakrishnan, S. D. Shibulal, K. Dinesh and Ashok Arora after they resigned from Patni Computer Systems.

Established in 1996, the Infosys Foundation supports programmes and organisations devoted to the cause of the destitute, rural poor, mentally challenged, and economically disadvantaged sections of the society. Its mission is to work in remote regions of several states in India. The Infosys Foundation works with local administration to achieve community development goals. They construct roads, provide drainage systems and electricity, and rehabilitate flood-affected victims in rural areas. The Foundation has donated more than Rs 40 crores for rural development and livelihood projects such as awareness campaigns on hygiene, sanitation, vocational training and entrepreneurship.

The Foundation took up sanitation and relief work at tsunami affected areas of Tamil Nadu and the Andaman Islands, earthquake-affected areas of Kutch, cyclone-devastated areas of Odisha, tribal areas of Kalahandi in Odisha and drought-hit areas of Andhra Pradesh. In Karnataka, it constructed 3,000 homes with better sanitation facilities for flood victims of Belgaum, Gulbarga, Dharwad, Gadag, Bagalkot, Bijapur, and Karwar. It donated healthy food for school going children that is midday meal programme of the Akshaya Patra Foundation, Bangalore, for poor children in North Karnataka and constructed 10,000 toilets in the backward districts of Karnataka.

Reliance Industries

Reliance Industries Limited is an Indian conglomerate holding company headquartered in Mumbai. The company is present in many business sectors across India including petrochemicals, construction, communications, energy, healthcare, science and technology, natural resources, retail, textiles, and logistics. It is the second-largest publicly traded company in India by market capitalisation and is the second largest company in India by revenue after the state-run Indian Oil Corporation. The company contributes approximately 14 per cent of India's total exports. The company was co-founded by Dhirubhai Ambani and his cousin Champaklal Damani in 1960s as Reliance Commercial Corporation. In 1965, the partnership was ended and Dhirubhai continued the business of the firm.

Reliance Foundation was set up in 2010 as an expression of its vision towards sustainable growth in India. Reliance's contribution to the community are in areas of health, education, infrastructure development (drinking water, improving village infrastructure, construction of schools etc.), environment (effluent treatment, tree plantation, treatment of hazardous waste), relief and assistance in the event of a natural disaster, and miscellaneous activities such as contribution to other social development organisations etc.

Reliance Industries has developed Community Medical Centres near most of its manufacturing divisions to provide comprehensive health services covering preventive, promotive and curative healthcare services to the community from neighbouring villages. The manufacturing divisions conduct regular health checkups for children in schools of their respective neighbouring regions. A unique joint initiative of Reliance and National Association of Blind, Project Drishti has undertaken over 9,000 free corneal graft surgeries for the visually challenged Indians from the underprivileged segment of the society.

The Primary Health Centre (PHC) at Dahej, Bharuch district, adopted by Reliance under the National Rural Health Mission Programme caters to the community health needs of 23 surrounding villages. Dhirubhai Ambani Hospital at Lodhivali, Maharashtra continues to play a significant role in improving the quality of life in surrounding communities. Reliance Industries has spent over Rs 700 crores of its net profit on corporate social responsibility last fiscal and significant sums went into healthcare and rural development initiatives.

Conclusion

Even before the concept of Corporate Social Responsibility came into practice the Tata Group has involved itself in philanthropic works. Organised philanthropic activities of Reliance industries started as late as 2010 with the starting of Reliance Foundation. However, most of the corporates in India are involved in philanthropic activities and among them many are involved in sanitation ventures both in rural and urban areas. In this connection, the words of Sudha Murthy, Chairperson of Infosys Foundation are inspiring. Mrs Murthy said the advice she got from J.R.D. Tata when she left her job to assist her husband Narayana Murthy to start up company, Infosys, which changed her life. He told her, "you are only trustee of money and it always changes hands. When you are successful, give it back to society that gave you so much goodwill".

References

Ghurye, G.S. 1969. *Caste, Class and Occupation.* Bombay: Popular Prakashan.

Gore, M.S. 1970. *Immigrants and Neighbourhoods: Two Aspects of Life in a Metropolitan City*. Bombay: Tata Institute of Social Sciences.

Gupta, Dipankar (ed). 1993. *Social Stratification.* Delhi: Oxford University Press.

Hutton, J.H. 1963. *Caste in India: Its Nature, Function and Origin* Bombay: Oxford University Press.

Lynch, Owen. 1974. *The Politics of Untouchability.* Delhi: National Publishing House.

Mahar, Michael J. 1969. *Untouchables in Contemporary India.* Tucson:The University of Arizona Press.

Ooman, T.K. 1994. Panchamas to Dalits: The Context and Content of Identity. *Times of India,* May 11.

Pais, Richard. 2004. *Scheduled Castes: A Study in Employment and Social Mobility.* Mangalore: Mangala Publications.

Shah, A.M. 1988. *Division and Hierarchy.* Delhi: Hindusthan Publishing Corporation.

CHAPTER 4

Scientific Methods in Sociology of Sanitation

Introduction

Sociology of sanitation is the scientific study of sanitation in society. Scientific study of sociology of sanitation reveals the depth and understanding of sanitation as a concept, method and perspective. The study of particular subject should be taken in way that the reader will get all answers to the problems or doubts regarding the subject. In the process of scientific study social scientists gain knowledge of a particular subject and they are able to interpret that knowledge for the better understanding of the social problems. Thus, social scientists should consider sociology of sanitation as a subject of study and it should follow the methods of sociological research which will generate accurate knowledge about the subject. The method followed in the study of sociology of sanitation is scientific. The scientific method of study consists of different steps. We should also follow a particular design for the study. The data can be collected from various sources.

4.1 Scientific Method

Scientific method is very essential in the study of sciences, both physical and social. It is a right procedure of investigation. It is a systematic effort to discover new facts and to test the old facts. Scientific method is a branch of study which is concerned with observed facts systematically classified and which includes trustworthy methods of discovery of truths. Scientific method is procedure or a mode of investigation by which scientific and systematic knowledge is acquired. It would be difficult to comprehend the nature and content of research without an appreciation of the method we designate as scientific. Research is an endeavour to discover answers to problems through the application of scientific methods to the knowable universe.

George Lundburg defines scientific method as one consisting of systematic observation, classification and interpretation of data.

According to Lastrucci, scientific method is an objective, logical and systematic method of analysis of phenomena, devised to permit the accumulation of reliable knowledge. It is a systematised form of analysis.

Scientific method differs from day-to-day generalisation. Scientific method lies in the degree of formality, rigourousness, verifiability and validity. According to Karl Pearson, scientific method consists of three important features i.e., (1) careful and accurate classification of facts and observation of their correlation and sequence; (2) discovery of scientific laws with the aid of creative imagination and (3) self-criticism.

Features of Scientific Method

Below important features of scientific method are examined:

1. *Reliance of Empirical Evidence:* The researcher is firmly committed to the belief that truth can be established on the basis of evidence that our sense organs can get at. The scientist believes that the sole source of knowledge is experience. So, empirical evidence is a source of knowledge acquired by means of observation or experimentation. For an empiricist, one can claim to have knowledge only when one has a true belief based on empirical evidence. The senses are the primary source of empirical evidence. This does not mean, the researcher accepts uncritically whatever the senses offer him. He applies reasoning to comprehend its true character.
2. *Objectivity:* Objectivity is the important feature of scientific method. Objectivity implies not involvement of subjective elements as hopes, desires, beliefs, prejudices, personal attitudes, feelings, motivations and even intuition. The phenomenon is to be observed in its real form without being affected by observer's

viewpoints. The researcher should not have any pre-conceptions about the subject matter under study. In the words of A.W. Green, objectivity is the willingness and ability to examine the evidence dispassionately. Objectivity is generally achieved by employing statistical methods and measurements. For example, by adopting random sampling to technique, it is possible to reduce subjectivity.

3. *Generality:* Scientific method believes that the world is regular and phenomena occur in patterns. Further, there are certain discernable uniformities in social behaviour which can be expressed as generalisations which are capable of explaining and predicting social phenomena. So, the conclusions drawn by the researcher by using scientific methods apply to all similar instances and situations. In the words of Wolf, science is not interested in with individual objects or individual groups of objects as such. It is primarily concerned with types or classes of objects and events of which the individual event or object is merely treated as a specimen. The aim of science is to trace the order in nature. To this end, science seeks to ascertain the common characteristics of types of objects and general laws or condition of events.
4. *Verifiability:* Scientific method presupposes that knowledge in order to be valid should consist of propositions that have been subjected to empirical tests and all evidence must be based on observation. Claims to knowledge must refer to concrete human experiences so that verification is possible. Science is, thus, empirical. Experience has come to represent the true test of science. One cannot establish true scientific facts unless one can experience them. Scientific method always aims at discovering facts as they are and not as they ought to be.
5. *Validity*: In social research, validity is the extent to which a concept, conclusion or measurement is well-founded and corresponds accurately to the real world. The validity of a measurement tool (for example, a test in education) is considered to be the degree to which the tool measures what it claims to measure. It is generally accepted that the concept of scientific validity addresses the nature of reality. Validity is important because it can help determine what types of tests to use, and help to make sure researchers are using methods that are not

only ethical, and cost-effective, but also a method that truly measures the idea or construct in question.

6. *Reliability*: The idea behind reliability is that any significant results must be obtained more than once i.e., it must be inherently repeatable. It indicates that other researchers must be able to perform exactly the same experiment, under the same conditions and generate the same results. This will reinforce the findings and ensure that the wider scientific community will accept the hypothesis. Without this replication of statistically significant results, the experiment and research have not fulfilled all of the requirements of testability.
7. *Ethical Neutrality*: It is a fact that the researcher is part of the society. So, the question is asked whether he can be ethically neutral. Despite this fact, social scientist should still strive for value neutrality. Ethical neutrality, as described by Max Weber, is the duty of sociologists to identify and acknowledge their own values and overcome their personal biases when conducting sociological research. In order to be value-neutral, sociologists must be aware of their own moral judgments and values, and avoid incorporating them into their research, their conclusions, and their teaching.
8. *Prediction*: Prediction is a statement about what will be observed before the actual event, a foretelling of some future happening. Prediction in research fulfills one of the basic desires of humanity, to discern the future and know what fate holds. In physical sciences the relationship between cause and effect is precise and therefore predictions are easy. Since social sciences are dealing with human beings and since human behaviour is complex a question is asked whether social scientists can predict the future. In spite of all these difficulties social scientists are able to make predictions.

4.2 Steps in Scientific Method

Generally, research is understood to follow a certain structural process. The researcher has to continue his research through a series of steps. These steps depend on the subject matter and researcher's knowledge and skills. The following eight steps are usually part of most formal research, both basic and applied.

1. *Selection of the Problem*

This is the first step in social research. It consists of the subject area of ones interest and following that subject area to conduct subject-related research. The subject area should not be randomly chosen since it requires reading a vast amount of literature on the topic to determine the gap in the literature the researcher intends to narrow. A keen interest in the chosen subject area is advisable. The research will have to be justified by linking its importance to already existing knowledge about the topic. The topic of research should not too wide or too narrow.

2. *Review of Literature*

After selecting the problem, the researcher should find background information regarding the topic. Generally, there will be some persons who have worked in the same topic or related topics. For this the researcher can make use of the library catalogs, article indexes and encyclopaedias. Bibliographies at the end of the articles and books can also be referred. Now internet is a great source of information. Additional background information may be found in lecture notes, textbooks and other readings.

3. *Formulation of Hypothesis*

Formulation of hypothesis is the foundation of all scientific research. A hypothesis is a possible answer to the problem. It gives direction to the enquiry and helps the researcher to draw specific conclusions. Later, if the hypothesis proves to be wrong, it can be discarded otherwise it becomes a conclusion which can be used by other researchers.

4. *Definition of the Concepts*

Next step is to establish working definitions of the concepts used in research. This can be done by describing a concept by relating it to other concepts and/or defining the variables and how they will be measured/ assessed in the study. Defining the concepts enables the researcher to translate the concepts into observable events to carry out the research.

5. *Research Design*

A research design is a plan comprising the researcher's decisions about the procedures, sampling, collection and analysis of data for a given study, which aims to fulfil the purpose of the study without a wasteful expenditure of time, energy and money. Designing the research ensures against its failure. It is economical in the long run, because it forestalls the possibility of a fruitless enquiry. The research designs differ according to the research purpose. The research designs are grouped under four broad categories. They are: Exploratory, descriptive, diagnostic and experimental.

6. *Gathering of Data*

Gathering of data consists of complex process of identifying a population, selecting samples and gathering information by using specific research instruments. Sampling is the process of selecting units (e.g., people, organisations) from a population of interest so that by studying the sample we may fairly generalise our results back to the population from which they were chosen. Next, the researcher based on the requirements has to choose his research tools i.e., the appropriate methods for collection of data. The methods may be observation, survey, interview or the use of a questionnaire. The instruments used for data collection must be valid and reliable.

7. *Analysis and Interpretation of Data*

After the collection of data it has to be processed and analysed, which in itself may involve several stages. The data received may be in qualitative in nature and it has to be transformed into quantitative. For this purpose, the data has to be coded by using the code key. Further, it has to be tabulated. The data so obtained has to presented in tables, figures and pictures. This will enable us to interpret the data.

8. *Report Writing*

Writing of the report is the final step in the research. Science is a public institution. Hence, the researcher is duty-bound to make his findings as also the method by which he arrived at these, known to the public. Reporting the research requires skills different from those needed in the earlier phases of research, since the purpose of a report is communication with the audience. The research report should highlight the problem of research, the research procedures consisting of the study design, sample, techniques of data collection etc., the results or findings and theoretical and practical implications. Finally, there should be a list of references of books, periodicals and other materials used in the study. Citing or documenting the sources used in research serves two purposes, it gives proper credit to the authors of the materials used, and it allows those who are reading the work to duplicate the research and locate the sources that have been listed as references.

4.3 Research Design

A research design is a plan of the proposed research work. It is a plan dictated mainly by practical considerations. It is a series of guide posts to keep one ahead in the right direction. To make research study more reliable and objective the use of research design is necessary. It is a plan, outline, and a blueprint specifying the objectives of study, sources, types of relevant information methods to be adopted for gathering and analysing the data. Research design is a blueprint like the design of the building prepared by an engineer before the construction of the building.

According to Johada and Cook, '*a research design is the arrangement of conditions for collection and analysis of data in a manner that aims to combine relevance to the research purpose with economy in procedure*'.

According to Fred N. Kerlinger, *'It is the plan, structure and strategy of investigation conceived so as to obtain the answers to research questions. The plan is the overall scheme or programme of research'*.

Generally, there are four types of research designs. Considering nature and types of the problem we classify different types of research designs. They are: exploratory, descriptive, diagnostic and experimental design.

Exploratory Design

It is a primary stage research. The exploratory or formulative design has the purpose of formulating the research problem for fresh investigations or of developing hypothesis. The main idea of this design is the discovery of facts and insights and to determine the scope and limits of research. Exploratory design presupposes that all sciences must have at the beginning had an approach which was purely exploratory. For example, when a doctor while examining the patient asks all sorts of questions and on the basis of this exploration he comes to a conclusion about the ailment.

In order to attain research objectives the following methods may be very helpful in exploratory research:

(1) *Survey of Literature:* It refers to the review of pertinent literature. The researcher has to survey the existing literature to see what has been done in the subject of the study, how it is done and

what conclusions were arrived at. It helps a researcher to find out the research gaps.

(b) *Experience Survey*: It refers to the survey of people. The informal interview with the experienced people of the area of research may be very useful and helpful in getting an insight into the subject and its various aspects.

(c) *Case Study:* Case study represents the analysis of examples. In a case study a unit is at first studied and explored. For particular problems certain cases may be found more appropriate than the others. The method aims at description as well as explanation of the unit it studies. Generally, it makes use of personal documents and case histories.

Descriptive Design

Descriptive design is concerned with detailed description of the phenomena, group or community. The main objective of descriptive design is to acquire knowledge. There are certain areas where knowledge has not properly developed. In such cases, the investigator has to confine himself or herself to descriptive design, which is more useful than the diagnostic design.

Descriptive design has three stages. They are: pre-field work, field work and data analysis.

Pre-Field Work: Usually all researchers have some general questions in mind when they enter the field. They are of two types i.e., substantive and theoretical. The substantive category is related to specific substantive issues in a specific setting. The second category is related to the basic sociological problems and broader theoretical issues.

Field Work: Field work mainly includes data collection. After the objectives have been determined, the methods of data collection have to be specified or designed. There are three methods of data collection namely, (i) The use of documents, (ii) Observation and (iii) Interviews or questionnaires. The relevance of a particular method of data collection will depend on the object of study. Each one of these methods can be divided into many types. The researcher has to consider a number of things such as the scope of the study, the types of the information needed, the degree of accuracy required and so on, and on this basis he or she has to select a proper method of data collection.

Data Analysis: The collected data must be properly processed and analysed. It has to be decided in the beginning whether the process of data collection would be a manual process or a mechanical process, and what types of tables are to be prepared. The nature and number of cross-tables is also essential to find out the relationship between two variables. The process of analysing the data includes coding the responses that is placing the data according to their categories, tabulating the data and necessary statistical computations.

Diagnostic Design

The diagnostic study is concerned with discovering and testing certain variables with respect to their association or disassociation. A diagnostic study is concerned with an existing social problem and its basic nature and cause. It is concerned with the case as well as the treatment. It is directed towards discovering what is happening, why is happening and what can be done about it.

Diagnostic design consists of the following: 1. The emergence of a problem, 2. A diagnosis of its cause, 3. Formulation of all positive remedies and 4. Recommendation for a possible solution. Data for diagnosis can be obtained mainly through case study method.

Case study method is concerned with everything that is significant in the history or development of the case. The purpose is to understand the life cycle, or an important part of the life cycle of an individual unit. The unit may be a person, a family, a group, a social institution or an entire community. This method probes deeply and intensively, analyses interactions between the factors that produce change or growth.

The characteristics of a good case study include an adequate data which is valid, continuous, carefully synthesised, confidential and which should be useful for follow up. The important methods used in case study are: interview, clinical observation and collaborative diagnosis.

Experimental Design

An experiment in the social sciences is not only different from but also more difficult than an experiment in the natural sciences. Experimental design is also called testing causal hypothesis. It is concerned with making experiment to find out the cause-effect relationship of the phenomenon under study. Experimental study is also known as the study of causal relationship. It is considered to be the highest stage in social research. Science tries to explain the phenomenon or to determine its causes.

According to J. S. Mill causation is the uniform antecedent. A cause is the invariable antecedent of an event. There may be many causes for an effect. In scientific research, we should determine the effect of particular variable. We generally study the relationship between two variables at a time by keeping causative variable constant.

Experimentation is an observation under controlled conditions. It means the phenomenon or the conditions should not be allowed to change while the experimentation is going on. In experimentation various types of evidences have to be collected, so that, alternative hypotheses can be tested and casual relationship be found out. Since a phenomenon is caused by many factors it is necessary to consider the effect of one variable at a time. Thus, one has to eliminate the other effects for the time being. This can be done by the required experimental design.

Before formulating the outline of the experimental design the researcher makes two important groups namely, (1) Experimental group and (2) The Control group. The experimental group is exposed to the experiment being made. It is exposed to assumed causal variable (independent variable). It is allowed to change by the acts of experiments. The control group is kept constant. That is, no change is made in it or no experiment is made on it (dependent variable). At the end of the experiment we compare both the groups in order to find out the results and effect of our experiment. The difference between the two groups is considered to be independent variable.

4.4 Sampling

Sampling is concerned with the selection of a subset of individuals from within a statistical population to estimate characteristics of the whole population. In any case, the sampled population and the target population should be similar to one another. Sampling is a tool that is used to indicate how much data to collect and how often it should be collected. This tool defines the samples to take in order to quantify a system, process, issue, or problem. Researcher can establish his or her hypothesis on the basis of a sample. Sampling i.e., selecting a sub-set of a whole population is often done for reasons of cost and practicality e.g., performing a crash test on every automobile produced is impractical.

The statistical research can be done in two ways i.e., survey method and through sampling technique. Under the survey method, the researcher studies each and every unit of the field of survey and derives conclusions by computing the sum of all the units. Under sampling technique, the scientist studies a fraction in the field of survey and this is known as sample survey. In this technique of survey some units are taken as representative of the whole field and the conclusions of these sample units are extended to the whole field.

Sampling has many advantages. It can save time and money. To Goode and Hatt, *a sample is a smaller representation of the larger whole.* Nan Lin defines it as *a subset of cases from the population chosen to represent it.*

Sampling is commonly used in social research. There are two types of sampling. They are: probability sampling and non-probability sampling.

Probability Sampling

Probability sampling is based on the theory of probability. In this sampling each element of the population has a chance of being selected. Some of the types under probability sampling are given below:

1. *Simple Random Sampling:* In simple random sampling the units of the universe are so arranged that the selection process gives equal probability of selection to every unit in that universe. So the researcher randomly selects the population under study. Simple random sampling is useful when the population is heterogeneous and large. Because, in this method the researcher picks up the elements randomly from the population and conducts his study. This can be done through lottery method or use of table of random numbers or through computer generated numbers.

2. *Stratified Random Sampling:* It is the stratum of a population under study. The usual and customary procedure is to select from each stratum in proportion to the contribution which that stratum makes to the total universe. Divide the population into "strata". There can be any number of these. Then choose a simple random sample from each stratum. Combine those into the overall sample. That is a stratified random sample.

3. *Systematic Sampling or Fixed Interval Method:* This method is alternative to random selection. Here first number is randomly selected samples are added at fixed intervals. For example, if you want to interview

20 students out of 300, divide 300 by 20 and you get 15. Select a number before 20 and go on adding 15 and select the required number.

4. *Cluster Sampling:* It is used when the population is clubbed into clusters, e.g., managers are clustered into one unit. In this case, a sample of managers could be obtained by taking a random sample of organisation investigating the managers in each of these organisation interviewing the managers on this is less costly and easier too.

5. *Multi-stage Sampling:* Sometimes the population is too large and scattered for it to be practical to make a list of the entire population from which to draw a simple random sampling. In such instances sampling is carried out in two or more stages. Here, at each stage, a sampling unit is a cluster of the sampling units of the subsequent stage.

Non-probability Sampling

It is based on the assumptions that proportionally all combinations of the item to be studied will be present in the sample. But there is no assurance that every such element has the chance of being included. The types of non-probability sampling are explained below:

1. *Convenience or Accidental Sampling:* In this sampling the researcher selects the sample units in a just 'hit and miss' fashion. For example, interviewing people who the researcher happens to meet. This also means selecting whatever units conveniently available. This method is also known as accidental sampling because the respondents whom the researcher meets accidentally are included in the sample.

2. *Purposive or Judgment Sampling:* It refers to the deliberate selection of sample units that conform to some pre-determined criteria. This involves selection of cases which we judge as the most appropriate ones for the given study. It is based on the judgement of the researcher or some expert.

3. *Quota Sampling:* Here, the researcher selects people according to some fixed quota like age, sex, class etc. That is, units are selected into a sample on the basis of pre-specified characteristics so that the total sample has the same distribution of characteristics assumed to exist in the population being studied. It is a method of stratified sampling in which the selection within the strata is non-random.

4. *Snowball Sampling:* This is a technique of building up a list or a sample population by using an initial set of its members as informants.

For example, if a researcher wants to study Indians in another county, he can interview one or two persons whom he knows and then ask them about others.

4.5 Methods of Data Collection

Data collection is one of the most important stages in social research. It is the process of gathering information on variables of interest, in a systematic manner that enables one to answer stated research questions, test hypotheses, and evaluate outcomes. Data collection starts with determining type of data required followed by the selection of a sample from a certain population. After that, one has to use a certain instrument to collect data from the selected sample. The data collection component of research is common to all fields of study including physical and social sciences, humanities, business, etc. While methods vary by discipline, the emphasis is on ensuring accurate collection of data.

Types of Data

Data is generally divided into: quantitative data and qualitative data.

Quantitative Data: Quantitative data is numerical in nature and can be mathematically computed. Quantitative data measure uses different scales, which can be classified as nominal scale, ordinal scale, interval scale and ratio scale. Nominal scale is used to categorise items into different groups, for example male and female, different examination grades, different races in a country, different types of companies, different shoe sizes and so on. The statistics that is used to analyse this type of data is mode. The second measure for quantitative data is the ordinal scale which other than providing information as the nominal scale does permit ranking of the data. Quantitative data is objective, data produced through a systematic process that is verifiable, replicable and in itself is not subject to interpretation. Quantitative data is data that can be measured numerically things that can be measured precisely - rather than through interpretation. Quantitative data can be measured. For example, length, height, area, volume, weight, speed, time, temperature, humidity, sound levels, cost, members, ages, etc.

Qualitative Data: Qualitative data are mostly non-numerical and usually descriptive or nominal in nature. This means the data collected are in the form of words and sentences. Qualitative data is information which does not present itself in numerical form and is descriptive, appearing mostly in conversational or narrative form. A good example of qualitative data is an answer that describes how good a certain type of massage feels. Such data cannot be accurately quantified. Qualitative data can be observed but not measured. For example, colours, textures, smells, tastes, appearance, beauty, etc.

Sources of Data

The sources of data can be divided into two types. They are primary data and secondary data.

Primary Data: Primary data is a type of information that is obtained directly from first-hand sources by means of surveys, observation or experimentation. It is data that has not been previously published and is derived from a new or original research study and collected at the source such as in marketing. In primary data the data is newly generated with efforts of the researcher and it is fresh. When someone refers to "primary data" they are referring to data collected by the researcher himself/herself. This is data that has never been gathered before, whether in a particular way, or at a certain period of time. Researchers tend to gather this type of data when they want the data and cannot be found from outside sources. Primary data actually follows secondary data because you should use current information before collecting more and one should be informed about what has already been collected on a particular research topic. The widely used methods of collecting primary data are: observation, experimentation, questionnaire and interview.

Secondary Data: Secondary data is all the information collected for purposes other than the completion of a research project and it's used to gain initial insight into the research problem. It is classified in terms of its source – either internal or external. Internal records are the records of agencies or institutions and statistics or reports issued by govenments or organisations are the external data. Secondary data is the data which is already available in the field and the researcher has to just refer to it. Secondary data can be published once, or it may be fresh. It might have been used by several researchers. If the time or hassle of collecting one's own data is too much, then secondary data may be more appropriate for the research. This type of data typically comes from other studies done by other institutions or organisations. Secondary data are collected from census, documents, personal diaries, sample survey reports, bibliographies, periodical indexes, abstracts, official statistics, directories and yearbooks, encyclopaedias and dictionaries, biographies and autobiographies, books and magazines, professional journals, newspapers and internet.

Important tools of data as historical method, observation, interview, questionnaire and case study will be discussed below.

4.5.1 Historical Method

Historical method of research is the process of systematically examining an account of what has happened in the past. It is not facts and dates or even a description of past events. The dynamic account of past events that involves an interpretation attempts to recapture the nuances, personalities and ideas and events. One of the goals of historical research is to communicate past events. Historical method is a method of social science that examines historical events in order to create explanations that are valid beyond a particular time and place, either by direct comparison to other historical events, theory building, or reference to the present day. Generally, it involves comparisons of social processes across times and places. It overlaps with historical sociology.

There are certain differences between history and sociology. The historian generally concerned with tracing a chronological sequence of the past events, while the sociologist is mainly interested in the functional relationships which exist between analytically distinct elements in the social systems. Secondly, while history concentrates on unique events, sociology is also concerned with regular or routine events. In spite of the differences the disciplines of history and sociology have always been connected.

The social researcher generally confines himself to three sources of historical data. They are: (1) documents and various historical sources to which the historian himself has access, (2) materials of cultural history and of analytical history, (3) personal sources of authentic observers and witnesses. When, how and under what circumstances to use any or all of these sources depends a great deal upon the discretion of the researcher, his interests, the scope of his study and the availability of these sources.

4.5.2 Observation

Observation is one of the important sources of collection of data. It refers to seeing or viewing. It implies the use of eyes rather than of ears and the voice. People go on observing something while they are awake. Most of such observations are casual. They have no specific purpose.

But observation in a method of data collection is different from such casual viewing or seeing. Observation is accurate watching and noting of phenomena as they occur with regard to the cause and effect or mutual relations. It is watching other person's behaviour or actions which actually happen without controlling it. For example, watching tribal religious rites, watching village festival and watching tribal marriage.

The rationale behind the use of observation in sociological research is that the sociologist should become party to a set of social actions sufficiently to be able to assess directly the social relationship evolved. The degree of involvement may vary considerably from being merely a watcher on the side lines to be deeply involved in and being a part of what is going on.

Observation has three components viz. sensation, attention and perception. Sensation is derived from sense organs. Attention is related to the ability to concentrate on the subject matter of study. Perception means understanding. It enables the mind to recognise the facts by identifying sensations. It also recognises the facts by drawing upon experience and introspection. The accuracy of observation, thus, depends on knowledge and experience.

According to Pauline V. Young, *observation is a systematic and deliberate study through the eye of spontaneous occurrences. The purpose of observation is to perceive the nature and extent of significant inter-related elements within complex social phenomena, cultural patterns or human conduct.*

Lindzey Gardener defined it as, *selection provocation, recording and encoding of that set of behaviours and settings concerning organisms in familiar surroundings which are consistent with empirical aims.*

Types of Observation

Observation can be divided into controlled and non-controlled observation. In each of these two there are two types:

Participant and non-participant.

1. *Controlled Observation:* Controlled observation is quite opposite of uncontrolled observation. In this method, an observer uses many techniques, tools and instruments such as maps, photos, tape recorders, graphs, samplings, sociometric scales and various

other projective techniques. Controlled observation is again divided into two namely, controlled participant and controlled non-participant observation.

2. *Uncontrolled Observation:* In the uncontrolled observation a sociologist does not make use of any type of tools. A researcher, especially experienced, observes the subject matter without the help of techniques and tools. Defining uncontrolled observation, Pauline Young says, 'in an uncontrolled observation we resort to careful scrutiny of real life situation making no attempt to use instrument of precision to check for accuracy of the phenomena observed'. It may also be divided into two viz. uncontrolled participant and uncontrolled non-participant observation.
3. *Participant Method:* In participant method the observer becomes a part of what is he observing. While observing, the other persons will not know that he is an observer. In this method, observer merges with a group itself and participates in all the activities of the group. Many sociologists and anthropologists made use of this method. For instance, William Foot White, Neel Anderson, Margaret Mead, Abraham Kardiner, P.V. Young, Verser Elmin and many others made use of participant observation technique in their studies. In this method observer uses different types of tools and techniques. He becomes a member of the group. This type of technique is very useful in small group research. Usually psychologists, sociologist, anthropologists and social psychologists, use this method.
4. *Non-Participant Observation*: In this method, no doubt an observer becomes a member of the group, at the same time he does not participate in all the activities which are done by the group. He does not merge with the group, but his purpose may be known by the group. In this method we require various social research techniques and tools, but at the same time we do not participate with the group. Social situation demands different types of observation.

In addition, there is disguised observation, structured and unstructured, direct and indirect, systematic and unsystematic and covert and overt observation. It is left to the researcher to make use of appropriate method. In spite of its demerits, observation is an important and indispensable method of data collection.

4.5.3 Interview

Interview is the most popular and commonly used direct method of data collection. In social sciences, it is universally used for the study of human behaviour, political behaviour, social and economic problems, attitudes etc. In this method one can find direct verbal interaction between the interviewer and interviewee. Through this process the interviewee provides such information to the interviewer. Professionals like doctors, lawyers, journalists and teachers make use of the interview method.

In the words of Fred N. Kerlinger, *the interview is a face-to-face inter-personal situation in which one person, the interviewer, asks a person being interviewed, the respondent, questions designed to obtain answers pertinent to research problems.*

According to Eckhardt and Ermann, *interviewing is a data collection procedure involving verbal communication between the researcher and respondent either by telephone or in face-to-face situation.*

Types of Interview

Interviews are generally grouped into structured and unstructured interviews.

Structured Interview: A structured interview or a standardised interview is a quantitative research method commonly used in survey research. The aim of this approach is to confirm that each interview is offered with exactly the same questions in the same order. This guarantees that answers can be reliably collected and that comparisons can be made with confidence between sample subgroups or between different survey periods.

Unstructured Interview: Unstructured interviewing involves direct interaction between the researcher and a respondent or a group. It differs from traditional structured interviewing in several important ways. First, although the researcher may have some initial guiding questions or core concepts to ask about, there is no formal structured instrument or protocol. Second, the interviewer is free to move the conversation in any direction of interest that may come up. Consequently, unstructured interviewing is particularly useful for exploring a topic broadly. However, there is a price for this lack of structure. Because each interview tends to be unique with no predetermined set of questions asked to all respondents, it is usually more difficult to analyse unstructured interview data, especially when synthesising across respondents.

Further, there are two methods of interview: direct interview and the indirect interview.

Direct Interview: Direct interview refers to that where the researcher will directly does interview with his subject with face-to-face contact.

Indirect Interview: In indirect interview the researcher and the subject will not be having any kind of face-to-face contact. Interview will take in the forms of telephone or letter or with the help of media.

There are other forms of interview as:

> *Focused Interview:* This is a semi-structured interview where the investigator attempts to focus the discussion on the actual effects of a given experience to which the respondents have been exposed. It takes place with the respondents known to have involved in a particular experience e.g., seeing a film, viewing a particular programme etc.
>
> *Clinical Interview:* Clinical interview is concerned with broad underlying feelings or motivations or with the course of the individual's life experiences. This sort of interview is used in social case work, prison administration, psychiatric clinics etc.
>
> *Group Interview:* Group interview is a method of collecting data in which number of individuals with a common interest interact with each other. Here, the interviewer acts as the discussion leader and he stimulates the group members to interact with each other.

Process of Interview

Interview is a complex process. It consists of the following stages: Preparation, introduction, developing rapport, carrying the interview forward, recording the interview and closing the interview.

4.5.4 Questionnnaire

Questionnaire is widely used for data collection in social research, particularly in surveys. It is a fairly reliable tool for gathering data from large, diverse, varied and scattered social groups. It is used in obtaining objective and qualitative data as well as in gathering information of qualitative nature. Questionnaire is a list of questions concerning an issue or problem. It is sent to persons and associations concerned requesting them to answer the questions to the best of their knowledge and ability.

A distinction is made between questionnaire, schedule and interview guide. A questionnaire is a tool or device for obtaining answers for a bunch of questions by the respondent who fills the form of questionnaire by himself or herself. Generally, the questionnaire is mailed to the informants who have to give answers in the manner specified in the covering letter of the questionnaire. A schedule refers to a form of questionnaire which is generally filled in by the researcher or the interviewer himself. An interview guide is a set of points, topics or matters which must be necessarily covered by an interviewer while conducting the interview.

According to Goode and Hatt, *questionnaire refers to a device for securing answers to questions by using a form which respondent fills in himself.*

In the words of Bogardus, *a questionnaire is a list of questions sent to a number of persons for them to answer and return.*

Types of Questionnaire

Questionnaire can be broadly classified into two types: structured and unstructured questionnaire.

Structured Questionnaire: Structured questionnaire contains definite, concrete and pre-ordained questions i.e., they are not prepared in advance. Answers to these questions are normally given with high precision without any vagueness and ambiguity. For instance, questions on age, marital status, number of children, nationality etc. Structured questionnaire is further divided into two: open ended and closed form. A closed form questionnaire is one in which questions are set in such a manner that it leaves only a few alternative answers. The open ended questionnaire is one in which the respondent has full choice of using his own style and diction of language, expression, length and perception. The answers may be free and spontaneous.

Unstructured Questionnaire: Unstructured questionnaire contains a set of questions which are not structured in advance and which may be adjusted according to the needs of question period. It gives scope for variety of answers. The unstructured questionnaire is used mainly for conducting interviews. It aims at securing from the respondent the maximum possible information.

Pictorial questionnaire is also used for collection of data, specially when they have to be gathered from children or illiterate persons. In a pictorial questionnaire, the selected alternative answers in the form of pictures are given and the respondent is required to tick the picture concerned.

Construction of Questionnaire

Proper care must be taken while constructing a questionnaire. Physical format should be presentable and attractive. An appeal in the beginning should include the purpose of study, the confidentiality of the data and instructions relating to answering the questions. The questionnaire must be short and questions should appear in proper sequence. The language used should be simple and understandable. The questionnaire should be divided into sections.

4.5.5 Case Study Method

Case study method is a method of exploring and analysing the life of a social unit. This unit may be a person, a family, an institution, a cultural group or even the entire community. The aim of case study method is to find out the factors that account for the behaviour patterns of the given unit and its relationship with the environment. This method probes deeply and intensively, analyses interactions between the factors that produce change or growth.

The characteristics of a good case study include that the researcher can take one social unit and studied intensely. Through this method an attempt is made to understand the complex factors that are operative within a social unit as an integrated totality. The approach of this method is qualitative and not quantitative. The data collected should be valid, continuous, carefully synthesised, confidential and which should be useful for follow up.

The case study method is a widely used systematic field research technique in sociology and anthropology. The credit of introducing this method goes to Frederic Le Play. Herbert Spencer used this method in his comparative study of different cultures. William Healey resorted to this method in his study of juvenile delinquents. The case study method received the necessary impetus and recognition as a systematic field research technique in sociology with the classic study of Thomas and Znaniecki, the Polish Peasant. In the course of this study, Thomas and Znaniecki made extensive use of life history documents and made them their chief instrument in reaching out to the actual experiences and attitudes of individuals and groups.

The major phases involved in the case study include recognition and determination of the status of the phenomenon to be investigated or the unit of attention. Secondly, it involves collection of data. The data can be collected through personal interviews, clinical observation and collaborative diagnosis. The purpose of this diagnosis is to assess factors such as resistances that may be encountered, the dynamics of the situation etc. Thirdly, diagnosis and identification of casual factors as basis for remedial or development treatment. Finally, application of remedial measures as treatment and therapy. Through follow-up programme the effectiveness of the treatment can be ascertained.

4.6 Processing and Analysis of Data

After the collection of data, the data has to be processed and analysed in accordance with the research plan. Processing of data implies editing, coding, classification and tabulation.

Editing

Editing of data is a process of examining the collected raw data to detect errors and omissions and to correct these errors when possible. Practically, editing involves a careful scrutiny of the completed questionnaires or schedules. Editing is done to assure that the data are accurate, consistent with other facts gathered, uniformly entered, as complete as possible and have been well-arranged to facilitate coding and tabulation.

Coding

Further, the data available has to be quantified for analysis for which coding is necessary. Coding refers to the process of assigning numerals or other symbols to answers so that responses can be put into a limited categories or classes. The purpose of coding is to translate unclassified data into symbols which may be counted and tabulated. For this, code keys have to be allotted. For example, in the question of the sex of the respondent, allotting one to males two to females.

Classification

Classification is the process of grouping of related facts and figures into classes. For example, in the above example classification is on the basis of sex. Classification may be taken up on the basis of age, education, place of residence, attitudes towards a particular topic etc. There are four major types of classification. They are: geographic, periodical, qualitative and quantitative. On the basis of geographical areas, the classification of data may be made as talukas, districts, towns, cities, tribal areas etc. Periodic classification is also known as chronological classification. This classification is done on the basis of time period. Qualitative classification is made on the basis of quality such as sex, colour, race, education, religion etc. Quantitative classification is done on the basis of number such as height, weight, number of marks and classes secured. Each of the items we have considered as a variable which can be compared with another.

Tabulation

Tabulation is the process of summarisation of mass data in the form of statistical tables for further analysis. It is an orderly arrangement of presenting the data in columns and rows. Tabulation conserves space and reduces explanatory and descriptive statement to a minimum. It facilitates the process of comparison. Further, it facilitates the summation of items and the detection of errors and omissions. Finally, it provides a basis for various statistical computations. Tabulation can be done manually or by mechanical or electronic devices.

Tables are of two types: frequency tables and correlation tables. Frequency tables indicate the number of times the variable occurs in the study. For example, the number of males and females in the study. In correlation tables one variable is correlated with another. For example, education and number of children. These are two-way tables. There can be three-way tables and manifold tables. Percentages are often used in data presentation for they simplify numbers, reducing them to 0 to 100 range.

Analysis of Data

Analysis of the data is the most skilled work of all the stages of the research. It is a task calling for the researcher's own judgment and skill. The steps envisaged in the analysis of data vary depending on the type of study. Statistical analysis helps a lot in making generalisations out of the results of sample surveys. It is also useful in testing the hypothesis. Statistical analysis is a matter of working out statistical distribution, constructing diagrams and calculating simple measures like averages, measures of dispersion percentages, correlation etc.

4.7 Report Writing

Writing of research report is the culmination of the research investigation. Though, it is a last step in research it is the most important. It is highly skilled work as interesting, fascinating and at the same time challenging. There is no standard criterion for the organisation of a report. The form depends on each investigation, problem, familiarity of the methods, nature and volume of facts etc.

Research report communicates as to what was done by the researcher. A research report should aim at the audience. The audience might be scientists, policy-makers, sponsors of research and general public. Secondly, the report should present the purpose of research. Further, the report should also consider the audience's communication characteristics. The researcher must maintain ethical responsibility in the report which aims at protecting the respondents in the study and providing accurate and complete information.

The research report should begin with an introduction dealing with the nature of problem and the scope of enquiry. The first step in research report is the formulation and development of research problem. Next, the methodology adopted should be mentioned. Further, is the presentation and analysis of the data leading to their interpretation. This is followed by presentation of findings. Here the researcher has to give all the evidence relevant to the research problem. The report closes with conclusions and recommendations. At the end, a summary of the investigation would be highly useful.

Outline of Research Report

Generally, the outline of a research report includes: Preliminary section, the main body of the report and the reference section. The preliminary section includes the title page, preface, table of contents, list of tables, figures and graphs. The body of the report includes introduction, review of literature, design of the study, principle findings and a summary. Introduction includes statement of the problem, definitions of important concepts, hypothesis to be tested, objectives, scope and significance of the study. The design of the study includes methodology, sources of data, sampling plan, tools and techniques employed, field work, data processing and analysis and limitations of the study. The last section includes references, appendices and index.

Conclusion

The scientific method used in sociology of sanitation is more or less same as sociology. It uses various methods as observation, interview, questionnaire, historical method and case study method in collecting data. The data so obtained is processed and analysed and the process culminates in the writing of the report.

References

Kothari, C.R. 1990. *Research Methodology: Methods and Techniques*. New Delhi: Wiley Eastern Limited.

Naganuri, P.G. 2010. *Research Methodology and Statistics*. Mangalore: Mangala Publications.

Raman A. 2003. *A Handbook on Research Process*. Chennai: S. Viswanathan Pvt. Ltd.

Rao, Ravindranath Y. and Kajekar, Duggappa. 2008. *Research* Methodology. Mangalore: Mangala Publications.

Sharma, B.A.V.; Prasad, Ravindra D. and Satyanarayana, P. 1983. *Research Methods in Social Sciences*. New Delhi: Sterling Publishers Private Limited.

Wilkinson, T.S. and Bhandarkar, P.L. 1982. *Methodology and Techniques of Social Research*. Bombay: Himalaya Publishing House.

CHAPTER – 5

Culture of Sanitation

Introduction

Sociology of sanitation as a branch of sociology is a vast subject. It also includes cultural dimension of sanitation. Any relations between people and their environment are embedded in culture. The relationship between culture and the sanitation is very close. The necessity of sanitation will be same throughout the world but the method of sanitation will vary from place to place, people to people and culture to culture. To deal with excreta might often be taboo connected to beliefs and traditions. Therefore, the respect for, assessment and integration of the cultural context of users such as religious or cultural beliefs, gender or generational differences in sanitation programmes are crucial to mitigate failure risks and promote sustainable solutions. So, it is important to study the culture of people if we want to study the sanitation and problems relating to sanitation.

Concept of Culture

Culture is a very broad term that includes all aspects as walks of life, modes of behaviour, philosophies, morals, manners, customs and traditions, religious, political, economic and other activities. It includes all that man has acquired in his individual and social life. Culture distinguishes human beings from animals. Most of the animal behaviour is instinctual whereas the behaviour of human beings is learnt behaviour. Human beings alone are able to communicate through language, have norms and other rules of society and are able to acquire and transmit knowledge. Man alone creates culture and lives in culture.

According to E.B. Taylor, *culture is that complex whole which includes knowledge, belief, art, morals, law, custom and any other capabilities and habits acquired by man as a member of society.*

Graham Wallas defines culture thus: *Culture is an accumulation of thoughts, values and objects, it is the social heritage acquired by us from the preceding generations through learning.*

Culture is not inherited biologically but learnt socially by man through the process of socialisation. It is social in the sense it originates and develops through social interaction and shared by the members of society. It is transmitted from one generation to next through the vehicle of language. Bierstadt calls culture 'the memory of human race' because culture is cumulative. In its cumulative capacity culture becomes richer and richer. Different parts of culture are inter-connected. For example, morality, religion, customs and beliefs. Though, sometimes there may be conflict in some elements of culture, soon the conflict will be resolved and there will be integration. Though culture is relatively stable it is subject to slow but constant change. Finally, culture is satisfying for the individuals and groups belonging to particular culture because it provides opportunities and means for the satisfaction of our needs and desires.

Culture is a complex process. It includes some important elements. According to Harry M. Johnson cognitive elements, beliefs, norms and values and signs, symbols are the important elements of culture. Cognitive elements refer to the knowledge of man as a member of society. Cultures of all societies include a vast amount of knowledge about the physical and social world. Secondly, people have beliefs in their cultures. Tested empirical knowledge and untested beliefs are elements of culture which go hand in hand. Norms are group shared standards of behaviour. Norms include customs, traditions, laws, legislations, rules etc. Values are higher order norms. Values may be said to be the measure of goodness and desirability. A sign includes the existence of a thing, event or condition in the past, present and future. For example, smoke is the sign of fire. Symbols are important in communication and expression. In all cultures, language is a symbol.

Cultural Diversity in India

India is a land of cultures. People have been living in India since thousands of years. The cultural origins of the Indian subcontinent can be traced back to the Indus Valley Civilisations. Since earliest times people started migrating to India. From twelfth century India came under Mughal rule. Since the late sixteenth century India was under the influence of the European powers till 1947 when India gained independence. All the people who came to India became one with the Indian culture. From this has evolved the composite Indian culture. This diversity has enriched our social life.

People of India are divided on the basis of region, religion, values, language, food habits, dressing patterns and the way of behaviour. People such as Hindus, Muslims, Buddhists, Sikhs, Christians, Jains, and Parsis etc., belonging to different religions live in India. We find diversity in the clothing and food habits of Indians. Clothing depends upon the climate, physical feature and traditions of the respective regions. There is diversity in our food habits too, due to climatic conditions, crops and other geographical factors. For example the people of Punjab eat *dal-roti* whereas people living in the coastal areas eat rice and fish. In respect of shelter, houses vary. In the rural areas, many houses have wattle and daub walls. Some houses have tiled roofs. While in urban areas they live in concrete house.

The Relationship between Culture and Sanitation

The relationship between culture and sanitation in Indian context is very close. Understanding the social habits of people is essential for the study of sanitation. Sanitation is the essential part of every person's life. It is the activity where every individual or group of people will follow in one or other way in their daily life in different forms. For example, a person who is born in a city washes his hands in the wash basin while a person born in the village washes his hands outside the house. In the study of culture of sanitation we will understand the relationship between culture and sanitation. Some of the components of culture of sanitation are associated with manual scavenging, the attitudes of people of different castes, beliefs and regions towards dirt and the problem of manual scavenging and suggest solutions for ending it.

5.1 Social Components in Scavenging and Cleanliness

Social components in scavenging and cleanliness are those elements which are responsible for scavenging activities and cleanliness in society. There are multiple components which have given rise to manual scavenging in the society. Manual scavenging is one of the important social problems in society.

The social habits of people towards cleanliness are very low in some primitive, ethnic, rural and slum communities of Indian society. A proper study of the components of manual scavenging and cleanliness can be understood by the study of social habits of the people. The social components of scavenging and cleanliness can be explained as below:

Caste System

The caste system can be considered as one of the important components of scavenging. The caste system is one in which the individual gets the status of his parents by birth. If an individual is born in Brahmin family he gets high social status and if he is born in an untouchable caste he gets lower status. The caste system not only gives low or high status to the individual, it also allots an occupation. The individual is supposed to take up the occupation of his parents. The caste system not only gives status to the individual in terms of his birth in a particular caste but also gives status to the occupation of the individual. The occupations too are graded. The occupations performed by upper caste people are given higher status and the occupation taken up by lower caste are given low status and they are despised.

The Untouchables suffered many disabilities in society. One of the important disabilities they suffered is that they had no right to choose their own occupation. They were not allowed to engage themselves in occupation which were reserved for the members of higher castes and were compelled to stick to their traditional occupations like scavenging, carrying the dead animal from the streets, sweeping, cleaning, leather works, herding swines, collecting wood for the funeral, carrying the message regarding the dead people, basket making etc. In the course of time, their occupations were passed on from generation to generation.

Though manual scavenging was abolished as late as 2013 by an Act of Parliament to provide for the prohibition of employment as manual scavengers and rehabilitation of manual scavengers and their families, manual scavenging still survives in parts of India without proper sewage systems. It is thought to be most prevalent in Gujarat, Madhya Pradesh, Uttar Pradesh, and Rajasthan. Some municipalities in India still run public dry-toilets. In addition, in all the town and city municipalities and city corporations the persons involved in sweeping the streets and carrying the dirt, to dumping yards are all Dalits. Though in many places the dirt is carried by trucks those fill the trucks and even the drivers are Dalits. No person of upper caste ventures into these jobs.

Culture

Culture is another component of scavenging. Culture refers to the ways of life. Culture differs from group to group. Cultural variations were found in the same group or community. Culture of the upper caste or class differed from the lower caste or class. If we examine the past Indian society we find different aspects of culture. The rich used to dress differently from the poor. Cultural value in the past was that the lower caste people were to subservient to upper caste people. The lower caste people in the past had to take care of the upper caste people by obeying their orders and do the menial jobs as cleaning their cloths, their houses, working in their fields, cleaning their faeces, cleaning animal waste etc. The culture of the upper caste people was to stay at home wearing good dress and ornaments. Thus, the culture consisted of upper caste or class people having toilet and bathroom facilities in the house or in premise while the lower caste people had to go to the open place for defecation. This culture of the past has continued to the present, both in towns and cities.

Lack of Education and Awareness

It is a fact that in the ancient times the lower castes could not be educated. Education was the monopoly of upper castes. After independence, the government has brought about reservation in education, employment and in politics. Because of reservation in education the Scheduled Castes can have entry into educational institutions and government is also providing books, uniform and other facilities. In spite of these provisions, most of the Scheduled Castes are not able to get benefits of these provisions. Legally, manual scavenging is abolished in the society. Yet, many of the scavengers continue in their professions to earn their living. Proper education and awareness against the evil practices of scavenging can only end this evil practice.

Social Domination

Domination refers to control of power over another or others. In the Indian society the upper castes had always dominated the lower castes. We can still observe the domination of the upper caste people over the lower caste people in many spheres in the country. Through the domination by the upper castes they have been able to select ritually pure occupations and higher paying jobs for them and leaving menial and less paying jobs to the lower castes. So, most impure job of scavenging is allotted to the most impure castes.

Social Deprivation

Social deprivation refers to denial of facilities to some sections of society. It is the limited access to some sections of people for socio-economic status or education. Socially deprived people lack basic freedom due to their low socio-economic status. The lower caste people are deprived of honest occupation being satisfied with scavenging activities. Since their wages are very low they are economically deprived and low social status is accorded to them.

Concepts of Karma and Dharma

The concepts of Karma and Dharma are intimately related to Hinduism and the caste system. Dharma signifies behaviours that are considered to be in accordance with the order that makes life and universe possible. The concept of dharma is a broad one. It includes duties, rights, laws, conduct, virtues and 'right way of living'. So, it is the duty of an Untouchable or Dalit is to do the duties of one's caste. According to the karma doctrine the course of life of every living being here and hereafter is determined by his karma or his deeds. A pious life leads to comforts, contentment and general well-being in the present life and re-birth in higher and better forms of existence. It also implies that a Dalit's life in the present world is the result of his past actions. So, these two concepts hold him back from changing his occupation. In addition to these concepts, there are concepts of '*papa*' and '*punya*'. *Papa* refers to punishment for bad deeds and *punya* refers to reward for good deeds. The scavengers' ideology is that since they do their dharma, duty of one's caste, they will get *punya*.

Basic Inferiority

In India, caste determines one's occupation. Caste occupation is passed on from generation to generation. A carpenter's son will become a carpenter so also a scavenger's son or daughter will become a scavenger. This aspect of caste is imbedded in the minds of people. A son or daughter of a scavenger will develop an inferiority psychology that they are destined to such jobs. This feeling of inferiority is also evident in other aspects of caste system. For example, we observe that senior members of Scheduled Castes are not entering the Hindu temples though younger ones now enter.

Due to this inferiority those involved in low or scavenging jobs lack in interest for any sort of development. They feel that they are meant for scavenging.

Exploitation

The caste system is a system of exploitation. The upper castes have exploited the lower castes for centuries. The scavengers were the lowest in the caste hierarchy and they were exploited the most. They were given low wages and nobody was bothered about their welfare. Society always looks down on them. Their touch would defile an upper caste person. During the time of the Peshwas, in Poona city the untouchables could not enter the city, for cleaning and scavenging, in the morning and in the evening because their long shadow if fell on an upper caste person would defile them.

Conclusion

Caste is the important component of scavenging. It has given lowest status to scavenging and to the people who are involved in scavenging. Due to the concepts of karma and dharma, culture and lack of education, scavengers continue in their profession. It is also because of domination, exploitation and the depressive psychology of the scavengers they continue in the profession.

5.2 Culture and Dirt Attitudes

Culture is that complex whole which includes knowledge, beliefs, art, morals, law, custom and any other capabilities and habits acquired by man as a member of society. In a particular culture, different people will have different attitudes towards different aspects in society. Similarly, they will have attitudes towards dirt. While some people like to be clean while others may not bother about cleanliness. Some others may not be able to be clean because of their bad economic condition. Attitudes are developed through the process of socialisation.

Attitudes

An attitude can be understood as a positive or negative evaluation of people, objects, event, activities, ideas, or just about anything in ones environment. According to Eagly and Chaiken an attitude is *"a psychological tendency that is expressed by evaluating a particular entity with some degree of favour or disfavour"*. According to psychologist

Alfred Jung, an attitude is a *"readiness of the psyche to act or react in a certain way"*. Attitudes are positive or negative. Negative attitudes are called as prejudices.

Researchers also suggest that there are several different components that make up attitudes. They are: emotional, cognitive and behavioural. Because of emotional component we feel about a person, object, issue or event. Cognitive component refers to one's thoughts and beliefs about the subject. Finally, a behavioural component indicates how our behaviour is influenced by our attitudes.

Attitudes form directly as a result of experience. They may emerge due to direct personal experience or they may result from observation. Social roles and social norms can have a strong influence on attitudes. Social roles relate to how people are expected to behave in a particular role or context. Social norms involve society's rules for what behaviours are considered appropriate. Attitudes can be learned in a variety of ways. For example, the children develop attitudes for junk food through advertisements in the T.V. or a teacher who bullies a student often may develop negative attitudes towards the teacher. In this way, both attitudes and prejudices are developed in the process of socialisation.

Attitudes towards Dirt

The attitudes towards sanitation and dirt depend on the culture. It may vary depending upon the geographical factors, availability of water, types of people on the basis of caste, religion etc. For example, in a place where there is shortage of water the attitude towards the dirt may be different than where there is availability of water. The attitudes may be different among Hindus and Muslims. Similarly, it is different among Brahmans compared to scavengers who belong to lowest caste. Attitudes towards dirt from the caste, religion and sex perspective are examined below:

Caste and Attitudes towards Dirt

Water is synonymous with life and, therefore, it is the most integral and inevitable part of each individual. Though water is required for drinking and cooking it is also essential for cleaning. In this connection, the Scheduled Castes have disabilities regarding access to water and sanitation. In rural India, there is discrimination regarding access to public water bodies and structures.

In India, more than 20 per cent of Dalits do not have access to safe drinking water. 48.4 per cent of Dalit villages are denied access to water source. Only 10 per cent of Dalit households have access to sanitation (as compared to 27 per cent for non-Dalit households), and the vast majority of Dalits depend on the goodwill of upper-caste community members for access to water from public wells. Dalit women stand in separate queues near the bore well to fetch water till the non-Dalits finish fetching water. Dalits are disentitled and not allowed to use taps and wells located in non-Dalit area. Regarding sanitation, 23.7 per cent of Dalit households have access to latrine facility as compared to 42.3 per cent for general households.

Dalits access to water is usually on the goodwill of dominant caste. The worst and most inhumane form of discrimination and untouchability is seen when it comes to water. Most of the violence starts for the very cause as Dalits try to access the public well or hand pumps. There are numerous case studies on violence against Dalits accessing water. So, the Dalits not only denied access to water they also become victims of violence.

Religion and Attitudes towards Dirt

Attitudes towards human waste are somewhat akin to attitudes towards dirt. The mental dispositions towards both physical necessities are the result of cultural norms. And one of the dominant universal influences of social behaviour is religion. Although the influence of religion on waste behaviour appears less obvious, it does exist.

Muslim Attitude towards Dirt: Islam is world's second largest religion. Islam is completely standing on the concept of purity. It is believed that the human excreta is a wastage and it is restricted one and polluted one. There are certain explanations in the Islamic preaching about the use of toilets. Followers of Islam consider purification of human body with the water except some situation as important. Muslim doctrine prescribes strict procedures regarding contact with faecal material. Only the left hand can be used for cleansing after elimination; the right is used for eating.

Moreover, the use of water for cleansing is specified that is a Muslim is obligated to use water to cleanse parts of the body through which impurities pass. This obligation has direct implications for planning toilet facilities. Having a toilet attached to the home is not prescribed by Islam.

In fact, they concede it as a sin to have toilet attached. But in urban areas people are forced to avoid such an attitude. As observed they use separate sandals for toilet and they concede that it is the place of saitan or demon. There are, however, Islamic societies using waterless toilets. In Yemen and Zanzibar, where waterless systems have been traditional, the users wash themselves away from the toilet opening. Since this has not posed a problem for traditional waterless systems, it might be an acceptable solution in other countries.

Hindu Attitude toward Dirt: Hinduism is the principle religion in India having a population of nearly 100 crores. The principle Hindu text, the Atharva Veda, clearly specifies the use of water for sanitation. It's been observed that the Hindus carry a brass vessel filled with water to a secluded spot away from running water, public roads, or temples. After defecation anal region is cleansed with water. Followers of the Atharva Veda are primarily Brahmans, consequently upper-caste Hindus consume more water for sanitary purposes than lower-caste Hindus especially the Untouchables, who traditionally carry away night soil.

India's lowest caste and people belonging to lower class defecates openly in public. The right hand is considered as pure and the left hand dirty because of its use. The Ganges is considered a holy river. But it is full of effluents from humans and industries. People bath, wash cloths and animals in this river. Sometimes half burnt corpses float in the current. It is the case with other holy rivers of India.

In Hindu culture, anything that leaves or is detached from the body is considered 'dirty'. If you were to carry out an act that secretes matter from your body, you must wash afterwards. This is not only related to shitting, but also nose-picking, cutting nails and getting ones hair cut. The toilet, therefore, is considered a dirty place and people that have a toilet in villages would not have it close to their house; others would just go somewhere to the fields. In cities, people are forced more or less to have a bathroom with toilet in the house, but it still considered a dirty place. In many places, people have separate pair of slippers to wear inside the bathroom; this is also practical as, in the absence of shower cabins or curtains, the floor is usually wet. As a consequence, cleaning toilets is considered a dirty task.

Women and Attitude towards Dirt

Open defecation is common in India. Open defecation is the practice of defecating outside and in public, in and around the local community, as a result of ingrained cultural patterns or having no access to toilets, latrines or any kind of improved sanitation. It is a practice widely considered to be at the heart of issues around sanitation worldwide. In India most of the rural people and people living in urban slums are involved in open defecation. It is a practice in Indian villages that men go to one side of the village and women go to another side for defecation.

In India, women suffer most because of lack of toilets. Both in rural and urban areas, women without toilets only go out to relieve themselves in the dark, because their gender ideology tells them that they cannot take the risk to be seen. There are instances, where women in order to avoid going to ease themselves reduce eating. For some women wait till the dark results in constipation and adapted diet and drinking habits, which give serious health problems. According to one estimate gynaecological and urinary tract problems run higher (almost one-third) among women who lack access to sanitation facilities. Evidence pointed out to conclusions that the absence of facilities is not merely because of poverty but also because of the cultural inhibitions and constraints regarding women's bodily functions. Further, women are not aware of these health problems nay some suffer silently.

According to the WHO, 65 per cent of the rural people defecate in the open. In this situation women appear to bear the brunt as they are mostly attacked and assaulted when they step out early in the morning or late in the evening. The gruesome rape and hanging of two teenage girls recently in the Uttar Pradesh proves how women have become the biggest victims of India's sanitation crisis. The two girls were going to the fields to defecate when they were raped and killed. Women living in urban slums of Delhi reported specific incidents of girls under 10 being raped while on their way to use a public toilet. Women in one slum said when they went out in the open to defecate they faced lewd remarks, physical gestures and rape when they relieved themselves in the bushes.

Dalit women are the worst affected with the lack of access to water and sanitation. Their connection with water resources is very intricate. A Dalit woman will have all the burden of household work in the family and she will be the one who is responsible to bring water to the family and therefore she is the one who will be facing discrimination at the first place. They even drop out from the school for this. While bringing water they will be facing verbal and physical abuse from the dominant caste and they will be under constant threat while collecting water from public wells and taps. They are also under constant threat while they go for defecation. Dalit women are forced to clean human excrement with their bare hands for little to no wages. As a result they have higher risk of occupational illness and health hazards.

5.3 Beliefs and Values Associated with Dirt

Belief is a state of the mind in which a subject roughly regards a thing to be true. People's beliefs may be true or may not be true. Yet people hold on to their views they regard it to be true. Values are higher order norms. Values can be defined as broad preference concerning appropriate courses of action or outcomes. As such, values reflect a person's sense of right and wrong or what "ought" to be. Beliefs and values tend to influence attitudes and behaviour.

Beliefs and values associated with dirt vary from group to group in India. It depends on the social structure of people and the attitude towards the sanitation. Among the first things you notice when you come to India is the repelling sight of people defecating in the open. Be it a rural village or the teeming city slums, you see people lined up besides railway tracks, fields, and rivers answering nature's call. Out of the estimated 2.6 billion people globally who have no access to proper sanitation, 638 million belong to India. According to the UN, more than 55 per cent of Indians practice open defecation. Even where local municipalities have constructed public toilets, the UN has questioned the utility of these services, terming them unhygienic and unusable and lacking in running water, drainage, and electricity.

Moreover, most manual scavengers have little choice in what they do for a living. Like most Indians, manual scavengers live according to the rigid stratification of the caste system. In other words, they dispose of human waste not because they want to, but because they are born into their particular caste. In a society where birth dictates one's job and livelihood, it is nearly impossible to find other opportunities; as a result, many are resigned to their fate: "You do what's assigned to you" is the usual refrain. People have negative and the neutral values for scavenging in society.

The most of the rural people defecate in the open area and they will not carry any sanitation care. Some of them walk with bare feet and just some amount of water to clean. Some of the families in rural India will be having a colour TV, the cell phone and dish connection but they will not be having a toilet. The attitude towards the toilet or sanitation is imaginable. The person who is quite rich or upper middle class in the rural society he also sometimes goes outside to defecate. The problem is the culture which they follow mostly will not allow them to construct a toilet within their house or nearby house. And the attitude of negligence and lack of knowledge makes them to ignore sanitation. In the early morning most of the spots are overused and for the majority of village folk, who walk barefoot to defecate, the experience they face every morning is unimaginable, it is disgusting in the rainy days. But people are not worried.

During the monsoons it is worse. In the dark when village people visit the water logged field overgrown with grass and floating with night soil, the danger of getting bitten by snakes and scorpions is also high even though rural families worried to construct a toilet, yet a toilet is not their priority. And surprisingly, it is also not the priority among millions of poor across India.

According to a UN study on sanitation, 563.7 million people in India have access to mobile phones while only 366 million have access to a toilet. The report estimates the cost of building a toilet is less than the cost of smart phone. Jack Sim, founder and president of the World Toilet Organisation (WTO) points out that the only way poor Indian families will prioritise toilets is through local entrepreneurs. "Train the poor to become sanitation entrepreneurs and sales agents," says Jack Sim, whose mission is to improve sanitation globally. Poor Indian society does not wish to construct a toilet or unless until any organisation or government initiates the project of constructing toilets.

In one of the villages of India which is situated in Ralegansiddi which is lead by Anna Hazare, people do public welfare jobs like constructing toilets by people's participatory labour, encourages people to construct toilets, wells and dams in the village. In fact, toilets have to be designed to be emotionally appealing so that they become status symbols and objects of desire amongst the poor, which is the only reason why poor are buying mobile phones and not investing in toilets.

Lack of proper sanitation is also a major cause of girls dropping out of school after adolescence. It is estimated that less than half of the 738,150 primary schools run by the governments across India have proper toilets. Only 28.25 per cent of all primary schools in the country have separate toilets for girls. According to Education World, the Human Development magazine, improper sanitation is the reason why only 63 million girls of the 102 million girls who begin schooling continue their education up to class VIII, i.e., secondary level education.

In Haryana, the number of rural households with toilets has risen considerably from 29 per cent in 2001 to an impressive 98 per cent in the last five years, women are doing just that. The "No Toilet, No Bride" campaign, launched by the Ministry of Rural Development, has resulted in the construction of approximately 1.71 million toilets across the state. The movement takes advantage of the fact that Haryana suffers from a warped sex ratio, a result of India's cultural preference for boys over girls. The scarcity of brides in the state helps prospective brides use their bargaining power to force their suitors to construct toilets for them before they marry. This is a good way of changing people's attitudes and values regarding sanitation. Ultimately, only if women decide to prioritise toilets can the policy-makers ensure their demand is fulfilled.

5.4 Problems of Scavenging

Manual scavenging refers to the removal of human excreta from unsanitary, dry toilets, i.e., toilets without the modern flush system. Manual scavenging involves the removal of human excreta using brooms and tin plates. The scavengers crawl into the dry latrines and collect the human excreta with their bare hands. The excreta are piled into baskets which scavengers carry on their heads to locations sometimes several kilometers from the latrines. Municipal records from 1870 show that the British organised municipalities in India which built roads, parks, public toilets etc. The British administrators organised systems for removing the night soil and employed bhangis, an untouchable caste.

Scavenging is a caste-based and hereditary occupation, which is handed down, as a legacy from one generation to the next. Manual scavengers belong to untouchable castes and are considered outcastes. Scavengers come in direct contact with human excreta and his/her hands are completely soiled. In a congested locality, the scavenger has to crawl through a narrow passage, pushing the basket with one hand, resting his body weight on the other to make his way up to the latrine chamber through a narrow opening. In the latrine, where the seat is deep inside, he/she has to stretch his/her hand to the fullest and thrust his/her head into the hole to clean the toilet. Their occupation is considered as ritually polluting.

Manual scavenging continues to exist in India, despite being unacceptable and hazardous as a method of disposal of human waste, despite scientific and technological advancement on various fronts that saves manual labour, and despite the availability of simple and low-cost alternatives which can eradicate the twin problems of manual scavenging and safe disposal of human excreta. It passes on from generation to generation. Culture of acceptance prevailing among them is also depriving them of their basic rights. Scavenging as a social problem in the nation like India we can observe several problems which are more highlighting in the present society.

Most of the municipalities in India are not equipped with the latest machines to clean the sewage system and therefore, sewage workers employed under compulsion to enter the underground sewerage lines through the manholes and cleanse them wherever the lines are clogged for whatever reason. The job of the sewer worker is to inspect and maintain the underground network pipes that make up sewerage system. Sewage workers have to remove solid substance wastes which is responsible for blockage of flow of fluid waste in sewage system. For that sewage workers regularly enter into manholes which contain very poisonous gases.

The working conditions of sewage workers are very dangerous; they are provided with a rope and bucket to clean the manhole manually. While working this, they have to face various poisonous gases which are harmful for their health and sometime it causes their life. Due to that, sewage workers usually have had cuts, injuries, irritation of eyes and suffered from skin rash and related health problems. The existing protective equipments are neither adequate nor up to the standard quality. Also, most of the sewage workers are not educated to use protective equipments. Most of sewage workers are recruited on contract basis and on daily wages. A large number of sewer workers die before retirement. While working on busy road area, there is always fear of accidents from moving vehicles.

The scavenging castes which were known by different names in different States like Bhangi, Balmiki, Chuhra, Mehtar, Mazhabi, Lal Begi, Halalkhor etc., in northern India; Har, Hadi, Hela, Dom and Sanei etc., in eastern India; Mukhiyar, Thoti, Chachati, Pakay, Relli etc., in Southern India; and Mehtar, Bhangias, Halalkhor, Ghasi, Olgana, Zadmalli, Barvashia, Metariya, Jamphoda and Mela etc., in Western and Central India, also made an effort to get united and have a common name. In 1911 census, some of them started returning as Adi Dharmi, Adi Dravida, Adi Karnataka and Adi Andhra.

Adi-Dravida and Adi Karnataka are the new names acquired by some Scheduled Caste groups in Karnataka to obliterate the stigma of untouchability. Generally, these groups belong to the lowest strata of Scheduled Caste society. According to Kakade, the idea that change of name would obliterate the stigma of centuries perhaps led the depressed classes to give up their old names and adopt new inoffensive and generic names like Panchamas, Adi-Dravida, Adi-Karnataka, Harijan etc. A study by the author in Mangalore has observed that mostly the Thotis have adopted the names of Adi-Dravida and Adi-Karnataka. According to the author, probably the process of sanskritisation in caste name is complete because in the socio-economic survey of 1993 conducted by Mangalore City Corporation not a single Scheduled Caste householder has given his caste name as Thoti.

Problems of manual scavenging can be classified into health problems, socio-economic problems, and the psychological problems.

Health Problems

Health problems are the important problems which are faced by the manual scavenger due to the contact with human disposal. The workers are affected by cardiovascular degeneration, infections like hepatitis and skin problems, prevalence of helicobacter, respiratory system problems. They are exposed to infections by hand-to-mouth contact. The manual scavengers are also highly affected by gastric cancer. Further, health hazards include exposure to harmful gases such as methane and hydrogen sulphide, cardiovascular degeneration, musculoskeletal disorders like osteoarthritis changes and inter vertebral disc herniation, infections like hepatitis, leptospirosis and helicobacter, skin problems, respiratory system problems and altered pulmonary function parameters. Women working unprotected are in grave danger of contacting countless diseases through their daily and close contact with human waste. Some of these diseases, in addition to TB, include: campylobacter infection, cryptosporidiosis, giardiasis, hand, foot and mouth disease, hepatitis A, meningitis (viral), rotavirus infection, salmonella infection, shigella infection, thrush and viral gastroenteritis.

Facing the dangers of daily contact, "ninety per cent of all manual scavengers have not been provided proper equipment to protect them from faeces borne illness," said a report (2007) on safety by Tata Institute of Social Sciences, Mumbai. This includes safety equipment like gloves, masks, boots and/or brooms. The use of hands by women manual scavengers, along with the certainty that they will have direct skin contact with human waste, is a very dangerous combination that is contributing to serious health conditions. Chronic skin diseases and lung diseases are very common among women manual scavengers.

Most of the municipalities in India are not equipped with the latest machines to clean the sewage system and therefore, sewage workers employed under compulsion to enter the underground sewerage lines through the manholes and cleanse them wherever the lines are clogged for whatever reason. The job of the sewer worker is to inspect and maintain the underground network pipes that make up sewerage system. Sewage workers have to remove solid substance wastes which responsible for blockage of flow of fluid waste in sewage system. For that sewage workers regularly entered into manholes which contain very poisonous gases.

The working conditions of sewage workers are very dangerous. They are provided with a rope and bucket to clean the manhole manually. While working this, they have to face various poisonous gases which are harmful for their health. Due to that, sewage workers usually have had cuts, injuries, irritation of eyes and suffered from skin rash and related health problems. The existing protective equipments are neither adequate nor upto the standard quality. Also, most of the sewage workers are not educated to use protective equipments. Most of sewage workers are recruited on contract basis and on daily wages. A large number of sewer workers die before retirement. While working on busy road area, there is always feared of accidents from moving vehicles.

Socio-Economic Problems

Manual scavengers are the vulnerable groups in the society. The caste system has pushed them to the work of manual scavengers and it will not bring them any kind of social status nay it will bring them social problems like social discrimination, social deprivation and suppression.

Manual scavenging has been practiced for long, unfettered by the complacent attitudes of society wedded to an abominable tradition. Manual scavenging as an occupation is entrenched in caste discrimination in the form of untouchability. The scavengers are social discriminated in all the sector of the society. Because of the tag of impurity people of higher caste will avoid them in the society. This kind of social discrimination can be observed in the present day also. The children of manual scavengers also will not get any status in the school or hospital or any other place. They are treated as untouchables in the society. Even now, in some of the villages the manual scavengers live outside the village.

The practice of scavenging is not only confined to cleaning of human excreta but also to people who clean the filth from urban sewer lines and the sweepers of railways. Society has generated a negative identity for these manual scavengers. These manual scavengers are socially deprived and harassed in the society. They are looked down by the people. They are kept away from the developmental opportunities. As a result the manual scavengers develop an inferiority complex.

Psychological Problems

Some of the manual scavengers get psychologically disturbed because of the suppression and the work which they are doing for a living. Since scavenging is considered to be the dirtiest job in the society the people who perform these jobs are accorded lowest or no respect. The psychological problems can also be observed in the school going children of the manual scavengers. These children face harassment from the upper caste children of the other community. Due to the domination and the harassment these children become mentally disturbed. They may also be prone to psychological disorder.

In spite of the continuous efforts by the governments, NGOs and others the practice of manual scavenging continues unhindered in gram panchayats, municipalities, cities and in railways affecting the physical and psychological health of the manual scavengers and their families. Concerted efforts are required to end this evil practice and liberate the manual scavengers.

5.5 Concepts of Purity and Impurity in Sanitation

Beliefs about ritual purity and impurity form some of the most pervasive themes in Hindu culture. These concepts are applied to matters of personal conduct, health and justice and are fundamental to untouchability. In fact, purity has little to do with cleanliness and hygiene, similarly impurity has little to do with dirt. The concepts of purity and pollution are central to the notion of caste in India.

In Hindu ideology, ritual purity or impurity constitutes the criterion generally accepted for justifying and explaining the rank of a caste in the caste hierarchy. The Brahmans at the top of the caste were considered pure. However, they could be polluted if they came into contact with an untouchable or if they were to accept food or gifts from them. By any chance, if a Brahman came into physical contact with an untouchable, he would consider himself polluted and would take a ritual bath and sometimes even wash his clothes to remove pollution. Other castes did their best to stay away from the untouchables.

The conception of purity and impurity is the key to the many of the apparent enigmas of the caste system and Ketkar regards it as the chief principle on which caste system depends. According to Ketkar, the Brahman is at the top of the society because he is more pure and sacred than other castes, while Mahar and Paraiyan are at the bottom because they are impure. Thus, purity is the pivot on which the entire system turns. Rank, social position, economic condition have no direct effect on the gradation from the standpoint of caste.

For Dumont, the opposition of pure and impure is the basis of understanding of caste, caste hierarchy and caste occupation. People whose traditional occupations put them in contact with leather, dead animals, toilets and sewers, and sweeping are usually associated with outcastes or Untouchables. At the other social extreme are Brahmins, who never have contact with such substances and, ideally, deal only with learning, books, or temple rituals and they are considered pure. Middle castes, which sometimes have contact with polluting substances in their traditional work, have an intermediate purity status. For example, barbers, who have contact with bodily substances as they cut people's hair, are seen as lower caste, though not untouchable.

Purity and impurity regarding sanitation is quite difficult to understand in general perspective. Purity is referred as it is the absence of impurity, and impurity is the absence of the purity. The purity concept can be referred in different aspects of social life. If purity is referred only cleanliness then it can be referred as only sanitation in humans. But purity and impurity in the society is wider in nature. Though ritual purity has little to do with cleanliness and hygiene and similarly ritual impurity has little to do with dirt in sanitation both ritual and physical impurity is present. Similarly those involved in sanitation such as sweepers and scavengers are impure, both ritually and physically because they live in unhygienic conditions. But now, because of the economic and social advancement made by some members of Scheduled Castes they have become physically pure.

In Hindu ideology and culture not only people were considered pure or impure, even occupations were considered pure and impure. The occupations such as learning and offering sacrifices were considered pure and were performed by the Brahmans whereas the occupations as sweeping, scavenging etc., were impure and were performed by the untouchables.

Not only people and occupations were considered pure or impure, but also the food they took. In India, food restrictions and habits are highly developed and indicate caste affiliation. For Brahmans, non-vegetarian food was anathema and so, they were vegetarians. Other Hindu castes were non-vegetarians. While middle order castes preferred mutton and chicken, lowest castes or untouchables also ate beef and pork. In addition, ingredients varied from caste to caste in their cooking, and the concept of purity remained fundamental to Hindu cooking.

In Hindu society strict rules were followed in order to keep maximum purity. The idea of keeping all pollutants away can be seen by the location of the kitchen in Indian houses. The kitchen is normally a separate room located at a slight distance from the main house in which shoes or any other leather items were not allowed near this space. Anything that was potentially a pollutant is to be kept away. Even low caste people were to be kept away from the food of higher castes for the low caste person would pollute the food by his/her touch. Only Brahmin cooking was acceptable to all, high and low castes.

A woman is seen as pollutant and contagious of pollution during her period. During a woman's period she would be banned from cooking or serving food because her impurity is very contagious during that time of the menstruation. It's not only what one did to keep the impurities away, but also what they ate to maintain a pure diet.

Ritual purity has been the cause of evil in society in the sense the pure people have started discriminating the people of the lower castes. They are not allowed to enter temples, public places, draw water from wells and ponds. They are forced to do menial and scavenging jobs nay they are exploited by the upper castes.

In the modern world people should not be worried about ritual purity instead they should be concerned with physical purity. It is essential to establish clean and healthy society. People should take initiatives to avoid unhealthy conditions in the society. If people want their environment to be clean they should keep their house clean. Since human and animal wastes affect the heath of the people, these have to be kept away where they do affect the health of the people.

5.6 Development and Sanitation

In the present day world sanitation has become a key to measure social and economic development of a nation. Access to sanitation has various impacts on the overall social and economic development of societies. Amongst other things, it contributes to reduction of poverty, alleviation of hunger, improving health and primary education, and environmental sustainability. Sanitation can be considered as one of the important element of development. Wherever there is no sanitation there are many social problems and wherever there is sanitation there is development. Lack of sanitation considered as the hindrance towards social development.

Following are some of the key development issues which are affected by improved access to water and sanitation.

Poverty

Poverty and sanitation are intimately connected. Since the people are poor they are not able to look after their economic needs including sanitation. The economic benefits of clean water and sanitation transform lives in poorest communities. As the focus shifts from survival to opportunity, people gain time and money to pursue economic and educational goals while enjoying an improvement in health and wellbeing. Household livelihood security depends on the health of its members, hence adults who are ill themselves or who must care for sick children are less productive. Illnesses caused by unsafe drinking water and inadequate sanitation generate health costs that can claim a large share of poor households' income. Often water has to be carried from long distances and time spent collecting water cannot be used for other livelihood activities.

Hunger

Every day 4,000 children die from illnesses like diarrhea, dysentery, and cholera caused by dirty water and unhygienic living conditions. We can't fight malnutrition without tackling the diseases that contribute to it. As an integrated approach to hunger, getting safe water, sanitation, and hygiene services to communities is the real need all over India and the world. Healthy people are better able to absorb the nutrients in food than those suffering from water-related diseases, particularly worms, which rob their hosts of calories. Water is a direct input to irrigation for expanded grain production. Reliable water sources support subsistence agriculture, home gardens, livestock, and tree crops and thus higher nutritional standards.

Education

Factors related to water, sanitation and hygiene affect children's right to education in many ways. In an atmosphere of poor health, children are unable to fulfil their education potential. For example, 400 million school-aged children a year are infected by intestinal worms, which sap their learning abilities. Schools partly determine children's health and well- being by providing a healthy or unhealthy environment. Although water and sanitation facilities in schools are increasingly recognised as fundamental for promoting good hygiene behaviour and children's well-being, many schools have very poor facilities. Conditions vary from inappropriate and inadequate sanitary facilities to the outright lack of latrines and safe water for drinking and hygiene. This situation contributes to absenteeism and the high drop-out rates of girls.

Household chores, such as fetching water, keep many girls out of school. Even if girls do manage to go to school, they are sent to fetch water when it is needed. Most other household chores – including cleaning latrines and garbage disposal – also fall to women and girls. When family members become sick (often due to hygiene-related diseases), girls are more likely to be kept home to care for them. Providing water closer to homes increases girls' free time and boosts their school attendance. All children need a sanitary and hygienic learning environment, but the lack of sanitation and hygiene facilities in schools has a stronger negative impact on girls than on boys. Girls need safe, clean, separate and private sanitation facilities in their schools. Sanitation at school helps the students to concentrate on the studies. Better sanitation reduces the problems with the growing children and reduces the problem of gender harassment at school level.

Gender Equality

Water is necessary not only for drinking, but also for food production and preparation, care of domestic animals, personal hygiene, care of the sick, cleaning, washing and waste disposal. Women and men usually have very different roles in water and sanitation activities. Men are usually more concerned with water for irrigation or for livestock. While women are often more direct users of water, especially in the household, men traditionally may have a greater role than women in public decision-making. Lack of access to safe water, sanitation and hygiene prevents women and girls from enjoying their right to live healthy and fulfilled lives and reach their potential.

Water sources and sanitation facilities closer to home put women and girls at less risk for sexual harassment and assault while gathering water and searching for privacy. Secondly, community-based organisations for water supply and sanitation can improve social capital of women. Further, improved water services give women more time for productive endeavours, adult education, empowerment activities, and leisure.

Child and Maternal Mortality

Sanitation and hygiene are key to child survival, development and growth. Higher rates of child survival are a precursor to the demographic transition to lower fertility rates; having fewer children reduces women's domestic responsibilities. Sanitation and safe water in healthcare facilities help ensure clean delivery and reduce neonatal deaths. Improved sanitation, safe drinking water sources, and greater quantities of domestic water for washing reduce infant and child morbidity and mortality. Mothers with improved water supply and sanitation services are better able to care for their children, both because they have fewer illnesses and because they devote less time to water-fetching and seeking privacy for defecation. Accessible sources of water reduce labour burdens and health problems resulting from water portage, reducing maternal mortality risks. Improved health and nutrition reduce susceptibility to anaemia and other conditions that affect maternal mortality.

Major Diseases

A system of sanitation provides the greatest health protection to the individual, the community, and the society. Human excreta have been implicated in the transmission of many infectious diseases including cholera, typhoid, infectious hepatitis, polio, cryptosporidiosis, and ascariasis. Undernutrition, pneumonia, worm infestations, are also associated with unsafe water, poor sanitation and hygiene resulting in reduced physical growth, weakened physical fitness and impaired cognitive function, particularly for children under the age of five. Infectious agents are not the only health concerns associated with wastewater and excreta. Heavy metals, toxic organic and inorganic substances also can pose serious threats to human health and the environment – particularly when industrial wastes are added to the waste stream.

Environmental Sustainability

Adequate treatment and disposal of excreta and wastewater contributes to better ecosystem management and less pressure on freshwater resources. Improved sanitation reduces flows of human excreta into waterways, helping to protect human and environmental health. Inadequate access to safe water and inadequate access to sanitation and other infrastructure are the defining characteristics of a slum.

Economic Benefits

Improved sanitation has positive impacts on economic growth and poverty reduction. According to a recent WHO study, every dollar spent on improving sanitation generates an average economic benefit of $7. People without toilets spend a great deal of time each day queuing up for public toilets. Similarly women would save time from bringing water from distant places if they had tapped water. Health and sanitation can reduce direct and indirect health costs. Money and time saved can be used for greater production. Money spent on sanitation in schools can improve education. Better toilet facilities in schools will reduce school dropouts and better education. Providing good drinking water for the citizens can improve their health. If an area or a country is clean people of other countries will visit it. So hygiene and sanitation can boost tourism and in turn tourism can bring about economic development of the country.

Conclusion

Sociology of sanitation as a branch of sociology includes cultural dimension of sanitation. Any relations between people and their environment are embedded in culture. Primarily, the concepts of purity and pollution are responsible for the problem of scavenging. In India, the social components of the caste system, cultural values, lack of education, social domination by the rich and powerful, social deprivation of the lower strata of society concepts of Karma and Dharma and exploitation have given rise to scavenging activities. The scavengers face health, social, economic, and psychological problems. Caste, religion and sex are the important agencies in the development of the attitudes, beliefs and values regarding sanitation and they are transmitted from generation to generation through the process of socialisation. In the present day world sanitation has become a key to measure of social and economic development of a nation. Lack of sanitation considered as the hindrance towards social development. Lack of sanitation is associated with poverty, hunger, lack of education, gender inequality, child and maternal mortality, diseases and economic deprivation.

References

Johnson, Harry M. 1966. *Sociology: A Systematic Introduction.* Bombay: Allied Publishers Private Limited.

Kakade, R.G. 1949. *Depressed Classes of South Kanara.* Poona: Servants of Indian Society.

Ketkar, S.V. 1990. *History of Caste in India.* Delhi: Low Price Publications.

Pais, Richard (Ed.). 2008. *Principles of Sociology.* Mangalore: Mangala Publications.

http://www.sswm.info/content/water-sanitation-and- development accessed on 9th September 2014

http://www.unicef.org/wash/index_schools.html accessed on 10th, September 2014

Chapter - 6

Reinvention of Sanitation in Modern World

Introduction

It is very important for the modern social developers to look into the past of the sanitation in the ancient society for better understanding the sanitation as a problem in the society. However, history presents very little information regarding the means employed in very early times for sanitation and for the protection of health. During these times the measures enforced in dealing with outbreaks of infectious disease depended chiefly upon the various theories of those in charge of this branch of public service. The plague and cholera were common diseases through which thousands of people died in Europe and in other countries.

In spite of the meagre information in history, historians are of the opinion that the sanitation facilities existed in the ancient society for the better health and use of the people. If we go to the ancient history of the world the use of toilet, sewage system can be observed and the construction of bathrooms and swimming pools arc so established they were used for hundreds of years.

In the words of Dr Bindeswar Pathak, unlike body functions like dance, drama and songs, defecation is considered very low. As a result very few scholars documented precisely the toilet habits of our predecessors. The Nobel Prize winner for Medicine (1913) Charles Richet attributes this silence to the disgust that arises from noxiousness and lack of usefulness of human waste. The more developed was the society, the more sanitised it became and vice versa.

6.1 Changes in Sanitation from Ancient to Modern

As Dr Bindeswar Pathak says, As long as man did not have an established abode, he did not have a toilet. He excreted wherever he felt like doing so. When he learnt to have a fixed house, he moved toilet to courtyard and then within his home. Once this was done, it became a challenge to deal with smell and the need was felt to have a toilet which can intake human wastes and dispose these out of the house instantly and, thus, help maintain cleanliness. Man tried various ways to do so i.e., chamber pots, which were cleaned manually by the servants or slaves, toilets protruding out of the top floor of the house or the castle and disposal of wastes in the river below, or common toilets with holes on the top and flowing river or stream underneath or just enter the river or stream and dispose of the waste of the human body. While the rich used luxurious toilet chairs or close stools the poor defecated on the roads, in the jungle or straight into the river.

Sanitation in the Ancient World

In the ancient world people were capable of designing quite sophisticated toilets. Stone Age farmers lived in a village at Skara Brae in the Orkney Islands; some of their stone huts had drains built under them and some houses had cubicles over the drains. By 2800 BC, private bathrooms, located on the ground floor, were found in many houses of the Harappa civilisation. 'Western-style' toilets were also made from bricks and used wooden toilet seats on top. In Ancient Egypt rich people had proper bathrooms and toilets in their homes. Toilet seats were made of limestone. Poor people made do with a wooden stool with a hole in it. Underneath was a container filled with sand, which had to be emptied by hand. Throughout most of our history, sanitation practices were practically nonexistent. Yet the history of sanitation dates back at least 7,000 years, to the Babylonians, Egyptians, Greeks, and Romans. 7,000 years ago the Babylonians discovered that contaminated water could cause disease. They brought in fresh water every day. 2,000 years ago the physician Hippocrates discovered that cleansing could prevent infection.

In the Indus Valley Civilisation (2,600-1,900 BC) streets were built on a grid pattern and networks of sewers were dug under them. Toilets were flushed with water. The ancient Indus Valley Civilisation of

Northwest South Asia, including Pakistan and parts of India, was prominent in hydraulic engineering, and had many water supply and sanitation devices that were the first of their kind. In Ancient and Medieval times, there were public toilets, but not the ones we have today. They pretty much looked like a bench with a hole in it, and a deep pit at the bottom of the hole where all the human waste would be kept in, occasionally was being shovelled out by unfortunate peasants or servants. Among other things, they contain the world's earliest known system of flush toilets. These existed in many homes, and were connected to a common sewerage pipe. Most houses also had private wells. The sewage was then led into cesspools, built at the intersection of two drains, which had stairs leading to them for periodic cleaning. Plumbing was done using earthenware plumbing pipes with broad flanges for easy joining with asphalt to stop leaks was in place.

Harappa, Lothal, and Mohenjo-Daro are three of the extensive archaeological excavations in the region of the Indus Valley Civilisation. They are noted for sophisticated public works that included sewage drainage systems, public wells, and private and public baths.

Sanitation in Ancient Rome

Sanitation in ancient Rome was a complex system similar in many ways to modern sanitation systems. A system of thirteen Roman aqueducts provided the inhabitants of Rome with water of varying quality, the best being reserved for potable supplies. Poorer-quality water was used in public baths and in latrines, which were an early form of toilet. Latrine systems have been found in many places, such as house steads, a Roman fort on Hadrian's Wall, in Pompeii, Herculaneum, and elsewhere that flushed waste away with a stream of water. Romans used sea sponges on a stick and dipped in vinegar after defecation.

The Romans had a complex system of sewers covered by stones, much like modern sewers. Waste flushed from the latrines flowed through a central channel into the main sewage system and thence into a nearby river or stream. It is estimated that the first sewers of ancient Rome were built between 800 and 735 BC. Drainage systems evolved slowly, and began primarily as a means to drain marshes and storm runoff. Around AD 100, direct connections of homes to sewers began, and the Romans completed most of the sewer system infrastructure. Sewers were laid throughout the city, serving public and some private latrines, and also served as dumping grounds for homes not directly connected to a sewer.

It was mostly the wealthy whose homes were connected to the sewers, through outlets that ran under an extension of the latrine.

In general, the poor used pots that they were supposed to empty into the sewer, or visited public latrines. Public latrines date back to the second century BC. Whether intentionally or not, they became places of socialisation. Long bench-like seats with keyhole-shaped openings cut in rows offered little privacy. The Romans recycled public bath waste water by using it as part of the flow that flushed the latrines. Terra cotta piping was used in the plumbing that carried waste water from homes. The Romans were the first to seal pipes in concrete to resist the high water pressures developed in siphons and elsewhere.

The system in Rome was copied in all provincial towns and cities of the Roman Empire, and even down to villas that could afford the plumbing. Roman citizens came to expect high standards of hygiene, and the army was also well provided with latrines and bath houses. Aqueducts were used everywhere in the empire not just to supply drinking water for private houses but to supply other needs such as irrigation, public fountains, and thermae. Indeed, many of the provincial aqueducts survive in working order to the present day, although modernised and updated.

Sanitation in the Middle Ages

After the fall of the Western Roman Empire in the fifth century AD sophisticated plumbing disappeared from Europe for centuries. In Saxon times, toilets were simply pits in the ground with wooden seats over them. However, in the middle ages monks built stone or wooden lavatories over rivers. At Port Chester Castle in the twelfth century monks built stone chutes leading to the sea. When the tide went in and out it would flush away the sewage. Medieval cities, castles and monasteries had their own wells, fountains or cisterns. Usually towns built a few modest latrines for the inhabitants, but these were mostly inadequate for the size of the population. The lack of proper sanitation increased the effects of epidemics in medieval towns in Europe.

Personal cleanliness in medieval times was hampered by a lack of access to fresh water supplies and frequent problems with sewage disposal in medieval towns. During medieval times, it was widely believed that bad smells were the cause of disease and so if the smell could be combated, the threat of disease was lessened. Town authorities across Europe made attempts to get rid of their rubbish and sewage, even if the link between waste and disease wasn't fully understood. In the late thirteenth- century, the Great Conduit of London supplied the city with clean water and in other towns, rivers were often used to carry away waste, to the detriment of those downstream.

Another problem was the lack of separation between industrial and domestic living areas. Many industries such as butchery, dyeing and tanning were carried out in or alongside living accommodation, meaning that dirt and strong, foul smells were part of everyday life. Waste from these industries often made its way back into the local water supply, further endangering health. The widespread practice of covering floors with a rush matting was another potential health hazard. Unless the floor covering was changed frequently (as in the wealthiest households), animal droppings and particles of food would rot within the rushes, spreading germs and disease.

Medieval times were truly the Dark Ages as far as sanitation was concerned. Towns were dirty and crowded, and disease and epidemics spread unchecked because of the lack of sanitation. Water was contaminated, and personal hygiene was virtually unknown. Tuberculosis, cholera, diphtheria, smallpox, yellow fever, all were rampant.

It is not surprising that health during the Middle Ages was poor and the mortality rates following illnesses were high. This was the period of the Crusades and battles for power. Siege warfare and constant battles were the norm in the Middle Ages. Knights and soldiers suffered from various health problems such as broken bones, wounds, abscesses and fractures. These were treated in unsanitary environments making the condition even worse. The only cure for toothache was having the tooth pulled - without anaesthetics. Dreadful amputations were performed by surgeons.

Sanitation in the Modern World

The fall of the Roman Empire also marked the end of this early sanitation culture. Due to lack of development flush toilets and sewage systems didn't exist in medieval Europe. Calls of nature or the faeces were simply poured into the gutters. This situation didn't change until the end of the sixteenth century, when the English poet Sir John Harington invented the first "modern" water closet – an undertaking assigned to him by his famous aunt, Queen Elizabeth I. Though Harington drew up a precise construction manual, the first water closet of our modern age fell into oblivion.

In spite of Harrington invention of a flushing lavatory with a cistern, the idea failed to catch on. People continued to use chamber pots or cess pits, which were cleaned by men called gong farmers. In 1775, Alexander Cummings reinvents the "water closet" and introduces the first S-trap to keep sewer odours from escaping. In 1885 Thomas, Twyford revolutionises toilet design by replacing the metal and wood contraptions with an all-porcelain design. In 1870, John Randall Mann patents a three-pipe water closet, developing a method to utilise the suction force of a siphon to aid the flush. There were public lavatories in the middle Ages and the sixteenth century.

The first modern public lavatory, with flushing toilets opened in London in 1852. Meanwhile Joseph Gayetty invented toilet paper in 1857. At first toilet paper was sold in sheets. It was first sold in rolls in the USA in 1890 and in 1928 in Europe. Soft toilet paper went on sale in 1942. However, after it was invented in the West toilet paper was a luxury. In the early twentieth century many families used newspaper.

However, flushing toilets were a luxury at first and they did not become common till the late nineteenth century. In the early nineteenth century working class homes often did not have their own toilet and had to share one. Sometimes one had to queue to use it. In the nineteenth century toilet pans were made of porcelain. They were usually decorated, embossed or painted with attractive colours. Seats were of wood and cisterns were often emptied by pulling a chain. At first toilet bowls were boxed in but the first pedestal toilet bowl was made in 1884. Meanwhile the vacant/engaged bolt for public toilets was patented in 1883. Also popular in the nineteenth century were earth closets. An earth closet was a box of granulated clay over a pan. When you pulled lever clay covered the contents of the pan. In rural areas flushing lavatories did not replace earth closets until the early twentieth century.

However, inside toilets were luxuries in the nineteenth century. In the late nineteenth century working class homes almost always had outside lavatories. About 1900, some houses were built for skilled workers with bathrooms and inside toilets. However, it was decades before inside toilets became universal. In nineteenth century in New York City, living conditions were as nearly as filthy as in the middle ages, and yearly epidemics swept through populations, killing many. The average life span was less than 40 years of age. But during the mid 1800's, it was discovered between germs and disease was proven. Soaps, disinfectants, and pharmaceuticals began to be developed, and it was first recognised that disease could be controlled. This began the Sanitation Revolution, and public health practices such as garbage collection, water treatment, public health departments and regulations, as well as personal bathing, became part of the culture. The death rate in children dropped, and the average life span increased over the years, upto age 74.

In the second half of the nineteenth century scientists, such as Louis Pasteur, began to recognise the relationship between disease and hygiene – as a result, the demands for more hygiene became increasingly louder. At a very early stage, ceramics specialist Villeroy and Boch saw the market potential of the sanitary-ware sector with its bathtubs, sinks, toilets and tiles. By 1870, Villeroy and Boch was already equipping public swimming baths, private bathrooms and hospitals with easy-care tiles. As early as the mid 1870s, the company was offering a small range of urinals and toilets. Developments made in the area of production methods and materials soon facilitated industrial production. Since Villeroy and Boch was able to produce sanitary ware in such large quantities, that these items became affordable for broad strata of society by 1899.

Sanitation at Present

Today, in rich countries we take toilets for granted yet in poor countries millions of people do not have hygienic toilets. Our word toilet is derived from the French word toilette, which means little cloth. In the seventeenth century it was a cloth cover for a dressing table, called a toilet table. If a woman was at her toilet it meant she was dressing and preparing her appearance. By the nineteenth century toilet room or toilet was a euphemism for a certain room. Our word lavatory comes from the Latin lavare meaning to wash. In the seventeenth century a lavatory was a place for washing. Later it became a euphemism for a certain room. Now, the word restroom is used for toilets in the developed countries. The word 'restroom' originated in the United States. Some Americans prefer restroom over bathroom because public restrooms rarely have bathtubs. The word 'washroom' is often used in the United States for a laundry room or utility room.

On board a ship the toilets are called the heads. Originally they were just wooden boards with holes cut in them hanging over the sides of the ships. They were placed at the head of the ship. On land there are many euphemisms for toilets. One is 'the smallest room in the house'. An old euphemism for going to the toilet was 'going to spend a penny' because public lavatories used to cost one penny to use.

In the modern world sanitation has taken importance in the health and the dignity aspects of human life. At present sanitation has taken changes into luxurious comfort, in earlier days it was only for the purpose of defecating, but at present it also gained importance as dignity. The concept of toilet has changed with its structure designs etc. The modern toilets are more attractive than the bed room of the people. People feel happy to decorate the toilets with fragrance etc. Some of the people use highly costliest material in the construction of the toilet.

Today, a wide selection of toilets can be found in a great variety of shapes and colours and offering additional comfort. They can be floor-standing or wall-mounted; a combination of toilet and cistern, or with pre-wall installation systems; washout toilets with ceramic ledges, or wash down toilets with direct access into the trap water. And there's even more: in recent years a whole series of innovations have been developed particularly in the area of sanitation. In view of the increasing scarcity of water resources, now companies offers modern, environment-friendly flushing systems, such as Omnia Green Gain or Aquareduct, which function with as little as 3.5 liters to 4.5 liters of water per flush. Extremely convincing qualities are also displayed by the ceramic surface finish, Ceramic Plus. It's easy-care properties help reduce the amount of water and cleaning agents needed. The Pure Air WC opens up a totally new dimension in WC comfort.

Without modern sanitation, life would be nightmarish. Human and animal waste would fester on the streets along with garbage and food scraps, producing a stench so foul that you'd want to keep your windows closed even in the sweltering heat of summer. The offensive odours and accumulating muck would be the least of your worries. However, preventable diseases such as cholera and yellow fever would be rampant, your life expectancy would be extremely short, and infant mortality rates would be staggeringly high.

The prime minister's Independence Day (2014) speech exhorted India Inc to adopt the mission of providing modern sanitation facilities nationwide. Just as the I-Day weekend got over, India Inc promised to spend big money to clean up India. TCS, Bharti, HUL, Aditya Birla Group, ITC, Adani and Dabur are among major companies that announced big CSR spends or promised to upgrade existing programmes for building sanitation facilities, especially for girl students and women in rural India. These announcements and promises look substantial. TCS, India's largest software services firm, said it will spend Rs 100 crore building sanitation facilities for girl students in 10,000 schools.

Swachh Bharat Abhiyan (Clean India Campaign) was officially launched on 2nd October, 2014 at Rajghat, New Delhi, where Prime Minister Narendra Modi himself wielded broom and cleaned a road. The campaign is India's biggest ever cleanliness drive and three million government employees and schools and colleges students of India participated in this event. This campaign aims to accomplish the vision of 'clean India' by 2nd October, 2019, 150th birthday of Mahatma Gandhi and is expected to cost over Rs 62,000 crores.

6.2 Modern Technology in Sanitation

Human society is facing the problem of sanitation right from its beginning. However, the sanitation practices have changed according to the will and the need of the community. Still, the societies specially the developing societies face the problem of disposal of human waste and the waste material generated in the society. Technology has played an important role in sanitation. Without the aid of technology it would be difficult for humans to solve the problem of disposal of human and animal waste.

It is important to discuss and evaluate the applicability of selected ancient water and sanitation systems for the contemporary developing world. Selected water and sanitation systems in ancient Mesopotamia, the Indus Valley, Egypt, Greece and Rome are briefly introduced and then discussed in the context of the developing world. One relevant aspect is that public latrines and baths were not only a part of daily life in ancient Rome but also a focal point for socialising. As such, they would appear to represent a model of how to promote use and acceptance of modern community toilets and ablution blocks.

Today, 2.5 billion people worldwide lack access to safe sanitation, causing serious health problems, and in some cases, death. Food and water tainted with faecal matter result in 1.5 million child deaths every year. Most of these deaths could be prevented with the introduction of improved sanitation, along with safe drinking water and increased hygiene. It was only in the sixteenth century that a technological breakthrough came about and which helped the human beings to have clean toilets in houses. This breakthrough did not come about easily and human race had to live in insanitary conditions for thousands of years.

The idea of implementing ancient water and wastewater technologies in the developing world is a persuasive one, since ancient systems had many features which would constitute sustainable and decentralised water and sanitation provision in contemporary terminology. Latest figures indicate 2.5 billion people do not use improved sanitation and 1.1 billion practice open defecation, thus there is a huge need for sustainable and cost-effective water and sanitation facilities, particularly in cities of the developing world.

Toilet Technologies

Technologies do matter, but it takes a lot more in the field of sanitation. In many countries, sanitation technologies are piloted. Some work well and go to scale, while others break down or do not deliver the services they were intended to provide. There are very few standards for assessment and introduction of technology at local levels.

Eighteenth century was a century of toilets. Despite invention of water closet by John Harrington in 1596 which was costing only six shillings and eight pence this was not adopted on a large scale for almost 182 years. The delays in actual use of invention are common in human history which Toffler calls as "Cultural Gap". During this period people used earth closet. In these toilets instead of water earth was used. So, the problem of cleaning remained. The world also saw development of Pan Closets - which like cigarette ash tray threw the material at the bottom. This too required manual cleaning. At the same time chamber pots, close stools, open defecation remained. In comparison to this, Harrington's toilet under the name Angrez was being used in France, though not introduced on a large scale in England. In 1738, Brondel introduced the valve type flush toilet. Alexander Cummings further improved the technology and gave a better device in 1775. In 1775, the Scottish inventor Alexander Cummings invented a water closet which presented the S-shaped trap still used to this day, and was awarded the patent for it.

Further, the world was yet to witness further technological developments. In 1870, S.S. Helior invented the flush type toilet, called Optims—an improvement over Blummer's design. From 1880 onwards, however, the emphasis has been more on aesthetics to make cisterns and bowls decorative. The bowls were so colourful that some suggested using these as soup bowls. It was in 1880 that the toilet curtains made their appearance. The trend was called the age of "Belleepoque" in France and Edwardian (opulence) in England. During 1890, we had the first cantilever type of toilet. Since then the world has not witnessed any significant technical change except some change in shape of toilets and reduction in quantity of water per use.

It was around 1900 that the institution of bathroom came in vogue in Europe. In India, the institution of Gushalkhana (bathroom) was established by the Mughal Kings in 1556. Oppressed by the heat and dust the Kings constructed luxurious bathing and massage facilities. But this was only for the rich. The ordinary citizens, however, lived in insanitary conditions. In contrast, the twentieth century has given a pride of place to toilet in the home rather these are more opulent, more spacious than any time in the past. While the provision of toilet in the house solved household problem of cleanliness but the challenge remained as to how to dispose of human waste at city level. This was also solved when the sewerage system was introduced. Haussmann in 1858 describes beautifully the sewerage system. He said that "the underground galleries which are the organs of the big city will work in the same way as organs of the body, without being revealed. The human waste was transported manually with the help of carts, at unhygienic atmosphere. The pure and fresh water, the heat and light will circulate like the various fluids whose movement and maintenance are necessary to ensure life. The secretions will not mysteriously like place there and maintain public health without disturbing the order of the city and spoiling its outer beauty". Around the same time the sewerage system was introduced at Calcutta - Capital of colonial India. However, its extension in the country was and remains slow as it is capital intensive and beyond the resource capacity of the economy even today.

In 1970, realising that sewerage facilities will remain out of the reach of the society at large, Sulabh International introduced a pioneer technology twin pour flush latrines and human excreta-based Biogas plants. They have constructed in the last 25 years over 6,50,000 toilets cum bath complexes and 62 human excreta-based biogas plants and are maintaining them. This gives an appropriate solution to dispose of and recycle human waste into fertilizer, electricity and gas which can be used in the kitchens.

Modern Technology in Sanitation

The sanitation technology is used all over the world according to their capacity and technology. In fact, lot depends on the geography regarding the appropriate sanitation technologies. The technologies used in the hilly regions may be less expensive and may not be used in the flat land topography. The application of sanitation technologies depends on the economic capacity of the public or the capacity of the government. For example, the technologies which are used for the purpose of sanitation in the Corporation of Mumbai may not be used in the municipality of Mangalore.

Some of the modern technologies in the field of sanitation which are used in the society are:

Hand-free Toilets: Long accepted as a great convenience for people with mobility or dexterity problems, to enable independent toileting, automatic shower toilets are also more hygienic. Almost 80 per cent of infectious diseases are passed on by human contact, and as only half of people wash their hands after using the toilet. Hands-free toileting without the need for toilet paper is a healthier option. Germs are passed by hand/ body contact, so removing that contact improves hygiene. Washing with water rather than wiping is also more effective, especially if you have a limiting physical or mental condition, and, for some, a religious consideration. And a combined unit takes up less space, and requires less cleaning than separate toilet and bidet.

Sewage Technology: Throughout the world different kinds of technologies are used to manage sewage water. The technologies like Advanced oxidation process, Aerated lagoon, Aerobic granular reactor, Aerobic granular sludge technology, Aerobic treatment system, Anaerobic clarigester, Anaerobic digestion, Anaerobic filter, API oil-water separator, Anaerobic lagoon, Batch filter technology, Belt filter, Bioconversion of biomass to mixed alcohol fuels, Bio filters, Bioreactor and septic tank etc. Septic systems are a type of onsite sewage facility (OSSF). In Europe, septic systems are generally limited to rural areas. Since a septic system requires a drain field that uses a lot of land area, they are not suitable for densely built cities. A septic tank is a key component of the septic system, a small-scale sewage treatment system common in areas with no connection to main sewage pipes provided by local governments or private corporations. Other components, typically mandated and/or restricted by local governments, optionally include pumps, alarms, sand filters, and clarified liquid effluent disposal means such as a septic drain field, ponds, natural stone fibre filter plants or peat moss beds. Periodic preventive maintenance is required to remove the irreducible solids that settle and gradually fill the tank, reducing its efficiency.

Sullage or Gry Water Technology: This is a household-based technology mainly for rural areas to treat grey water that comes from the kitchen sink and bath for re-use. A kit designed to treat household waste water for reuse could be one of the ways to tackle water scarcity in rural areas. The kit consists of two large PVC barrels about 1.2 m high, each able to contain up to 200 liters of water, pipes and sand. Before reaching the barrels, the waste water goes through a separate filter where things like small bits of food are removed. The barrels are filled with sand; there is an anaerobic digestion of the organic matter when the water goes through the sand filter and becomes cleaner.

Drainage Technology: Drainage technology allows the flow of waste water through open or underground pipes to the sea or the tanks of filtration. In the hilly region it is easy to supply the drain water to sea. In the flat region the electronic pumps or machinery pumps are used for the flow of waste water.

Street Cleaning Technology: A street sweeper or street cleaner may refer to either a person's occupation, or a machine that cleans streets. A street sweeper cleans the streets, usually in an urban area. Street sweepers have been employed in cities since sanitation and waste removal became a priority. A street-sweeping person would use a broom and a shovel to clean off litter, animal waste and filth that accumulated on streets. Later, water hoses were used to wash the streets. Modern street sweepers are equipped with water tanks and sprayers used to loosen particles and reduce dust. The brooms gather debris into a main collection area from which it is vacuumed and pumped into a collection bin or hopper. A regenerative air street sweeper uses forced air to create a swirling effect inside a contained sweeping head and then uses the negative pressure on the suction side to place the road debris inside a hopper. Debris is removed from the air by centrifugal separation and reused, keeping particulate matter inside the hopper.

Application of Technology

The technology assessment framework is now under development and examines key criteria such as the performance of the technology, the market potential, whether the technology can be applied widely, support required from government and private sector institutions and sustainability of the technology over time. There is a need for innovators and creative thinkers to solve the sanitation challenge. And technology is one part of the puzzle. In addition to improving technology, we need to reflect on what we know already, understand what sanitation options people want and strengthen the enabling environment for sanitation services that last. This means investing in formative research and behaviour change, strengthening governance and accountability, working on better supply chains as well as in technology that is not only innovative, but also appropriate.

The second challenge is that there are a lot of reasons why existing technologies fail, that are related to the technology, but not (only) technical: the technology is unaffordable for the poorest, construction materials are not available, local workmanship is of low quality, etc. And thirdly, to ensure that technologies are used, we need to understand what consumers want. It's households who make the decision to invest in a toilet. The process of technology introduction, demand creation and hygiene behaviour change is a crucial factor in determining if the technology will be taken up.

In 2011, the Gates Foundation launched the Reinvent the Toilet Challenge – a programme created to design toilets that capture and process human waste without piped water, sewer or electrical connections, and transform waste into useful resources, such as energy and water, at an affordable price. This India toilet challenge is the second effort targeted to a specific country and is a testament to the research and development capabilities in India. One uses microwave energy to transform human waste into electricity. Another captures urine and uses it for flushing. And still another turns excrement into charcoal. The Reinvent the Toilet Challenge is designed to spur innovation and bring creative thinking to solve the problem of dealing human waste.

6.3 Prevention is Better than Cure

Sanitation is the only way for better life in the modern world. As the society is developing the threat for human life is increasing in different forms. The threat of human waste is one of the important things which humans cannot ignore. So the management of human waste in a particular manner may help humans to live better life in the society. Lack of sanitation should not become a reason for unhealthy atmosphere in the society.

Considerably, we can say that it is better to prevent something before it turns into a problem. So, modern society has to understand the importance of sanitation and the meaning of prevention is better than cure.

Prevention is better than cure is a wise saying which has come down to us since the ages. It holds true for ever. The wisdom of the saying lies in the fact that a little effort in the early phase of a problem helps to solve it before it becomes too difficult to be solved. This principle is always observed by wise people to succeed in life. Those who do not observe this principle generally suffer even if they are intelligent. The saying prevention is better than cure means that it is easier to prevent an illness than to treat it. Treatment can be costly, life-changing and sometimes damaging. Therefore, it is often more beneficial from a health, happiness and financial aspect to prevent something rather than allowing oneself to fall ill if there are preventative measures that can be taken.

We have all grown up hearing the adage, 'Prevention is better than cure' since our very childhood as - brush your teeth to protect them from decaying; wash your hands before eating food to avoid a stomach upset; do not eat uncovered street food; get vaccinated against diseases like polio; get rid of stagnant water to stay clear of malaria and dengue; exercise to stay fit; and so on. No one wants to argue with these time-tested measures, which if followed can reduce one's chances of contracting a disease; forget about trying to find a cure later. One of the aims identified of engaging people more closely in their personal health and well-being is to increase the number of quality of life years they experience; preventing illness and prolonging life.

In India, how can anyone ignore the subject of toilet when the society is faced with human excretions of the order of 900 million liters of urine and 135 million kilograms of faeces matter per day with totally inadequate system of its collection and disposal? The society, thus, has a constant threat of health hazards and epidemics. As many as 600 out of 900 million people do open defecation. Sewerage facilities are available to no more than 30 per cent of population in urban areas and only three per cent of rural population has access to pour flush latrines. Seeing this challenge, the subject of toilet is as important if not more as other social challenges like literacy, poverty, education and employment. Rather, subject of toilet is more important because lack of excremental hygiene is a national health hazard while in other problems the implications are relatively closer to only those who suffer from unemployment, illiteracy and poverty.

The containment and treatment of human excreta – combined with hand-washing – protects humans from harmful bacteria, viruses and helminthes. Sanitation dramatically reduces cases of diarrhea, cholera, typhoid and worm infections. This particularly guards children from additional malnutrition and stunted growth. Without such illnesses, the body is more resilient against acute respiratory diseases, like pneumonia. Sanitation protects the health of AIDS patients with a weakened immune system. By preventing unnecessary death and disease, sanitation alleviates the psychological burden of permanent fear for loved ones from many families and communities. Safe sanitation and clean water can save the lives of 5,000 children under the age of five per day.

Preventive Measures of Poor Sanitation

Poor sanitation is the reason for health problems or social problems like open defecation. In fact, poor sanitation is the result of ignorance of the people and the lack of social measures for the development of sanitation. Though water treatment and handling practices in the community were generally good, insufficient hygiene and sanitation may contribute to an increased risk of infectious disease transmission in an already economically and socially disadvantaged community. Improvements in water, sanitation and hygiene practices and infrastructure may be one of the most important and cost-effective methods for decreasing the burden of infectious diseases worldwide. Fortunately, most of these diseases are preventable with improvements in water, sanitation and hygiene practices and infrastructure. Increases in hand washing alone decrease the prevalence of diarrheal disease by 42 per cent, while improvements in hygiene cause a reduction of 33 per cent and sanitation a reduction of 36 per cent, according to rigorous studies in developing countries.

Some of the important measures can be followed for the prevention of poor sanitation are highlighted below:

Construction of Toilets in the Required Area: Toilet has been one of the important requirements of human beings in the society. It is very important to have a toilet for the personal use. The requirement of toilet in the public places is more. So, wherever the requirement of public toilet is there, the public authority should take proper measures to construct toilets to prevent unhealthy environment.

Construction of Sewage or Drainage System: Construction and maintenance of drainage system for the purpose of waste water is one of the important things to be taken care off. Mismanagement of waste water can lead to several diseases which will spoil the life of the public. So, construction of waste water drainage in a systematic and scientific way is important in the present society.

Providing Drinking Water Facilities: It's been observed that people are facing the problem of drinking water and due to bad drinking water people are getting sick. Providing safe, clean drinking water can avoid the chances of getting sick. The requirement of safe drinking water is the first need of the society. Panchayats, town and city municipalities and city corporations should consider it as a priority issue.

Proper Disposal of Human and Animal Waste: Human and animal waste is threatening which has to be taken care off. Use of latest technology to dispose of human and animal waste should be used. It should not be left to the river or the canals by which people get disease. Management of human and animal waste can help to establish better environment. Both people of rural and urban areas should be helped in this regard.

Creating Awareness about Sanitation: Lack of awareness about sanitation among people is also one of the important reasons for bad sanitation in the society. When people get awareness about sanitation and the importance of sanitation they will try to avoid unhealthy condition in their surrounding for better health. Generation of awareness among people is also considered as one of the important aspect of human society. Both adults and children should be educated. The children could be educated in the schools.

In the society it is not the problem of sanitation which is causing health problems or any other social problems in that matter, it is the ignorance of people and the negligence among the people leading towards health issues in the society. Thus, it is understood that one should take responsibility to prevent unhealthy surroundings by not contributing to pollution and developing better sanitation system in the society. The movement started by Present Prime Minister, Narendra Modi, 'Swachha Bharath Abhiyan' is a right step in this direction. All people, irrespective of caste, religion, region and political party should co-operate in this venture.

6.4 Sanitation as Business

Business is an organisation or economic system where goods and services are exchanged for one another or for money. Every business requires some form of investment and enough customers to whom its output can be sold on a consistent basis in order to make a profit. Businesses can be privately owned, not-for-profit or state-owned. Sanitation as business is nothing but using sanitary system for the purpose of business. Providing a toilet facility by collecting money can be called as sanitation business. The process of better society in the name of sanitation is established and in the name of collecting money business is accomplished. Nowadays, it is observed in the society that the public toilets are also managed by the private organisations for better maintenance. It is true that the paid toilets are clean comparatively to the free toilets.

The use of sanitation in different ways for generation of finance is called as business. Sanitation business now turned as income generating business in the modern world. Nowadays, people are collecting the human and the animal waste by paying money for it. The use of human and animal waste in generating biogas and fertilizers are generating more income to the society.

The case study titled "Making night soil-based biogas plants viable in Maharashtra's Pune district" has been written by Dr S V Mapuskar in India Infrastructure Report, published in 2007 by United Nations Children's Fund (UNICEF). It presents Dehu village of Maharashtra's Pune district, where some families allow their neighbours to use their toilets for a nominal maintenance charge making attached biogas plants economically viable. The strategy has also eased the village Panchayat's responsibilities for human night soil management and reduced environmental pollution due to open defecation. The experience in Dehu has shown that there are about 75 family-owned human night soil-based biogas plants in Dehu providing kitchen fuel for villagers and it has been calculated that the installation of the 75 biogas plants in Dehu village has reduced the demand for LPG gas in the village by about 100 domestic LPG cylinders per month. The health benefits are also significant as faecal pollution is reduced.

Following are some of the ways through which sanitation can be turned into business.

Paid toilets: In order to maintain better sanitation levels government and nongovernmental organisations are establishing paid toilets in the public places and the slum areas wherever it is necessary. These public toilets charge nominal amount for the use. More than that, it is the requirement of toilet of the public makes them to pay. And thus, it is turned as a business nowadays.

Biogas plants: Biogas plants generate gas for domestic use with the use of human and animal waste which generates income for the family. Earning money with the waste (biogas) generates income and also helps in establishing sanitation in the society. The toilets which are constructed for human defecation can be used for income generation also. There are so many companies which have made building biogas plants as business for the homes in rural areas.

Sanitary Arts and Designs: No one has given any thought to the toilet as a piece of art, but in terms of business it is yes. Sanitary designs are the important aspects in the field of sanitary business. The art of sanitary system is nowadays gaining more attention in upper middle class society. The people are paying lakhs of rupees for just paintings and sanitary fittings. Some of the families wish to install toilet fittings which are imported; they feel happy to have imported items in the toilet. These attitudes of people have helped to establish sanitation as business in the society. Sanitary items are generating more income for the people. Sanitation was necessity, but now it has turn to a dignity.

Every business needs an investment. Sanitation is low margin business in the society. You invest fewer amounts and get assured profit throughout the life. There is no fear of decreasing demand; there will be always demand as it is a necessity for the people. So, sanitation has turned as better business in the metropolitan cities like Delhi, Kolkata, Mumbai, and Bangalore. Sanitation can be considered as faster growing business in the society, with lesser skill and lesser investment with assured profits. Moreover non-governmental institutions are taking more interest in the sanitation business than the government, though they are non-profit organisations.

6.5 Sanitation as Dignity

Dignity refers to the state or quality of being worthy of honour or respect. In general, the term has various functions and meanings depending on how the term is used and on the context. Dignity is the social status which will uphold the personality in the society on the basis of his economic assets and socio-political power. Dignity of a person can also be measured on the basis of his job which is more socialistic in nature.

We can observe two kinds of dignity when we are referring to sanitational dignity; one is the sanitational commodities which will increase the human value in the society, and the other one is the dignity of human labour in the field of sanitation. Dignity with commodity is more economic in nature; dignity with labour is more socialistic in nature. Let us understand sanitation as dignity in both the ways: dignity in terms of commodities as well as dignity of labour in sanitation work.

Dignity of labour in sanitation deals with the social status of the sanitation labourers, as they have low status in the society. The dignity of sanitation labour is too low as found in the caste hierarchy. Though Martin Luther says, 'All labour that uplifts humanity has dignity and importance and should be undertaken with painstaking excellence'. According to Max de Pree, American businessman and writer, we need to give each other the space to grow, to be ourselves, to exercise our diversity. We need to give each other space so that we may both give and receive such beautiful things as ideas, openness, dignity, joy, healing, and inclusion.

Sanitation as dignity can gain a wider meaning when it is considered in terms of economical aspect; the attitude of the people is contributing to the dignity through sanitation. Considerably, people are not only using sanitation for the purpose of health, they maintain well designed sanitary system like bath tubs, imported showers, basins, and some electronic sensor type of water taps etc., people think that the expenditure on sanitary system can upgrade the status of the people in the society, thus the dignity is improved. Sanitation has a strong connection not only with personal hygiene but also with human dignity and well-being, public health, nutrition and even education.

Sanitation contributes to gender equality, access to education and dignity. It also enhances dignity, privacy and safety, especially for women and girls. It improves convenience and social status. Sanitation in schools enables children, especially girls reaching puberty, to remain in the educational system. Restricted toilet opportunities increase the chance of chronic constipation and are making women vulnerable to violence if they are forced to defecate during nightfall and in secluded areas. In some areas, it is considered that having a toilet at home is more important than any gold assets, basically a women needs toilet more than anything else. Providing improved sanitation facilities is equal to liberating women and girls and also providing substantial benefits for the whole community.

Toilet facilities provide privacy and prevent women from experiencing abuse while defecating openly. As domestic caretakers of the sick in many societies, women benefit the most from a healthy community. Thus, women can defecate with dignity at home with a toilet facility. Their own health is safeguarded while they gain time to further their education and contribute to their family's well-being. Clean toilets contribute to poverty eradication by protection of one's health and ability to work. Good school sanitation is essential for keeping children in school– particularly girls during menstruation.

Sanitation is considered as a part of dignity with changing modern society. The concept of dignity not only related to the exterior parts of the house like car etc. It is also related to the interior part of the house. It is a common practice when the groom's side visits girl's house during proposal to visit the house and also see the toilet. It is also the case when girl's side visit groom's house. In such instances, both the families take care to see that both the house and toilets are clean.

Nowadays, Indian families are considering sanitation as dignity and they are spending more amounts of money on the toilet and bathroom than the hall where people come and go. Sanitary systems are getting costlier as it is considered as dignity and also the development of sanitary system is taking place not only with the notion of necessity but dignity. On an average the Indian middle class family spends nearly 1.5 lakh on their sanitation itself at home. In some of the homes of Mumbai and in large cities, people are using golden plated toilet fittings for the use.

Sanitation saves lives and the faster we act the more lives we can save. A child's life could be saved every 20 seconds, if safe drinking water and basic sanitation were available. This improvement could reduce 80 per cent of all sickness and disease; it could save more lives per year than are lost due to war. The dramatic health improvements would permit more dignified lifestyles – providing each man, woman or child with more time to work, learn or care for the family. Urinating and defecating are basic human needs just like eating, drinking, sleeping or breathing. Every human being should be able to fulfil that need in dignity. Sanitation provides privacy and protects everyone in the community. It is time we recognise the potential of sanitation for human development and act concertedly to make a difference.

References

http://en.wikipedia.org/wiki/Sanitation_in_ancient_Rome

http://www.villeroyboch-group.com/en/about-villeroy-boch/our- stories/the-history-of-the-toilet-sanitations-ups-and-downs.html

Chapter – 7

Environmental Sanitation

Introduction

Environmental sanitation refers to the sanitation in the environment in which we live. It is aimed at improving or maintaining the standard of basic environmental conditions affecting the well-being of people. It is the environment in which an individual lives, interacts with others and satisfies his basic physical and social needs. So, the responsibility of environmental sanitation begins from the individual. The individual cannot be separated from the society. The environment in which the individual lives i.e., where the group or the community lives is important. Since man is an integral part of the group or society the individual is equally responsible as the group for the environment in which he/they live. The individual and the group are also responsible for the sanitation in the group. So, it is very important to understand what is environmental sanitation and the dimension of environmental sanitation.

Environmental sanitation is a set of actions geared towards improving the quality of the environment and reducing the amount of disease. By doing so, we hope that living conditions will improve and health problems will decrease. The management of water, solid waste, and industrial waste, as well as the topics of pollution of various types fall under the umbrella of environmental sanitation. It is said that environmental sanitation is very vital for any nation. So, in order to live in a world free from diseases, we must embark on task of cleaning our houses, neighbourhoods and public places. Health experts have indicated that the initiative has drastically reduced the burden of malarial diseases and other health related problems.

The definition of environmental sanitation is quite simple. Environmental sanitation simply refers to *'cleaning the environment for better human life'*. It also refers to proper maintenance of trash and garbage to support a healthy environment. Environmental sanitation is the control of environmental factors that form links in disease transmission. Subsets of this category are solid waste management, water and waste water treatment, industrial waste water treatment and noise and pollution control.

According to the World Health Organisation (WHO), there are four areas that must be reviewed in order for environmental sanitation to be effective: planning, water supply, sanitation, and hygiene education.

What is Environmental Sanitation?

Environmental sanitation is a set of actions geared towards improving the quality of the environment and reducing the amount of disease. These actions include:

1. Getting clean and safe water supply.
2. Breathing clean and safe ambient air.
3. Disposal of efficient and safe animal, human, and industrial waste.
4. Protection of food from biological and chemical contaminants.
5. Adequate housing in clean and safe surroundings.

By doing so, the hope is that living conditions will improve and health problems will decrease. The management of water, solid waste, and industrial waste, as well as the topic of pollution and noise control, all fall under the umbrella of environmental sanitation. Moreover, environmental sanitations are activities aimed at improving or maintaining the standard of basic environmental condition affecting the well-being of peoples.

Importance of Environmental Sanitation

Environmental sanitation are activities that are aimed at improving the standard of basic environmental conditions that affect the well being of people. Some of the important facts about environmental sanitation are human excreta always contain large number of germs, when people become infected with diseases such as cholera, typhoid and hepatitis A, their excreta will contain large amounts of the germs, and during the rainy season excreta may be washed away by rain water and can run into wells and streams. Environmental sanitation involves both household and environmental sanitations. Household sanitation also involves household food safety, and the maintenance of clean living conditions which do not promote the spread of disease. This includes general cleaning in our places where we keep food. Without environmental sanitation, many would become sick and die.

Disease occurs when a disease causing agent gets into the body and invades our body defences. Some of our family members get sick as the weather changes, or when they got caught up with so much stress. There are so many factors to consider. Even mothers who just stay at home could get ill just by cleaning the house or by disposing the trashes. In reality, disease chooses no one and everyone is capable of getting ill. These things are our environmental factors which gives a huge impact on the infectious agents and transmission of disease.

- Disposal of human excreta
- Sewage
- Household wastage
- Water drainage Domestic water supply
- Housing

People tend to forget to put these environmental factors in consideration with regards to prevention of diseases. Improper disposal of human excreta could give people different illnesses such as hepatitis A, and other gastrointestinal tract diseases. Faeces, or human wastes harbours lots of harmful micro-organisms that when it enters into the body, it could definitely cause an illness to a person, same as true with the other household wastes. The water drainage, if not properly maintained and cleaned could be a possible cradle of vectors and disease causing insects. Serious health problems may result when contaminated water is ingested into the body because it may lead to poliomyelitis, etc. Water that is not properly treated could contain harmful bacteria that might cause an illness. We are all living in a world full of responsibilities but the big point here is, we also have a responsibility in ourselves for improper environmental sanitation. Realising that every person deserves good health is the key before recognising the problem in having a good environmental sanitation. This is because environmental sanitation plays an important role in the development of diseases in humans.

7.1 Levels of Sanitation Individual, Household and Community

Environment sanitation begins with the individual and moves with the community. Environmental sanitation comprises disposal and treatment of human excreta, solid waste and wastewater. It also comprises the control of diseases and also the provision of washing facilities for personal and domestic hygiene. All these, aim at improving the quality of life of the individuals and contributing to social development. There are different factors to consider in achieving a better and cleaner environment.

Environmental sanitation is not just about the beliefs and practices. It also comes from the influences of the economic aspects. What are the things we usually do to maintain the cleanliness of our homes? Are these practices being utilised in the community? It is important to remember that different beliefs and practices must be altered for a better environment. As a person especially if you are a mother, you must be responsible in every single thing that you do. Cleanliness starts with you. Personal hygiene is the first step in helping environmental cleanliness to develop. You can never teach your children or your friends to be clean if you yourself wake up and go to school or work without even taking a bath or brushing your teeth. You cannot say to people that you are environmentally aware if you, yourself throw trash in any place you wish. Even the manner of eating and washing is part of the personal hygiene. Self discipline is a key towards a successful sanitation of the environment.

Maintaining a clean environment requires nothing but a person's discipline and dedication in having a good hygiene. Next to that is household cleanliness. Cleanliness must be maintained in all the time inside the house especially in the sensitive areas such as bathroom, and kitchen because it is in these places where harmful micro-organisms are often found. Different disease causing organisms live in food and various bathroom surfaces and so it is necessary that proper sanitation is practiced. Once you had developed cleanliness within yourself, it is now time to teach others about this by being a good example and starting to clean your own homes. After that, having a clean community would be the next step. Proper waste disposal and maintaining cleanliness all throughout the community particularly in the streets and sidewalks are essential towards a healthier community.

Environmental sanitation depends on social and cultural practices and beliefs and these have to be considered in planning interventions. To allow for transmission of infectious agents they have to be present in the immediate human environment, exposure has to take place, and transmission has to occur by uptake of the agents through unsafe practices. To interrupt the transmission, environmental sanitation can act on reducing exposure to infectious agents by limiting contact to wastes or polluted media, and by changing hygiene and socio-cultural practices.

Individual Sanitation

The practices of environmental sanitation can be defined as the daily habits of humans within the environment in his living. It may begin from his house and it may end in the larger group of society. It may begin in the morning and may continue until he goes to bed. Environmental sanitation is the co-operation with the environment for establishing better sanitation in the society.

Sanitation and personal hygiene are important for keeping food safe. Healthy volunteers need to practice good personal hygiene and use clean surfaces, equipment, and utensils when preparing food. People with a cold, flu or have symptoms such as diarrhea, vomiting or sore throat can spread disease through the food they handle. If you have an infected cut, burn or wound on your hand, do not work in the preparation of food. There are thousands of ways for individual sanitation in the society, but the thing is how we are promoting environmental sanitation through individual sanitation. The environmental sanitation can be promoted in the means of proper disposal of waste generated by an individual. The care taken in the disposal of waste can enhance environmental sanitation.

Household Sanitation

House is the beginning of environmental sanitation. In fact, the environmental sanitation should begin from the house where people live and produce environmentally harmful garbage or waste. It is very important to take care of the waste which is generated in the house for better environment. Otherwise, it may become a threat to the environment. Household-centred environmental sanitation challenges conventional thinking about sanitation; it proposes inclusive planning and implementation of environmental sanitation services, which depart radically from the centralised policies and planning of the past. The approach places the household and its neighbourhood at the core of the planning and decision-making process. Environmental sanitation involves behaviours and actions of individuals as well as the technical expertise of environmental sanitation facilities to improve sanitation. Stakeholders can plan conservation and reuse of water, rainwater, and recycling of sanitation products. In this connection, the following aspects are important:

- Human dignity, quality of life, and environmental security of the individual are at the centre of this approach, which is responsive and accountable to the needs and demands of people in the community setting.
- Decision-making involves participation of all stakeholders, especially the consumers and providers of services.
- Waste is considered a resource (to be diluted as little as possible), and its management forms part of an integrated water resource, nutrient flow, and waste management process.
- Solutions to environmental sanitation problems are sought first in households and communities, working into larger domains if solutions cannot be found (e.g., town, district, catchment and city).

Applying household-centred environmental sanitation in communities relies not only on the willingness and ingenuity of individuals within a community or town, but on all decision-makers in the field – elected and appointed municipal planners along with sector specialists, working with staff of NGOs and community organisations.

Community Sanitation

Community refers to a group of people living in a geographic area and having community sentiment. People by living in the same geographic area come to have attachment for the area and the people living in that area. These people use or consume different kinds of commodities for their living and comfort which sometimes leads to waste. The proper care or management of the waste which is generated by the group is the responsibility of the same group. As the individual practices of sanitation will help the individual and the sanitation of family helps the family, the sanitation of the community will help the community for its own growth and development.

A sanitation improvement programme should help people to help themselves. Government programmes must involve community members in local planning, organisation and implementation. The whole community should take part in some way or the other, especially the women and children. With appropriate training programme should support the development of local government, especially in rural areas.

If the community fails in the responsibility of sanitation then it becomes a burden for the government to maintain environmental sanitation. Often the community functions like religious or national festivals generate large amount of waste in the society. In such instances it becomes a herculean task to manage the waste. Community sanitation begins from the grass root level of the individual and the family. If an individual or the family takes responsibility of sanitation, then waste generated by the individual or the family will not turn as a burden for the community.

Sanitation in Public Places

Where a large number of people are using one area, such as bus station or school, especially when they are eating food from the same source, there is a greater risk of the spread of diseases such as cholera, hepatitis A, typhoid and other diarrheal diseases. Lack of sanitation in public places may cause environmental pollution which leads to diseases. These places vary in the number of people using them, the amount of time that people spend there and the type of activity that occurs in the area, but all public places need to have adequate sanitation and hygiene facilities.

Responsibility for the provision of sanitation facilities in public places is not always obvious, especially where these are informal gathering places. It is vital, however, that an agency monitors the sanitation facilities in public places on behalf of the users. Ideally, this should be part of the role of the ministry of health, or its equivalent. Special attention should be paid to the adequacy of facilities, their availability to the public, and the conditions of their operation.

There are several basic rules for sanitation in public places:

1. There should be sufficient toilet facilities for the maximum number of people using the area during the day. This normally means one toilet compartment for every 25 users. The toilet facilities should be arranged in separate blocks for men and women. The men's toilet block should have urinals and toilet compartments; the women's block toilet compartments only.

The total number of urinals plus compartments in the men's block should equal the total number of compartments in the women's block.

2. Toilet facilities should not be connected directly to kitchens. This is in order to reduce the number of flies entering the kitchen and to reduce odours reaching the kitchen. It is important that people using the toilet facilities cannot pass directly through the kitchen.
3. There must be a hand washing basin with clean water and soap close to the toilet facilities. There should be separate, similar facilities near to kitchens or where food is handled.
4. There must be a clean and reliable water supply for hand washing, personal hygiene and flushing of toilet facilities. The water supply should meet quality standards and be regularly tested to ensure that any contamination is discovered quickly and that appropriate remedial action is taken.
5. Refuse must be disposed of properly and not allowed to build up, as it will attract flies and vermin.

Responsibilities for cleaning sanitation facilities should be very clearly defined. Dirty facilities make it more likely that people will continue to use the facilities badly or not at all. Clean facilities set a good example to users. It is important to make sure that information about health is available in public places. Such information should be displayed in an eye-catching, simple and accurate way. Where appropriate, large posters with bright colours and well chosen messages, put up in obvious places, are effective. Health and hygiene messages may be passed on to the public using such posters in public places.

Waste Management

Waste management is the collection, transport, processing or disposal, managing and monitoring of waste materials. Waste management is the collection, transport, processing or disposal of waste materials, usually ones produced by human activity, in an effort to reduce their effect on human health or local aesthetics or amenity. Environmental experts have indicated that environmental conditions of a given area may be affected by waste management, the process used to dispose of garbage. How waste is disposed of varies based on living conditions and the accepted standard of living in a geographical area. While some communities provide wastewater treatment and trash collection, others do not, which reduces the ability to control the well-being of the environment and its people. When waste is not removed and treated properly, pollution may lead to the spread of disease; when proper disposal and treatment methods are followed, disease and pollution can usually be reduced.

Solid Waste Management

Every day, people throw away a large amount of garbage, which is usually referred to as solid waste. In many countries, some form of solid waste management system has been put in place. Some common ways to dispose of the garbage include incarceration, which is the burning of waste, or landfills, which are places to store waste. In the United States and Europe, both of these methods are commonly used to manage solid waste. The disposal of refuse can have a significant effect on the health of communities. Where refuse is not disposed of properly, it can lead to pollution of surface water, as rain washes refuse into rivers and streams. There may also be a significant risk of groundwater contamination. Refuse disposed of in storm drains may cause blockages and encourage fly and mosquito breeding. It is, therefore, very important that household waste is disposed of properly.

Disposal of solid waste is most commonly conducted in landfills, but incineration, recycling; composting and conversion to bio-fuels are also avenues. In the case of landfills, advanced countries typically have rigid protocols for daily cover with topsoil, where underdeveloped countries customarily rely upon less stringent protocols. The importance of daily cover lies in the reduction of vector contact and spreading of pathogens. Daily cover also minimises odour emissions and reduces wind-blown litter. Likewise, developed countries typically have requirements for perimeter sealing of the landfill with clay-type soils to minimise migration of leach ate that could contaminate groundwater.

For incineration options, the release of air pollutants, including certain toxic components is an attendant adverse outcome. Recycling and bio-fuel conversion are the sustainable options that generally have superior life cycle costs, particularly when total ecological consequences are considered. Composting value will ultimately be limited by the market demand for compost product.

Industrial Waste Management

Environmental sanitation is not limited to the pollution of water and the improper disposal of household. When factories or businesses dispose of chemical and physical waste in ways that directly affect the environment, it is often referred to as industrial pollution. For example, while the actual dumping site may occur several miles away from a main source of water, drainage and rainfall can cause chemicals and physical waste to mix with the water supply and pollute it. Some countries have developed a system to properly dispose of industrial waste and help protect the environment; as with household waste, some of these systems incorporate incarceration and landfills into their management strategies.

7.2 Problems of Environmental Sanitation in India

Environmental sanitation envisages promotion of health of the community by providing clean environment and breaking the cycle of disease. It depends on various factors that include hygiene status of the people, types of resources available, innovative and appropriate technologies according to the requirement of the community, socio-economic development of the country, cultural factors related to environmental sanitation, political commitment, capacity building of the concerned sectors, social factors including behavioural pattern of the community, legislative measures adopted, and others. India is still lagging far behind many countries in the field of environmental sanitation.

The unsanitary conditions are appalling in India and need a great sanitary awakening similar to what took place in London in the mid-nineteenth century. Improvement in sanitation requires newer strategies and targeted interventions with follow-up evaluation. The need of the hour is to identify the existing system of environmental sanitation with respect to its structure and functioning and to prioritise the control strategies according to the need of the country.

Environmental sanitation comprises both a change in behaviour and facilities to form a hygienic environment. However, significant numbers of people worldwide lack access to adequate water, sanitation, drainage, and solid waste disposal services. It has been defined by the Water Supply and Sanitation Collaborative Council as Interventions to reduce people's exposure to disease by providing a clean environment in which to live, with measures to break the cycle of disease. The latest statistics reveal that 1.1 billion people still do not have access to safe drinking water, and 2.4 billion people do not have access to adequate sanitation.

Furthermore, research has shown that in many urban areas of developing countries, less than 50 per cent of the municipal solid wastes are collected and only an insignificant fraction is disposed off appropriately. This not only increases the rate of diseases and mortality, but also slows down the economic progress of hundreds of millions of people in developing countries. At the same time, the world's natural supply of freshwater is subject to increasing environmental and economic pressure. These priorities are particularly important because of issue of water constraints, environment-related health problems, rapid population growth, inequitable distribution of water resources, issues related to administrative problems, urbanisation and industrialisation, migration of population, and rapid economic growth. Following are some of the important causes lack of environmental sanitation in India.

Lack of Social Responsibility: People are so busy in working for their livelihood that they won't get any time for social welfare. Some time, they are not ready to spend their time in something which is not their personal problem. There is an absence of social responsibility among the people of society. It's been observed that the permanent residents of the society are worried about the environmental sanitation, but the migrant group of people are not worried of public problem because for the reason that they may not be there after a few years.

Lack of Social Awareness about Sanitation: People are lacking about the knowledge of environmental sanitation. Though a child is supposed to learn from the family about sanitation, often the parents themselves lack the knowledge of sanitation. The knowledge about sanitation and awareness of their social responsibility may help the people to keep society clean.

Lack of Education: Education often enhances the desire for a better life. Education is the only way for acquiring knowledge in the society. Similarly, knowledge of sanitation is acquired in the process of socialisation or education. If at all society wants people to keep its environment clean then it should be implemented through education.

Over-crowded Population: Environmental sanitation is a bigger challenge where there is large number of population settled in a particular area without proper sanitation facilities. In urban areas or in the slums of the cities the problem of environmental sanitation arises. The migrated people come and settle down in places which are already congested. Lack of toilet facilities force them to defecate in the open which will pollute the environment and generate disease among the people.

Present Scenario

Poor countries due to lack of financial resources will not be able to maintain sanitation which will spoil the environment. As per estimates, inadequate sanitation cost India almost $54 billion or 6.4 per cent of the country's GDP in 2006. Over 70 per cent of this economic impact or about $38.5 billion was health-related. Evidence suggests that all water and sanitation improvements are cost-beneficial in all developing societies.

Sectoral demands for water are growing rapidly in India owing mainly to urbanisation and it is estimated that by 2025, more than 50 per cent of the country's population will live in cities and towns. Population increase, rising incomes, and industrial growth are also responsible for this dramatic shift. National Urban Sanitation Policy 2008 was the recent development in order to rapidly promote sanitation in urban areas of the country. India's Ministry of Urban Development commissioned the survey as part of its National Urban Sanitation Policy in November, 2008. In rural areas, local government institutions in charge of operating and maintaining the infrastructure are seen as weak and lack the financial resources to carry out their functions. In addition, no major city in India is known to have a continuous water supply and an estimated 72 per cent of Indians still lack access to improved sanitation facilities.

A number of innovative approaches to improve water supply and sanitation have been tested in India, in particular in the early 2000s. These include demand-driven approaches in rural water supply since 1999, community-led total sanitation, public–private partnerships to improve the continuity of urban water supply in Karnataka, and the use of microcredit to women in order to improve access to water.

Total sanitation campaign gives strong emphasis on information, education, and communication, capacity building and hygiene education for effective behaviour change with involvement of Panchayati Raj institutions, community-based organisations and nongovernmental organisations. The key intervention areas are individual household latrines, school sanitation and hygiene education, community sanitary complex, anganwadi toilets supported by rural sanitary marts and production centres. Though the main goal of the Government of India was to eradicate the practice of open defecation by 2010, it was not feasible now and extended to 2017. To give fillip to this endeavour, Government of India has launched Nirmal Gram Puraskar to recognise the efforts in terms of cash awards for fully covered Panchayat Raj institutions and those individuals and institutions who have contributed significantly in ensuring full sanitation coverage in their area of operation. The project is being implemented in rural areas taking district as a unit of implementation.

Providing private excreta disposal would be expected to reduce diarrhea by 42 per cent, while eliminating excreta around the house would lead to a 30 per cent reduction in diarrhea. The findings suggest that improvements in both water supply and sanitation are necessary if infant health in developing countries is to be improved. They also imply that it is not epidemiologic but behavioural, institutional, and economic factors that should correctly determine the priority of interventions. Morbidity and mortality due to waterborne diseases have not declined commensurate with increase in availability of potable water supply. More importantly, young children bear a huge part of the burden of disease resulting from the lack of hygiene. India still loses between 0.4 and 0.5 million children under five years due to diarrhea. While infant mortality and under five mortality rates have declined over the years for the country as a whole, in many states, these have stagnated in recent years. One of the reasons is the failure to make significant headway in improving personal and home hygiene, especially in the care of young children and the conditions surrounding birth.

Challenges for Environmental Sanitation

1. Prevention of contamination of water in distribution systems,
2. Growing water scarcity and the potential for water reuse and conservation,
3. Implementing innovative low-cost sanitation system,
4. Providing sustainable water supplies and sanitation for urban and semi-urban areas,
5. Reducing disparities within the regions in the country and
6. Sustainability of water and sanitation services.

7.3 Public Toilets, Organisation and Functioning

Sanitation services are necessary to support urban stability, enable social balance, economic growth and development and are imperative for the improvement of urban public services. In the absence of proper sanitation, people suffer from high levels of infectious, contagious, water borne, air borne and vector borne diseases leading to high incidences of morbidity and mortality. This directly affects the ability of a country to maintain an efficient economy and implies great personal suffering among infected individuals and their families. Thus, improving environmental health is the most cost-effective means of enhancing people's health and welfare.

Although there have been several national initiatives to increase sanitation coverage in India, a substantial part of urban population, especially in slums, has no adequate sanitation facilities made available to them by the government or public machinery. In cities, as on-site sanitation option, Municipal Corporations have constructed community toilets. These are required for slums and pavement dwellers, rickshaw pullers and the floating population and, therefore, they serve a purpose.

Community toilets not only provide sanitation facility but at the same time have a demonstrative effect as well. The people using these become habitual users of toilets, and in turn realise the need for individual household toilets. Community toilets, thus, are the tools for bringing behavioural changes amongst the public residing in the slum areas as well as in generating a demand for the use of the individual toilets. Large and sizable investment has been made for the construction of community toilets, which have become either hazardous, unhygienic or abandoned due to poor construction and planning, or lack of water supply or lack of proper maintenance. At the same time, it must be understood that community toilets are specifically important for slums, especially where it may not be possible to construct individual household toilets due to the non-availability of space. Under these circumstances not only the construction but devising measures for strengthening operational and maintenance aspect of the community toilets becomes all the more important. This scenario necessitates initiatives not only in the construction but over and above in the operation and maintenance of community toilets.

Community Led Total Sanitation (CLTS) in India is mostly used within the framework of Government of India's Total Sanitation Campaign (TSC), which was launched in 1999. TSC provides for subsidies, now called incentives, to below poverty line households in rural areas of the country. CLTS is reportedly in use now in 16 of 35 states in India. Since its introduction in Ahmednagar and Nanded districts of Maharashtra in 2002 on a pilot basis, CLTS has been reportedly used in varying degrees across 135 districts in the country so far, particularly since 2006. As per a rough estimate, around five million people have gained access to safe sanitation following CLTS interventions across rural India.

Himachal Pradesh and Haryana are the two states where CLTS has been used in all the districts. In the remaining 14 states, the percentage of districts where CLTS has been used ranges from 6 to 86 per cent in the states of Uttar Pradesh and Meghalaya respectively. While Himachal Pradesh remains the only state where state sanitation strategy of 2005 adopts CLTS principles of no-subsidy and community ownership of the sanitation agenda, Haryana is a state which has underplayed the provision of subsidy in TSC to support those who have tried to make the sanitation drive community led using the CLTS approach, as in the districts of Panipat and Sirsa.

In Himachal Pradesh and Haryana where CLTS has been used in all the districts of the state, results have been remarkably better with around 60-70 per cent increase in sanitation coverage over a period of four to five years during 2006-2010. In states of Meghalaya, Maharashtra, and Madhya Pradesh, where CLTS has been introduced in few of the districts, rate of increase in sanitation coverage has been in the range of around 30-40 per cent during the same period. In the state of Bihar, where there is provision of subsidy both for above poverty line and below poverty line households with no CLTS activity so far, the rate of increase in sanitation coverage has been only around 20 per cent in that period.

But beyond these figures, there is a growing body of experience and evidence, mainly of a qualitative nature, from across states of Himachal Pradesh, Haryana, Maharashtra and Meghalaya, which suggests that CLTS has helped achieve faster and more sustainable results on the ground.

CLTS has been used in three urban centres as well that include: Kalyani near Kolkata in West Bengal (2005-07); Raigad near Mumbai in Maharashtra (2008); and Nanded in North-Western Maharashtra (2011-ongoing). Kalyani Municipal Area has the distinction of being the first city to have 52 slums, which have become open defecation free using the CLTS approach. The process in Kalyani was facilitated by Kamal Kar, the innovator of the CLTS approach, and his team. CLTS in Raigad was used to trigger urban communities into action with its focus on safe disposal of solid waste.

Nanded is the first city in India to use CLTS to engage with communities for the preparation of a comprehensive city sanitation plan, which is currently in its implementation phase. Around 100 communities with an average population of 1000 people have been triggered into action since April 2011. These communities have mobilised themselves to stop open defecation, make their locality garbage free, and undertake the responsibility of keeping the city drains clean. Supported by Nanded-Waghala City Municipal Corporation, this process is currently being facilitated by Knowledge Links and Feedback Foundation.

Water for Asian Cities Programme, a collaborative initiative between UN-HABITAT and Asian Development Bank (ADB), is supporting the implementation of the water and sanitation related targets in Asian cities and promoting new/innovative investments in the urban water and sanitation sector. In India, Water for Asian Cities Programme is supporting the ADB financed Madhya Pradesh Urban Administration and Development Project in cities of Bhopal, Gwalior, Indore and Jabalpur for the improvement and expansion of urban water and sanitation services. This is a joint publication of UN-HABITAT and the Directorate of Urban Administration and Development, Government of Madhya Pradesh and analyses status of community toilet in terms of its infrastructure, operation and maintenance, uses and payment of user charges. It also examines where community toilets are well maintained and the users are paying for charges and examined the possibility of involving user/community groups and enhancement of their capacity for handing over operation and management. In fact, the chances of success of these groups are more when women are actively involved.

The community toilets in municipal areas are maintained by the corporations through their health departments. Some of the community toilets have been constructed and are being maintained by "Sulabh International" on a "pay and use basis". The upkeep of the community toilets constructed by Municipal Corporation has been dismal, with the conditions turning so unsanitary that people prefer open defecation to using the community toilets. Many community toilets have also become non-functional on account of a variety of reasons ranging from non-availability of water to lack of maintenance.

The possible reasons for non-use of community toilets are:

- Faulty construction, not conforming to norms of availability of sustainable water supply, ventilation, natural lighting etc.,
- Lacking in special provision for children and handicapped/ disabled persons,

- Lacking in safety and security for women,
- Lack of operation and maintenance and financial issues,
- Insufficient funds for running the system,
- Non-availability of funds for augmentation, rectification and up gradation of facilities,
- Non-consultations with community on design and location of community toilets,
- Lack of motivation and non-generation of felt need towards sanitation,
- Lack of public health and hygiene education among poor sections of society,
- Lack of sensitisation on gender issue.

Status of Infrastructure in Community Toilets

The uses of the community toilets also depend on the availability of infrastructure facilities such as water, bathing facility, effluent disposal in sewer line or in septic tank. Availability of water has not been ensured in all the community toilets. Their limited use is also explained by the lower availability and accessibility, apart from poor maintenance in terms of irregular or no water supply, bad sanitary condition and lack of proper drainage are major issues. Providing a bathroom also does not appear to be the norm with less than half community toilets in Bhopal and only two community toilets in Gwalior providing them.

Status of Maintenance of Community Toilets

The community toilets have been grouped under various categories depending upon status of operation and maintenance. It is evident from the study that 22 out of 28 community toilets in Bhopal, two out of two community toilets in Gwalior, 32 out of 40 community toilets in Indore and 10 out of 12 community toilets in Jabalpur are maintained and used on payment basis. Therefore, for ensuring proper utilisation of community toilcts, services based on user charges appears to be an important factor.

There are examples where community toilets are well-maintained and the users are paying for charges. The Sulabh International has constructed several community toilets in slum areas. They charge 50 paise per use. A family of five can purchase a monthly card for Rs 20. The operation cost of the community toilets maintained by Sulabh International is estimated as Rs 6000 per month having 10 seats in the complex, which is being met through user charges. Therefore, any policy option on operation and maintenance of community toilets should primarily be focused on raising the contributions from users for meeting the operation and maintenance.

Involving user groups in maintenance is another measure tried successfully in southern part of the country. The chances of success of these groups are more when women are actively involved. This was learnt from the experiences of Tiruchirappalli Municipal Corporation in Tamil Nadu. The women of the area were involved in construction of community toilets. The women group was formed to take up the maintenance responsibility of the community toilet under pay and use system. The women group soon could be able to earn money out of the toilet maintenance and further invested the money in renovation of an abandoned community toilets nearby which was earlier used by men. They replaced the damaged water closets in the men's community toilet and attended other repair and renovation works in the toilet. The men of the area started using the renovated community toilet and avoided open defecation in the slum. For children, the community has decided to construct a separate toilet adjacent to the pay and use latrines meant for men and women. They could design and construct a child friendly toilet. The child friendly toilet is being used by the girls and boys of the slum who are below six years old. Therefore, community participation especially of women has great chance of successful operation and maintenance of community toilets.

Sanitation is an issue that starts from individual and spreads to community. Therefore, interpersonal communication measures with strong interactive mode will facilitate the effective communication to bring desired behavioural changes. This will include enhancing knowledge regarding hygiene and sanitation and encouraging conversion of the knowledge into practice. Communication campaign for awareness creation and demand generation should clearly give the following messages:

- The beneficiaries will own the community toilets, rejuvenated or constructed;
- The Municipal Corporation will not maintain the community toilet;
- Information regarding its operation and maintenance cost, replacement cost etc.

- Full operation and maintenance and replacement cost are to be borne by the beneficiaries.

Working of Community Toilets

The idea of building community toilets is good, it is important that these toilets should be maintained well. This could be done at the organisational level or at the community level. In this, the community based organisations will provide a link between the community and the Municipal Corporation of the area. The community mobilisation will result in the formation of committees and groups. The members of these will act as the pressure groups in meeting the demands and solving community issues. Women will be involved as they are primarily responsible for the overall health of the family. The women living in the slums would have to be counselled for active participation in promoting efforts for securing hygiene conditions in their localities.

When the demand for community toilets has been expressed explicitly, then the community workers must play their role in institutionalisation of such community activities by mobilising and registering the community and organising them as Community Water and Sanitation Committee (CWASC) or Self Help Group (SHG). Further, the implementation of initiative of rejuvenation of community toilet will start with gathering of the baseline data by a physical survey of the community toilets in the area in question illustrating the location and condition of sanitation.

The Municipal Corporation will take the services of NGOs having experience in outreach. These NGOs will be responsible for activities like community mobilisation through communication, information, education and communication, Human Resource Development (HRD), capacity development, social mobilisation etc.

The NGOs will organise all trainings and capacity building activities and determine key behaviours and perceptions regarding sanitation, hygiene, and water use, operation and maintenance etc. The NGO will be responsible for bringing specialist consultants from the fields of communication, and sanitation and hygiene education. The services of NGOs would also be utilised for demand generation, rehabilitation works, and setup operation and maintenance arrangements as well as for ensuring that people actually make use of the toilets.

The community through the CWASC or SHG would have to enter into an memorandum of understanding with the Municipal Corporations agreeing to contribute towards cost of rejuvenation, while the SHG would have to bear full cost of operation and maintenance and post-construction management of the sanitary complexs, while the Municipal Corporation would have to rejuvenate the defunct community toilets on the request of the community and extend full support to remove all the infrastructural deficiencies including water supply. The community group would also have to work out the modalities, how to share the revenue generated, as well as find ways and means to increase their savings, for the furtherance of their collective goals, i.e., the maintenance and smooth functioning of the system to be put in place. The community would have to be authorised to levy user charges for the operation and maintenance of the facilities.

Operators of the community toilets will either be families chosen from the communities or an individual who would have to be paid for it. For that to materialise a mutually agreeable system would have to be worked out. Since most of these facilities also provide other businesses on the site, like corner shop or café, revenue generation would not necessarily be a problem. Each toilet maintenance operator would have to sign an individual contract with CWASC/SHGs covering his or her conditions of employment, including monthly salary and rewards for achieving the target revenues.

7.4 Sanitation and Safe Drinking Water

The rural population of India comprises more than 700 million people residing in about 1.42 million habitations spread over 15 diverse ecological regions. It is true that providing drinking water to such a large population is an enormous challenge. Our country is also characterised by non-uniformity in level of awareness, socio-economic development, education, poverty, practices and rituals which add to the complexity of providing water. The health burden of poor water quality is enormous. It is estimated that around 37.7 million Indians are affected by waterborne diseases annually, 1.5 million children are estimated to die of diarrhoea alone and 73 million working days are lost due to waterborne disease each year. The resulting economic burden is estimated at $600 million a year. The problems of chemical contamination are also prevalent in India with 1, 95,813 habitations in the country are affected by poor water quality. The major chemical parameters of concern are fluoride and arsenic. Iron is also emerging as a major problem with many habitations showing excess iron in the water samples. The provision of clean drinking water has been given priority in the Constitution of India, with Article 47 conferring the duty of providing clean drinking water and improving public health standards to the State. The government has undertaken various programmes since independence to provide safe drinking water to the rural masses. Till the tenth Plan, an estimated total of Rs 1,105 billion spent on providing safe drinking water. One would argue that the expenditure is huge but it is also true that despite such expenditure lack of safe and secure drinking water continues to be a major hurdle and a national economic burden.

While no comprehensive study on equity issues relating to water supply, sanitation, and health has been conducted for the country as a whole, common equity issues that plague the sector in most developing countries also hold true for India. In addition, comprehensive studies on the economic value of the water and sanitation sector in India also do not exist.

It is important to reiterate the need for Rural Water Supply and Sanitation [RWSS] and Urban Water Supply and Sanitation [UWSS] agencies to operate hand-in-hand with their health and education counterparts to jointly monitor indicators of RWSS, UWSS, health, education, poverty, and equity in order to make significant headway in the respective sectors. Existing health promotion and education programmes should be made more effective and geared towards achieving behaviour changes needed to improve hygiene.

On one hand, the pressures of development is changing the distribution of water in the country, access to adequate water has been cited as the primary factor responsible for limiting development. The average availability of water is reducing steadily with the growing population and it is estimated that by 2020 India will become a water stressed nation. Groundwater is the major source of water in our country with 85 per cent of the population dependent on it.

A recent study highlighted that policy shift to include better household water quality management to complement the continuing expansion of coverage and upgrading of services would appear to be a cost-effective health intervention in many developing countries. Most of the interventions (including multiple interventions, hygiene, and water quality) were found to significantly reduce the levels of diarrheal illness, with the greatest impact being seen for hygiene and household treatment interventions. Interventions to improve water quality at the household level are more effective than those at the source. Unfortunately, in developing countries, public health concerns are usually raised on the institutional setting, such as municipal services, hospitals, and environmental sanitation. There is a reluctance to acknowledge the home as a setting of equal importance along with the public institutions in the chain of disease transmission in the community. Managers of home hygiene and community hygiene must act in unison to optimise return from efforts to promote public health. A recent survey through in-depth interviews with more than 800 households in the city of Hyderabad in India concluded that, even if provided with market (not concessional) rates of financing, a substantial proportion of poor households would invest in water and sewer network connections.

The role of the WHO Guidelines for Drinking Water Quality emphasises an integrated approach to water quality assessment and management from source to consumer. It emphasises on quality protection and prevention of contamination and advises to be proactive and participatory, and address the needs of those in developing countries who have no access to piped community water supplies. The guidelines emphasise the maintenance of microbial quality to prevent waterborne infectious disease as an essential goal. In addition, they address protection from chemical toxicants and other contaminants of public health concern.

Progress on Sanitation and Safe Drinking Water

Some 2.4 billion people, one-third of the world's population, will remain without access to improved sanitation in 2015, according to a joint WHO/UNICEF report. Faster progress on sanitation is needed and both organisations call for a final push to meet the Millennium Development Goal sanitation target. At the end of the International Drinking Water Supply and Sanitation decade (1981-1990), WHO and UNICEF established a Joint Monitoring Programme for Water Supply and Sanitation.

UNICEF's long standing support for improving water supply, sanitation and hygiene stems from a firm conviction and based on sound evidence that these are central to ensuring the rights of children. In fact, it is essential for children to survive, grow and develop into healthy and fulfilled citizens of the world. In the broader context, UNICEF's activities in water, sanitation and hygiene contribute to the achievement of the Millennium Development Goals.

Adequate, well-maintained water supply and sanitation facilities in schools encourage children to attend school regularly and help them achieve their educational goals. Inadequate water supply and sanitation in schools are health hazards and affect school attendance, retention and educational performance.

In fact, both water supply and sanitation are necessary if infant health in developing countries is to be improved. It implies that it is not epidemiologic but behavioural, institutional, and economic factors that should correctly determine the priority of interventions. Another study highlighted that water quality interventions to the point-of-use water treatment were found to be more effective than previously thought, and multiple interventions (consisting of combined water, sanitation, and hygiene measures) were not more effective than interventions with a single focus. Studies have shown that hand washing can reduce diarrhea episodes by about 30 per cent. This significant reduction is comparable to the effect of providing clean water in low-income areas.

Lack of safe water supply, poor environmental sanitation, improper disposal of human excreta, and poor personal hygiene will help to spread diarrheal diseases in India. Since diarrheal diseases are caused by 20–25 pathogens, vaccination, though an attractive disease prevention strategy, is not feasible.

National water policies are shifting to community-based management approach because local authorities are in daily contact with users, of whom about 50 per cent are women. Historically, national policy shifted from attention to distribution of investments in the water sector to reorganisation of water agencies and to building up the capacity of private or voluntary agencies. The local context allows for more efficient and effective responses to local conditions. Local institutions and groups are better equipped to solicit local participation. Local water resource planning is very important in strengthening the economic and individual capacity of poor people in underdeveloped areas.

The 2001 Census reported that 68.2 per cent of households in India have access to safe drinking water. According to latest estimates, 94 per cent of the rural population and 91 per cent of the people living in urban areas have access to safe drinking water. Data available with the Department of Drinking Water Supply shows that of the 1.42 million rural habitations in the country, 1.27 million are fully covered, 0.13 million are partially covered and 15,917 are not covered. However, coverage refers to installed capacity, and not average actual supply over a sustained period or the quality of water being supplied which is the most essential part.

While accessing drinking water continues to be a problem, assuring that it is safe is a challenge by itself. Water quality problems are caused by pollution and over-exploitation. The rapid pace of industrialisation and greater emphasis on agricultural growth combined with financial and technological constraints and non-enforcement of laws have led to generation of large quantities Water Aid's vision is of a world where everyone has access to safe water and sanitation. Conventional practices of monitoring water quality rely on output as a means for quality assurance. Such practices are not timely enough to prevent consumption of contaminated water and do not give sufficient information to identify the source of contamination.

Water Supply and Sanitation

As per the Ninth Plan Working Group document, the coverage of urban population for drinking water and sanitation could not be raised as planned due to a rapid rise in urban population and inadequate plan outlay, besides the marked shift in the priority from urban to rural sector.

The issue of adequate quantity, quality and the distance of the nearest available source is emerging to be the most contentious issue with regard to urban water supply. Per capita water supply grossly varies from 40 litres per capita per day (lpcd) to 200 lpcd. As per the White Paper on Drinking Water presented by the Maharashtra government, 78 per cent of cities and towns in the state had water supply below normal. Water quality monitoring and surveillance is a rare phenomenon, except in the case of few privileged metropolitan cities. As the traditional water sources are all drying up, transporting water from far off places is becoming a common feature and is thus becoming an expensive affair.

Industries (large, medium and small-scale) located in the urban centres are not only large consumers of freshwater, but also contributors to the pollution of air, water and land. Lack of sufficient quantity of freshwater and high costs of supply (for example, in Bangalore, the cost of one kilolitre of freshwater for Industries is around Rs 60) from the Public Water Supply System for industrial processes has triggered off unsustainable tapping of groundwater aquifers. Many industries today are 'purchasing' water from private suppliers since their aquifers have gone dry.

Another aspect of concern is the discharge of liquid effluents over land and surface water from industrial sources. While most of the large-scale industries have effluent treatment plants, innumerable small and medium scale industries have not yet invested in the treatment of their factory effluents. This has led to the pollution of surface and ground water sources in urban centres. In Bangalore, many small-scale industries (tanneries, metal fabrication, etc) on the banks of the Vrishabhavathi river, discharge their untreated effluent into this river. While this is not only unaesthetic (as it gives out a foul smell), some people even irrigate vegetable gardens with this highly polluted water on the riverbanks. The contaminated vegetables are then sold in the city.

Another serious problem is the lack of maintenance in water supply and sanitation, leading to contamination of ground water sources in most of the cities and towns today. The main cause of contamination of groundwater and surface water is the improper discharge of sewage. More than half of the cities have no sewage treatment facilities. In class-I cities, only five per cent of the total wastewater is collected, of which only 25 per cent is treated. Poor infrastructure facilities for proper collection, transportation, treatment and disposal of solid wastes also are further adding up to the problem.

References

http://www.who.int/water_sanitation_health/hygiene/envsan/en/

http://www.who.int/water_sanitation_health/hygiene/emergencies/envsanfactsheets/en/index2.html

http://www.wisegeek.org/what-is-environmental-sanitation.htm

http://www.seefed.eu/waste-management.html

http://observer.gm/africa/gambia/article/essential-benefits-of-environmental-sanitation

http://www.ncbi.nlm.nih.gov/pmc/articles/PMC3299104/

http://cn.unhabitat.org/downloads/docs/4180_99251_Policy%20 Paper-3.pdf

file:///C:/Users/Admin/Downloads/drinking-water-quality-rural- india.pdf

CHAPTER – 8

State and Sanitation in India

Introduction

Sanitation means much more than building toilets. The most important requirement for safe sanitation, of course, is getting rid of human excreta, dirty water and household refuse. Also crucial are the way people think and behave, and whether they have hygienic and healthy habits. Sanitation improvement is a bigger process, aimed at the individual, the home and the community, which must include health and hygiene education as well as sustainable improved toilet facilities, water supply and methods of removal of dirty water and household refuse.

Providing, improving and maintaining satisfactory sanitation affects all members of society. This policy must apply in all situations: in rich and poor communities, in rural and urban areas, and whether sanitation is for individual households or provided as a system for an entire community. As a policy document, the White Paper provides a foundation on which we can build future sanitation improvement programmes. It is not an implementation manual but provides detailed information where this is necessary to help readers to understand the reasoning behind the policies. It contains sufficient information to be a complete policy; but aims to be flexible enough to allow local structures to decide what approaches are best for them, within the national framework.

The major aim of national policy on community sanitation is to improve the health and quality of life of the whole population. Improved sanitation facilities will reduce the incidence of disease, but only if there is improved hygiene practice and behaviour as well. Health department personnel at local level will play an important part in the promotion and education activities that are essential for success. The sanitation programme should check that health is really being improved and modify health education approaches if necessary.

8.1 Sanitation Policies, Planning and Programmes

Historically, the Indian society has often given high priority to sanitation. Excavations from the Indus Valley Civilisation and Harappa reveal ingenious solutions to facilitate waste water conveyance through underground drainage systems. Sanitary engineering, as far as 5000 years ago, was at a developed stage. Such visions on improved sanitary practices continued across the reign of various dynasties – like the Mauryas, Guptas or the southern kingdom of Vijayanagara – that ruled the subcontinent. Even from an ideological point of view, various social reformers of India propagated the importance of sanitation. From Patanjali's philosophy to writings of Vivekananda and the Gandhian concept of sanitation, the emphasis on sanitation was integral to India's cultural foundation.

It was in 1986 that the government launched the Central Rural Sanitation Programme (CRSP), the first nationwide sanitation programme. It was restructured in 1999, with a shift from a high subsidy to a low subsidy model. The supply driven approach was altered to a demand driven model with increased emphasis on public participation. In 2001, the same programme was overhauled with the introduction of the Total Sanitation Campaign (TSC), which carried forward the demand driven approach focusing on awareness building. The CRSP was restructured in 1999, with a shift from a high subsidy to a low subsidy model. The supply driven approach was altered to a demand driven model with increased emphasis on public participation. In 2001, the CRSP was overhauled with the introduction of the Total Sanitation Campaign (TSC), which carried forward the demand driven approach focusing on awareness building. As a fillip to the TSC, the Nirmal Gram Puraskar (NGP) was launched, to recognise the achievements and efforts of Gram Panchyats towards full sanitation coverage. In 2007, TSC was renamed Nirmal Bharat Abhiyan (NBA). It was not until the inception of the National Urban Sanitation Policy (NUSP) in 2008, that urban sanitation has been allotted focused attention at the national level. In 2014, Nirmal Bharat Abhiyan (NBA) was transformed into Swachh Bharat Mission (SBM) by Prime Minister Narendra Modi.

Central Rural Sanitation Programme (CRSP), 1986

In realisation of the importance of sanitation for improving the quality of life and its impact on productivity, Ministry of Rural Development has been making concerted efforts to ensure total sanitation coverage. The 'Central Rural Sanitation Programme' (CRSP) launched in 1986 aims at improving the quality of life of the rural poor and to provide privacy and dignity to women in rural areas. This was intended to supplement the efforts of the States. The programme provided for 100 per cent subsidy for construction of sanitary latrines for Scheduled Castes, Scheduled Tribes and landless labourers and subsidy as per the rate prevailing in the States for the general public.

Based on the feedback received on implementation of the programme from the States, UNICEF and voluntary organisations, the programme was revised by the Government of India in March 1991. For the construction of individual sanitary latrines, liberal subsidy at the rate of 95 per cent for Scheduled Castes/Scheduled Tribes and people below the poverty line and 80-90 per cent for general public were provided. The programme also provided for construction of village complex with bathing facilities, hand pumps, latrines, drainage facilities, washing platform etc, upto five per cent of the outlay could be utilised towards administrative cost and another 10 per cent for training of masons, awareness and health education. The contribution by the States from their own funds was limited to one-third of the assistance received from the Central Government.

The programme has since been further revised in September 1992, and the strategy outlined in the Eighth Five Year Plan. The revised programme aims at generation of felt need and peoples' participation. The subsidy pattern has been changed limiting to 80 per cent for persons below the poverty line for individual household latrines. For exclusive sanitary complex for women, the subsidy will be limited to 70 per cent the balance 30 per cent being the contribution by the Panchayats/ beneficiaries. For other sanitation facilities in the village the subsidy will be 50 per cent balance cost being met by the Panchayats. The revised programme aims at an integrated approach of rural sanitation. The concept of sanitary marts for supply of materials required for construction of sanitary latrines and involvement of voluntary organisations in publicity campaign and execution of the programme are also the new elements. At least 10 per cent of the total funds are to be channeled through voluntary organisations. The subsidy will be shared equally by the Central and the State Governments.

Another salient feature of the revised programme is to develop at least one model village covering facilities like sanitary latrines, conversion of dry latrine, garbage pits, soakage pits, drainage, pavement of lanes. Sanitary latrines in village institutions, cleanliness in ponds, tanks, clean surrounding around hand pumps and other drinking water sources.

Central Rural Sanitation Programme was restructured in the year 1999 exhibiting a paradigm shift in the approach and Total Sanitation Campaign (TSC) was introduced.

Total Sanitation Campaign (TSC), 1999

The Central Rural Sanitation Programme was a supply driven, high subsidy and infrastructure oriented programme. As a result of these deficiencies and low financial allocations, the CRSP had little impact on the gigantic sanitation problem. The experience of community-driven, awareness-generating campaign based programmes in some states and the results of evaluation of CRSP, led to the formulation of the Total Sanitation Campaign (TSC) approach in 1999.

The main objectives of the TSC are to:

- Bring about an improvement in the general quality of life in the rural areas.
- Accelerate sanitation coverage in rural areas.
- Generate felt demand for sanitation facilities through awareness creation and health education.
- Cover schools/Anganwadis in rural areas with sanitation facilities and promote hygiene education and sanitary habits among students.
- Encourage cost-effective and appropriate technologies in sanitation.
- Eliminate open defecation to minimise risk of contamination of drinking water sources and food.
- Convert dry latrines to pour flush latrines, and eliminate manual scavenging practice,wherever in existence in rural areas.

Strategy

The strategy is to make the programme 'community led' and 'people centred'. A "demand driven approach" is adopted with increased emphasis on awareness creation and demand generation for sanitary facilities in houses, schools and for cleaner environment. Alternate delivery mechanisms are adopted to meet the community needs. Subsidy for individual household latrine units has been replaced by incentive to the poorest of the poor households. Rural school sanitation is a major component and an entry point for wider acceptance of sanitation by the rural people. Technology improvisations to meet the customer preferences and location specific intensive campaign involving Panchayati Raj institutions, co-operatives, women groups, self-help groups, NGOs etc., are also important components of the strategy. The strategy addresses all sections of rural population to bring about the relevant behavioural changes for improved sanitation and hygiene practices and meet their sanitary hardware requirements in an affordable and accessible manner by offering a wide range of technological choices.

Components

The important components of the programme include:

- Provision of individual household latrines: Incentive of Rs1500—Rs 2000 in case of hilly and difficult areas and Rs 700 for each toilet is given by Central and State Governments respectively to BPL households after they construct and use toilets. APL households are motivated to construct toilets with their own funds or by taking loans from SHGs, banks, cooperative institutions etc.
- Provision of toilets in schools and anganwadis with the cost shared by Central and State Governments in the ratio of 70:30.
- Construction of community sanitary complexes.
- Assistance to production centres of sanitary materials and rural sanitary marts.
- Solid and liquid waste management.

Implementation

Implementation of TSC was proposed on a project mode and was implemented with a district as unit. The TSC project cycle in the project districts was expected to take about four years or less for implementation.

Evaluation

The Programme Evaluation Organisation of Planning Commission was entrusted to conduct in 2013 an independent evaluation of TSC programme in order to assess its socio-economic impact. The study tried to assess the impact of the ongoing TSC programme in terms of reduction in open defecation and build-up of toilet facilities at the household level. In spite of 14 years of the implementation of the programme it was surprising to see the existence of open defecation in rural India to the extent of 72.63 per cent, a stupendous figure.

The study further showed that the role of Rural Sanitary Marts/ Production Centres as alternative delivery mechanism to "encourage cost effective and appropriate technologies for ecologically safe and sustainable sanitation" is insignificant. Further, it appeared that the Rural Sanitary Marts/Production Centres mechanism has been adopted in letter but not in spirit in most states, with many states not even opting for this mechanism.

The study finds that policy variables such as TSC awareness and awareness of water-borne diseases due to squalid sanitary practices emerge as significant factors impacting the household level open defecation and toilet availability. With greater awareness, households are likely to exhibit improved sanitary and hygienic behaviour, construct toilets and reduce open defecation. The effect of incentive on households' toilet availability is also found to be positive and significant.

Moreover, well-designed, functional toilet facilities are also a step ahead in reducing open defecation, which is a very straight-forward and expected outcome. Other variables like water availability and education are important determinants of availability of household toilet provision and open defecation. The study also finds that educational attainment is an important determinant of sanitation practices and hygienic behaviour. Families with better levels of educational attainment are more likely to refrain from open defecation. Also, adequacy of water in the area where the toilet is to be constructed is a prerequisite for effecting reduced open defecation.

Although in general, we may expect the practice of open defecation to come down with higher income households, the study finds that Above Poverty Line (APL) families with higher income may have a greater tendency towards open defecation vis-à-vis Below Poverty Line (BPL) families. This is because our study establishes the interaction effect between BPL households and TSC incentive given for toilet construction. Hence, the former may have a higher proclivity towards toilet construction to avail the incentive and hence the tendency towards open defecation may be lower in such families.

From a policy point of view, however, tweaking in important policy variables is necessary to engender desired outcomes. Predominantly, a massive surge in awareness campaigns about the TSC programme and educating the masses of the ills of poor sanitary habits is the first important step in this direction. This may be done through information, education and communication initiatives, garnering increased community participation and Zilla Parishad and/or Self Help Group support, among others. Further, since household education may forestall obnoxious sanitary practices and unhygienic behaviour, the most educated household members/representatives may be separately trained on this initiative so that the positive spillovers can trickle down to the less-educated family members.

In fact, the role of Gram Panchayat level policy variables such as Panchayat Raj institutions role, Village level Water Sanitation Committee, Motivators and Grievance Redressal Mechanism cannot be overemphasised. Panchayat Raj institutions involvement in institutional arrangement for monitoring and supervising the various works under the TSC as well as contributing funds for construction released activities is also found to be important. Information, education and communication activities for motivating households to construct latrines and induce healthy and sustainable sanitation outcomes with the help of various aids like wall graffiti, street plays, folk media, Gram Panchayat meetings and rallies, development of micro plan in Gram Panchayat, hoardings, demonstration activities etc., deserve attention.

Nirmal Gram Puraskar (NGP), 2003

Government of India has been promoting sanitation coverage in a campaign mode to ensure better health and quality of life for people in rural India. To add vigour to its implementation, Government of India launched an award-based Incentive Scheme for fully sanitised and open defecation free Gram Panchayats, Blocks, Districts and States called "Nirmal Gram Puraskar" (NGP) in October 2003 and gave away the first awards in 2005 as a component of its flagship scheme TSC. Nirmal Gram Puraskar till 2011 was given by Ministry of Drinking Water and Sanitation, Government of India at all levels of Panchayat Raj institutions that is Gram Panchayat, Block Panchayat and District Panchayat.

It has now been decided that with the transition to Nirmal Bharat Abhiyan, selection of Gram Panchayats to award Nirmal Gram Puraskar from the year 2012 shall be taken up by the States, while selection of the Blocks and District Panchayats shall continue to be with the Centre. These guidelines have accordingly been formulated.

A Gram Panchayat will be eligible to apply for the NGP on the following grounds:

1. Gram Panchayat has adopted a resolution to ban open defecation within its entire area inclusive of all habitations and villages.
2. All habitations within the Gram Panchayat jurisdiction have access to water for drinking and sanitation purposes.
3. The Gram Panchayat has achieved objectives for all components as approved in the District Project.

National Urban Sanitation Policy (NUSP), 2008

India has the second largest urban system in the world with 310 million people and 5,161 cities and towns. Urbanisation has become irreversible with the urban population expected to reach 575 million by 2030 at the current rate of growth. The transition to an urban society, however, has neither been accompanied by a corresponding increase in the supply of basic urban services such as water supply and sanitation services, city roads, and public utilities such as street lights and pavements; nor by adequate supply of land and housing.

The Government of India, Ministry of Urban Development developed the "National Urban Sanitation Policy" in 2008. The vision of the policy is that all Indian cities and towns become totally sanitised, healthy and liveable and ensure and sustain good public health and environmental outcomes for all their citizens with a special focus on hygienic and affordable sanitation facilities for the urban poor and women. The focus of the policy is on awareness generation and behavioural change by generating awareness about sanitation and its linkages with public and environmental health amongst communities and institutions and also promoting mechanisms to bring about and sustain behavioural changes aimed at adoption of healthy sanitation practices.

Policy Goals

The overall goal of this policy is to transform Urban India into community-driven, totally sanitised, healthy and liveable cities and towns. The specific goals are:

A. Awareness Generation and Behaviour Change: This includes:

(a) Generating awareness about sanitation and its linkages with public and environmental health amongst communities and institutions;

(b) Promoting mechanisms to bring about and sustain behavioural changes aimed at adoption of healthy sanitation practices.

B. Achieving Open Defecation Free Cities: All urban dwellers will have access to and use safe and hygienic sanitation facilities and arrangements so that no one defecates in the open. In order to achieve this goal, the following activities shall be undertaken:

(a) Promoting access to households with safe sanitation facilities (including proper disposal arrangements);

(b) Promoting community-planned and managed toilets wherever necessary, for groups of households who have constraints of space, tenure or economic constraints in gaining access to individual facilities;

(c) Adequate availability and 100 per cent upkeep and management of Public Sanitation facilities in all Urban Areas, to rid them of open defecation and environmental hazards.

C. Integrated City-Wide Sanitation: This refers to re-orienting institutions and mainstreaming sanitation:

(a) Mainstream thinking, planning and implementing measures related to sanitation in all sectors and departmental domains as a cross-cutting issue, especially in all urban management endeavours;

(b) Strengthening national, state, city and local institutions (public, private and community) to accord priority to sanitation provision, including planning, implementation and operation and maintenance management;

(c) Extending access to proper sanitation facilities for poor communities and other unserved settlements.

Secondly, it includes sanitary and safe disposal of wastes. Specifically, 100 per cent of human excreta and liquid wastes from all sanitation facilities including toilets must be disposed of safely. In order to achieve this goal, the following activities shall be undertaken:

(a) Promoting proper functioning of network-based sewerage systems and ensuring connections of households to them wherever possible;

(b) Promoting recycle and reuse of treated waste water for non-potable applications wherever possible will be encouraged;

(c) Promoting proper disposal and treatment of sludge from on-site installations (septic tanks, pit latrines, etc.);

(d) Ensuring that all the human wastes are collected safely confined and disposed of after treatment so as not to cause any hazard to public health or the environment.

Finally, it includes proper operation and maintenance of all sanitary installations. Specifically,

(a) Promoting proper usage, regular upkeep and maintenance of household, community and public sanitation facilities;

(b) Strengthening urban local bodies to provide or cause to provide, sustainable sanitation services delivery.

Activities

In order to achieve these goals, the following activities shall be undertaken:

1. Promoting access to households with safe sanitation facilities (including proper disposal arrangements);
2. Promoting community-planned and managed toilets wherever necessary, for groups of households who have constraints of space, tenure or economic constraints in gaining access to individual facilities;
3. Adequate availability and 100 per cent upkeep and management of Public Sanitation facilities in all Urban Areas, to rid them of open defecation and environmental hazards.

It lays out a vision for urban sanitation in India. It instructs states to come up with their own detailed state-level urban sanitation strategies and City Sanitation Plans. It moots the idea of totally sanitised and open-defecation cities as a target and the setting up of a multi-stakeholder City Sanitation Task Force to achieve this. Environmental considerations, public health implications and reaching the unserved and urban poor are given significant emphasis in the policy. Funding options are laid out including direct central and state support including through existing schemes, public-private partnerships, and external funding agencies. It directs that at least 20 per cent of the funds should be earmarked towards servicing the urban poor. The Centre also plans to institute awards to the best performing cities, reminiscent of the Nirmal Gram Puraskar awards for villages.

The National Urban Sanitation Policy takes into account all the elements of environmental sanitation, i.e., solid waste management; generation of industrial and other specialised/hazardous wastes; drainage; as also the management of drinking water supply, generating awareness of the benefits of a hygienic and clean environment and thereafter brings about behaviour change, elimination of open defecation, integrated citywide sanitation, safe disposal and proper operation and maintenance of all sanitary installations are some of the goals of the project. Special focus has been given to hygienic and affordable sanitation facilities for the urban poor particularly for the urban poor and women and will ensure improved cleanliness in cities and towns.

The National Urban Sanitation Policy envisages transforming all the towns and cities of India into 100 per cent sanitised, healthy and livable spaces, ensuring sustained public health and improved environmental outcomes for all its citizens. The exact contents of this framework may be adapted to suit the state's urban sanitation strategy and used for its cities. To assist in thinking through the challenge, some core building blocks are outlined. The policy focuses on achievements of outcomes rather than on mere construction of infrastructure, and emphasises building capacities at the city level.

Nirmal Bharat Abhiyan (NBA), 2012

The Nirmal Bharat Abhiyan (NBA) is a comprehensive programme to ensure sanitation facilities in rural areas with broader goal to eradicate the practice of open defecation. In fact, the programme of Total Sanitation Campaign started in 1999 was renamed as Nirmal Bharat Abhiyan in April, 2012. The objective is to accelerate the sanitation coverage in the rural areas so as to comprehensively cover the rural community through renewed strategies and saturation approach. The revised approach emphasised more on Information, Education and Communication (IEC), Human resource development, capacity development activities to increase the awareness among rural people and generation of demand for facilities for rural sanitation.

The salient features of the revised guidelines are:

1. Accelerating the sanitation coverage in the rural areas is advocated so as to comprehensively cover the rural community through saturation approach to create Nirmal Gram Panchayats.
2. Implementation of NBA is proposed with 'Village Panchayat' as the base unit. Village Panchayats where all habitations have access to water are to be taken up on priority.
3. Accelerate sanitation coverage in rural areas to achieve the vision of Nirmal Bharat by 2022 with all Village Panchayats in the country attaining nirmal status.
4. Incentive as provided under the scheme for construction of individual household latrines has been extended to all BPL households and APL households restricted to SCs/STs, small and marginal farmers, landless labourers with homestead, differently abled and women headed households.
5. The incentive amount for construction of one unit of individual household latrines has been increased from Rs 3,200 to Rs 4600. The Central share out of this is Rs 3200 and State Government share is Rs 1400. Minimum beneficiary share shall be Rs 900.
6. The schools which are not yet covered under Sarva Shiksha Abhiyan and Anganwadi centres in the rural areas will be provided with proper sanitation facilities and proactive promotion of hygiene education and sanitary habits among students will be undertaken.
7. Appropriate convergence with MGNREGS has been provided.
8. All houses constructed by the beneficiaries under Indira Awas Yojana (IAY) or any other State rural housing Scheme which did not have toilets shall also be eligible for the incentive for creation of sanitation facilities.
9. Solid and Liquid Waste Management may be taken in the proposed and existing Nirmal Gram Panchayats.

Swachh Bharat Abhiyan, 2014

Swachh Bharat Abhiyan was announced by Prime Minister of India Narendra Modi on Indian Independence Day and launched on 2nd October, 2014, Gandhi Jayanti. On this day, Modi addressed the citizens of India in a public gathering held at Rajghat, New Delhi and asked everyone to join this campaign. Later on this day, Modi himself swept a parking area at Mandir Marg Police Station followed by pavement in Valmiki Basti, a colony of sanitation workers, at Mandir Marg, near Connaught Place, New Delhi. This campaign aims to accomplish the vision of 'Clean India' by 2nd October, 2019, 150th birthday of Mahatma Gandhi and is expected to cost over Rs 62000 crore.

The drinking water and sanitation ministry will implement the programme in rural areas while the urban development ministry will do the same in urban areas. The 'Nirmal Bharat Abhiyan' will be restructured into the 'Swachh Bharat Mission' with two sub-missions-'Swachh Bharat Mission' (rural) and 'Swachh Bharat Mission' (urban). Budgetary provisions for the two sub-missions will be provided separately in the demand for grant of the ministries of drinking water and sanitation (for rural) and ministry of urban development (for urban).

The programme includes elimination of open defecation, conversion of insanitary toilets to pour flush toilets, eradication of manual scavenging, municipal solid waste management, bringing about a behavioural change in people regarding healthy sanitation practices, generating awareness among citizens about sanitation and its linkages with public health, strengthening of urban local bodies to design, execute and operate systems to fulfil these objectives and creating and enabling environment for private sector participation in capital expenditure and operational expenditure. The urban component of the programme consists of providing individual household toilets, community and public toilets and municipal solid waste management in all 4,041 statutory towns.

On 14 November, 2014, the birthday of Pandit Jawaharlal Nehru, the first Prime Minister of India, the Union Minister of Women and Child Development Smt Maneka Gandhi launched the National Bal Swachhta Mission in New Delhi. The Bal Swachha Mission is a part of the nationwide sanitation initiative of 'Swachh Bharat Mission' launched by the Prime Minister on 2nd October, 2014.

8.2 Liberation and Rehabilitation of Scavengers

Introduction

Manual scavenging refers to the removal of human waste/excreta (night soil) from unsanitary, "dry toilets", i.e., toilets without the modern flush system. Manual scavenging involves the removal of human excreta using brooms and tin plates. The excreta are piled into baskets which scavengers carry on their heads to locations sometimes several kilometers from the latrines. Manual scavenging is said to have started in 1214 in Europe when the first public toilets appeared. Manual scavenging is a caste-based and hereditary profession, which is handed down, as a legacy from one generation to the next; "manual scavenging" has been an age-old routine for this community, which is untouched by technological advancement in sanitary practices. Not only does the prevalence of this culture seem antediluvian, but what is worse is the fact that those born in this community are considered agents of pollution due to their background of social hierarchy, based on birth. They are the most oppressed and suppressed class of Indian society - hated, ostracised, vilified and avoided by all other castes and classes. The appalling hardship, humiliation and exploitation they face, have no parallel in human history. The practice started in the Pauranic period continued in the Buddhist, Mauryan, Mughal and British periods.

Life of Scavengers

Manual scavenging is considered one of the lowest, polluted and most degrading occupations. Scavengers come in direct contact with human excreta and his/her hands are completely soiled. In a congested locality, the scavenger has to crawl through a narrow passage, pushing the basket with one hand, resting his body weight on the other to make his way up to the latrine chamber through a narrow opening. In the latrine, where the seat is deep inside, he/she has to stretch his hand to the fullest and thrust his/her head into the hole to clean the toilet. The scavenger has to bend forward into the narrow space to clean excreta from the toilet antechambers. In latrines, which have no receptacles, human excreta drops directly on the floor, which, with passage of time, wears the brickwork that becomes patchy and uneven. In most cases, the sidewalls are also without cement plaster; with the result, the excreta get stuck up everywhere on the sidewalls and also on the floor. The scavenger, while cleaning, has to scratch the floor and sidewalls to do maximum cleaning. It is a common sight to see scavengers, mostly women, moving with excreta on the head, stored in bamboo-baskets, or in leaking drums, with the muck trickling down over face and body. Passers-by avoid such persons. If a scavenger comes in close proximity, he or she is showered with a hail of abuse. In many places, latrines are so constructed that the users do not even see their own excreta. They simply squat, perform, and go away without even caring to know who cleans their toilets. No human degradation could be more cruel and inhuman than the one suffered by scavengers.

Manual scavengers are India's hidden communities, crammed into slums and largely forgotten as the country marches forward as the world's largest democracy. They are shunned by society, often banned from entering temples or accessing the same water pumps as higher castes - rules that are enforced by verbal abuse and violence. Today, activists estimate there are 3,00,000 manual scavengers in India, despite repeated high-level commitments to stamp out the practice. The latest census in 2011 showed there are still around 8,00,000 Indian households with dry latrines that are cleaned manually.

Background of the Scheme

The National Scheme of Liberation and Rehabilitation of Scavengers and their Dependents mark the convergence of several public initiatives over a period of four decades preceding its introduction in 1992. The first initiative taken by the erstwhile State of Bombay resulted in the submission of a report on the living conditions of scavengers in 1952. The major recommendations contained in the report were circulated by the Government of India to the State Governments for wider application in 1955. In its report submitted in 1955, the first Backward Classes Commission also recommended measures for the alleviation of the sub-human living conditions of scavengers. These recommendations were again brought to the notice of the State Governments in 1956. The Government of India also constituted a Central Advisory Board of Harijan Welfare in 1956, which had reviewed the working and living conditions of scavengers in the country and had recommended that the Government introduce a Centrally Sponsored Scheme for the alleviation of their condition. A Centrally Sponsored Scheme was accordingly introduced in the Third Five Year Plan in pursuance of various recommendations. This scheme, however, failed primarily because it merely sought to shift the mode of carrying night soil from the head to a wheel-barrow and the handling of the wheel-barrow proved impractical. The scheme was discontinued during the Fifth Five Year Plan following the realisation that the practice of scavenging was inextricably linked with the evils of a stratified social structure.

A Committee was then appointed in 1965 by the Government of India to examine the question of abolition of customary rights of the scavengers. In its report, the Committee recommended the dismantling of the customary rights structure under which non-municipalised cleaning of private latrines was passed on from generation to generation of scavengers in the form of a hereditary right. The recommendations of the Committee though circulated to the State Governments failed to evoke any response.

Thereafter, the National Commission on Labour recommended in 1968-69 a comprehensive legislation for regulating the working, service and living conditions of scavengers. During the Gandhi Centenary Year (1969), a special programme for converting dry latrines to water-borne flush latrines was undertaken. A pilot project with the same objective was undertaken during the Fifth Five Year Plan. The conversion scheme failed principally because it had no element of subsidy and the State Governments failed to generate the necessary internal resources. The scheme was, therefore, deleted from the Sixth Five Year Plan.

The first major initiative in the direction of consolidating and spearheading a concrete proposal was taken in 1980 with the Ministry of Home Affairs introducing a scheme for conversion of dry latrines into sanitary latrines and rehabilitation of liberated scavengers and their dependents in dignified occupations in selected towns. The scheme was dovetailed into the then existing Centrally Sponsored Implementation of the Protection of Civil Rights Act Scheme as one of the measures for the removal of untouchability. The thrust was urban and the central grant was dependent on a matching grant being provided by the State Governments.

The scheme was taken up in two towns of Bihar initially and was subsequently extended to Andhra Pradesh, Assam, Kerala, Maharashtra, Rajasthan, Tamil Nadu, Tripura and Uttar Pradesh. The scheme was operational in sixteen States by the end of the Sixth Five Year Plan period. The scheme succeeded in converting about one lakh dry latrines into water-borne flush latrines and rehabilitated 5,000 scavengers in alternative employment in seventy towns. The scheme was thereafter transferred from the Ministry of Home Affairs to the Ministry of Welfare in 1985. A task force constituted by the Planning Commission in July 1989 estimated that there were 76 lakh dry latrines in the country. By 1991, Rs 82 crore had been released as central assistance for implementing the scheme in 490 towns. The efforts resulted in the conversion of 10 lakh dry latrines into water borne sanitary latrines and around 17,000 unemployed scavengers were rehabilitated in alternative trades and occupations.

Following a review of the working of the scheme in 1991, the Planning Commission decided to bifurcate the scheme: the Ministries of Urban Development and Rural Development being made responsible for conversion of dry latrines and the Ministry of Welfare being made responsible for the rehabilitation of scavengers. The National Scheme of Liberation and Rehabilitation of Scavengers and their Dependents was introduced by the Ministry of Welfare on 22nd March, 1992. Under the Act, the States could formulate schemes to further the objectives of the law, but no reference to the national scheme was made.

Objectives of the Scheme

The objective of the scheme is to liberate scavengers and their dependents from their existing hereditary and obnoxious occupation of manually removing night soil and filth and to provide for and engage them in alternative and dignified occupations within a period of five years.

While Ministry of Urban Development will implement the programme of conversion of dry latrines into water borne flush latrines to liberate the scavengers from their obnoxious occupation, the Ministry of Welfare is entrusted with implementation of Scheme for their rehabilitation in an alternative occupation.

The Scavenger is one who is partially or wholly engaged in the obnoxious and inhuman occupation of manually removing night soil and filth. The dependent of a Scavenger is one who is a member of his/her family or is dependent on him/her irrespective of the fact whether he is partially or wholly engaged in the said occupation.

The Scheme would cover primarily all scavengers belonging to Scheduled Caste community and scavengers belonging to other communities engaged in servicing specifically dry latrines, to eliminate the practice of manual scavenging. Persons engaged in cleaning occupations other than dry latrines are not eligible for assistance under the scheme.

Women form a bulk of the work force engaged in manual scavenging and continue to be engaged so after men of the family have shifted to more dignified professions. First priority, therefore, should be given to rehabilitation of women.

The Scheme comprises of the following components: (i) Time-bound programme for identification of scavengers and their dependents and their aptitude for alternative trade through a survey. (ii) Training in identified trades for scavengers and their dependents at government training institutions. (iii) Rehabilitation of scavengers in various trades and occupations by providing subsidy.

Organisation of the Scheme

The organisation of the scheme was at four levels i.e., at Central government level, District level and at Town/Mohalla level.

The Ministry of Welfare is the implementing as well as nodal agency at the national level. There is central Monitoring Committee under the Chairmanship of the Secretary, Ministry of Welfare, with representatives from the Ministries/Departments of the Urban Development, Rural Development, Labour, Education, Banking, Small Scale Industries, Planning Commission and the State Governments which meets once in three months to evaluate the implementation of the scheme and to take collective action.

Secretary in-charge of Scheduled Castes Welfare in the State is responsible for the implementation of the scheme. He co-ordinates the implementation of the scheme with the Central Government as well as with Departments of the State Government. The State-level Scheduled Castes Development and Finance Corporation is the chief agency for the implementation of the scheme.

The District Collector/District Magistrate/Deputy Commissioner of the district is responsible for overall implementation of the scheme. The District Managers/Assistant Managers of the State Scheduled Castes Finance and Development Corporations are responsible for the day-to-day implementation of the scheme.

At the local level, the State Government/District Officer/District Collector constitutes a small Committee for each town wherever the number of scavengers may be about 100 or more than 100. The District Officer may constitute suitable representative Mohalla Committees with appropriate persons/officers as Chairpersons and convenors. The local body level Committee and the Mohalla Committees help in the identification of scavengers and provide forum for discussions or initiating corrective action in the implementation of the programme.

Evaluation

The Employment of Manual Scavengers and Construction of Dry Latrines (Prohibition) Act, 1993 was adopted by sixteen States as of

April 2002, but there was no evidence of its enforcement in any of the States. The Scheme did not even mention the existence of the Law. Lateral support to the Scheme through liberation (i.e., conversion of dry latrines into water-borne ones) of scavengers was not aligned with the progress of rehabilitation measures.

Surveys for identification of scavengers and their dependents necessary to locate, specify and particularise the beneficiaries and their needs were often not methodologically sound and results varied widely. Even the definition of Scavenger was not on any settled basis by the survey agencies of the States which resulted in inclusion of ineligible persons in the list of beneficiaries. Reliable base-line data were not available even after ten years of the implementation of the scheme.

Targets for training were not communicated by the Ministry to the States which resulted either in targets not being prescribed by the States or in targets being determined only on ad hoc basis. Consequently, shortfall in training coverage was as high as 68 per cent and targets set for the Eighth Plan were not achieved even at the end of the Ninth Plan. No special curriculum was developed for training of scavengers though it was recognised that occupational shift in low-skill areas would require special measures.

The Ninth Plan efforts showed lesser rehabilitation numerically than the Eighth Plan period. The targeting exercise was largely hypothetical as it did not take into account the year-wise progress though there was 61 per cent shortfall in achieving targets for rehabilitation. Rehabilitation efforts were characterised by misapplication of resources, emphasis on low- cost projects for availing of cash benefits without income generation and mismatches between skills and occupations.

During 1999-2000, a new thrust area in the form of the Sanitary Mart Scheme was identified and Rs 130.05 crore were released for the purpose. However, this scheme failed as only 14 per cent of the targeted Marts could be set up during the period.

District Collectors were to act as key functionaries for coordinating with training institutes, financial institutions and various departments of State Governments executing welfare schemes. However, their role was confined largely to survey and identification of beneficiaries. The responsibility of the scheme was transferred to Scheduled Castes Development Financial Corporations, which were not accountable to the

District Collectors in the normal course of their functioning. These organisational mismatches adversely affected the implementation of the scheme.

During the Ninth Plan period, the initial budgetary commitment of Rs 421.50 crores was scaled down to Rs 249.15 crores representing a decrease of 41 per cent. Funds for implementation of the scheme continued to flow to the Scheduled Castes Development Financial Corporations notwithstanding substantial unspent balances. Large quantum of funds was released at the very end of the financial year resulting in either hurried spending or notional spending for balancing the accounts. The desired financial support of State Governments was not available.

There was hardly any workable monitoring machinery at the Ministry, State and District levels. Monitoring Committees were either not formed or were not functioning properly.

Impact assessment of the Scheme by Audit revealed poor performance along all the critical parameters, i.e., identification of scavengers, training of beneficiaries, rehabilitation, monitoring and evaluation of progress of implementation of the Scheme.

8.3 Sanitation in Karnataka

Karnataka is a state in South West India. It was formed on 1st November, 1956, with the passage of the States Reorganisation Act. Originally known as the State of Mysore, it was renamed Karnataka in 1973. The capital and largest city is Bangalore. Karnataka is bordered by the Arabian Sea and the Laccadive Sea to the west, Goa to the north-west, Maharashtra to the north, Telangana to the north-east, Andhra Pradesh to the east, Tamil Nadu to the south-east, and Kerala to the south-west. The state covers an area of 191,976 square kilometres or 5.83 per cent of the total geographical area of India. It is the seventh largest Indian state by area. With 61,130,704 inhabitants at the 2011 census, Karnataka is the eighth largest state by population, comprising 30 districts. Kannada is the most widely spoken and official language of the state.

The state has three main geographical zones: (1) The coastal region of Karavali, (2) The hilly Malenadu region comprising the Western Ghats and (3) The Rayaluseeme region comprising the plains of Deccan Plateau. In Karnataka 83 per cent are Hindus, 11 per cent Muslims, 4 per cent Christians, 0.8 per cent Jains and 0.7 per cent Buddhists.

A Profile of Karnataka – 2011

Population of Karnataka	6,11,30,704
Male population	3,10,57,742
Female population	3,00,72,963
Density	319
Literacy	75.61
Male Literacy	82.84
Female Literacy	68.45
Literates	4,10,29,323
Illitarates	1,32,45,580
Illiterates (Males)	47,21,430
Illiterates (Females)	85,24,150
Sex Ratio	968

Karnataka is one of first states to ban manual scavenging. It was banned in 1970 by Basavanappa, the Minister for Social Welfare, Government of Karnataka. It is estimated that there are as many as 8,000 manual scavengers earn their living by clearing human waste. On 20th July 2010, Manual scavengers from the Bhangi caste in Savanur had covered themselves with human excreta to protest their impending eviction and a denial of water by the Town Municipal Corporation of Savanur.

Availability of Toilet Facility

At the start of the twenty-first century the violation of the human right to clean water and sanitation is destroying human potential on an epic scale. In today's increasingly prosperous and interconnected world more children die for want of clean water and a toilet than from almost any other cause. Exclusion from clean water and basic sanitation destroys more lives than any war or terrorist act (HDR, 2006). Eventhough Karnataka state claiming that in IT and technology it is one of the developed states, its position in basic human services is lagging behind considerably especially in water, sanitation, primary health, electricity and roads. This is evident from the information provided in Table 1.

Table 8.1: Availability of Toilet Facility in Karnataka

Source: HH-Series Tables, Census of India 2011.

It is evident from the Table 8.1 that almost three-fourth (71.58%) of rural households do not have toilet facility within its premises. It is disgusting to view that almost half of the households in Karnataka lack toilet facility within their easy reach. Therefore around three crore people of Karnataka do not have toilet facility within their premises. As a result 92.15 per cent of them have to defecate in open places. Further information provided in Table 8.2 reveals that only 22 per cent of the rural people have improved sanitation facility in their houses.

Table 8.2: Brief Outline of Sanitation Facility in Karnataka

Sl. No.	Sanitation Facility	Rural	Urban	Total
1.	Improved Sanitation	22.0	59.3	32.4
2.	Flush to sewer/septic/pit	20.3	56.3	30.4
3.	Not improved	40.7	78.0	67.7
4.	No toilet/open space	76.8	26.3	62.7

Source: DLHS-3 Karnataka.

Bathing Facility and Drainage Connectivity

Gloomy picture can also be seen in the facility of bathing and drainage connectivity. Almost one-fourth of them do not possess this facility within their house or premises. It is also perturbing to underscore that 3.6 per cent of the urban households in the state do not have bathing facility within their premises. Most of the poor slum dwellers face this indispensable requirement of routine life (Table 8. 3).

Table 8.3: Households Having Bathing Facility

Region	*Total Households*	*Number of Households having Bathroom facility with the premises*	*Enclosure Without Roof*	*Number of households not having Bathroom facility within the premises*
Rural	78,64,196 (100.00)	49,85,101 (63.38%)	12,63,205 (16.06)	16,15,890 (20.55%)
Urban	53,15, 715 (100.00)	48,74,674 (91.70%)	2,49,269 (4.69%)	1,91,772 (3.60%)
Total	1,31,79,911 **(100.00)**	**98,59**,775 (74.80%)	15,12,474 (11.47%)	18,07,662 (13.71%)

Source: HH-Series Tables, Census of India 2011.

Information about drainage connectivity reveals that 'Open Indian Style' is visible in the State. Majority of rural households (87.26 per cent) do not have connectivity to their drainage. It is alarming to notice that only 12.61 per cent of urban households in Karnataka have closed drainage facility to their houses. And roughly same percentage of households manages without any drainage facility (Table 8.4).

Table 8.4: Drainage Connectivity for Waste Waster Outlet

Sl. No.	*Region*	*Closed Drainage*	*Open Drainage*	*No Drainage*
1.	Rural	30,05,430 (8739%)	29,11,757 (63.82%)	45,18,789 (87.26%)
2.	Urban	4,33,650 (12.61%)	16,51,008 (36.18%)	6,59,277 (12.74%)
	Total	34,39,080 (100.00)	45,62,765 (100.00)	51,78,066 (100.00)

Removal of Human Waste

One of the most hazardous aspects of human social life is removal human waste/excreta by using brooms, tin plates and baskets from dry latrine and carrying it to disposal grounds some distance away. It is evident from the 2011 census is still removed manually in Karnataka. Development in science and technology is not in a position to eradicate this horrendous task to night soil removal by human. In fact in 1970s itself the state of Karnataka passed a law to ban manual scavenging. It is terrible to know that still people are utilising the help of human only to remove human excreta in Karnataka. 7,740 cases have been reported in Karnataka as per Census 2011 (Table 8.5)

Table 8.5: Night Soil Disposition in Karnataka

Sl. No.	Region	Night soil disposed into open drain	Night soil removed by human	Night soil serviced by animal
1.	Rural	9,328 (15.10%)	2,052 (26.51%)	13,388 (46.18%)
2.	Urban	52,474 (84.90%)	5,688 (73.49%)	15,607 (53.82%)
	Total	61,802 (100.00)	7,740 (100.00)	28,995 (100.00)

Source: HH-Series Tables, Census of India 2011.

Magnitude of Sanitation Deprivation in Karnataka

One of the perceptible problems pertaining to hygiene in the state is the continuation of rural and urban disparities. Whereas most of the urban areas inevitably have done to maintain cleanliness and hygiene, villages in Karnataka suffer from these provisions. The problem of sanitation is not uniformly distributed in the state. Some districts have achieved almost complete sanitation, others performed dismally.

Table 8.6: Availability of Toilet Facility in Gulbarga Division

Division/ Districts	Region	Total Households	Number of Households having latrine facility within the premises	Number of household not having latrine facility within the premises
Bidar	**Rural**	2,37,380	20,983	2,16,397
	Urban	76,141	51,822	24,319
	Total	3,13,521	72,805	2,40,716
Raichur	**Rural**	2,64,274	26,397	2,37,877
	Urban	95,063	47,929	47,134
	Total	3,59,337	74,326	2,85,011
Koppal	**Rurnl**	2,13,217	25,565	1,87,652
	Urban	46,179	22,366	23,813
	Total	2,59,396	47,931	2,11,465
Gulbarga	**Rural**	3,11,531	13,911	2,97,620
	Urban	1,53,714	1,04,881	48,833
	Total	4,65,245	1,18,792	3,46,453
Yadgir	**Rural**	1,61,665	6,938	1,54,727
	Urban	38,759	15,585	23,174
	Total	2,00,424	22,523	1,77,901
Bellary	**Rural**	2,91,383	35,296	2,56,087

	Urban	1,90,321	1,20,814	69,507
	Total	4,81,704	1,56,110	3,25,594
Gulbarga Division CHK Region)	**TOTAL**	20,79,627 (100.00)	4,92,487 **(23.68%)**	15,87,140 (76.32%)

Table 8.7: Availability of Toilet Facility in Belgaum Division

District.	*Region*	*Total Households*	*Number of Households having latrine facility within the premises*	*Number of households not having latrine facility witliin the premises*
Belgaum	**Rural**	7,08,069	1,31,009	5,77,060
	Urban	2,55, 756	1,85,216	70,540
	Total	9,63,825	3,16,225	6,47,600
Bagalkot	**Rural**	2,38,746	17,187	2,21,559
	Urban	1,16,631	49,626	67,005
	Total	3,55,377	66,813	2,88,564
Bijapur	**Rural**	3,07,984	15,516	2,92,468
	Urban	97,092	57,784	39,308
	Total	4,05,076	73,300	3,31,776
Gadag	**Rural**	1,37,799	12,732	1,25,067
	Urban	77,803	32,936	44,867
	Total	2,15,602	45,668	1,69,934
D hat wad	**Rural**	1,57,960	36,449	1,21,511
	Urban	2,14,094	1,75,642	38,452
	Total	3,72,054	2,12,091	1,59,963
Haveri	**Rural**	2,54,181	71,774	1,82,407
	Urban	71,275	49,646	21,629
	Total	3,25,456	1,21,420	2,04,036
Uttar Kannada	**Rural**	2,26,803	1,14,752	1,12,051
	Urban	93,109	75,091	18,018
	Total	3,19,912	1,89,843	1,30,069
Belgaum Division	**TOTAL**	29,57,302 (100.00)	10,25,360 (34.67%)	19,31,942 (65.33%)

Source: HH-Series Tables, Census of India 2011.

Regional Deprivations in Health and Hygiene

Economically, Karnataka is one of the developed states in India. This state is known for its progress in IT/BT sector. But this development largely confine to Bangalore only. Regional disparities are completely obvious in the state not only in economic field but also in human development aspects. Regional deprivations are also seen in the availability of sanitation facility. For administrative purpose Karnataka state has been divided into four divisions. They are in Northern Karnataka-Gulbarga and Belgaum and in South Karnataka - Mysore and Bangalore. Information about Division-wise disparities in sanitation same has been given in Table 8.8.

Table 8.8: Availability of Toilet Facility in Bangalore Division

District.	*Region*	*Total Households*	*Number of Households having latrine facility within the premises*	*Number of households not having latrine facility within the premises*
Chitradurga	**Rural**	2,82,019	53,839	2,28,180
	Urban	72,124	53,303	18,821
	Total	3,54,143	1,07,142	2,47,001
Davangere	**Rural**	2,72,929	81,363	1,91,566
	Urban	1,31,911	1,06,683	25,228
	Total	4,04,840	1,88,046	2,16,794
Tumkur	**Rural**	4,95,885	90,868	4,05,017
	Urban	1,40,509	1,15,953	24,556
	Total	6,36,394	2,06,821	4,29,573
Bangalore	**Rural**	2,07,628	1,55,366	52,262
	Urban	21,69,428	20,99,233	70,195
	Total	23,77,056	22,54,599	1,22,457
Kolar	**Rural**	2,26,245	57,664	1,68,581
	Urban	1,04,745	84,011	20,734
	Total	3,30,990	1,41,675	1,89,315
Chikkaballapur	**Rural**	2.20,309	50,677	1,69,632
	Urban	62,002	52,280	9,722
	Total	2,82,311	1,02,957	1,79,354
Bangalore Rural	**Rural**	1,62,398	1,22,643	39,755
	Urban	62,347	56,946	5,401
	Total	2,24,745	1,79,589	45,156
Ramanagara	**Rural**	2,00,171	56,142	1,44,029
	Urban	59,623	52,749	6,874
	Total	2,59,794	1,08,891	1,50,903
Shimoga	**Rural**	2,57,060	1,58,828	98,232
	Urban	1,45,079	1,27,301	17,778
	Total	4,02,139	2,86,129	1,16,010
Bangalore Division	**TOTAL**	52,72,412 (100.00)	35,75,849 (67.82%)	16,96,563 (32.17%)

Source: HH-Series Tables, Census of India 2011.

Table 8.9: Availability of Toilet Facility in Mysore Division

District	*Region*	*Total Households*	*Number of Households having latrine facihty within the premises*	*Number of households not having latrine facihty within the premises*
Udupi	**Rural**	1,74,548	1,45,909	28,639
	Urban	71,765	68,899	2,866
	Total	2,46,313	2,14,808	31,505
Chikimglur	**Rural**	2,15,334	1,16,556	98,778
	Urban	56,839	50,813	6,026
	Total	2,72,173	1,67,369	1,04,804
Mandya	**Rural**	3,54,049	97,526	2,56,523
	Urban	72,529	62,292	10,237
	Total	4,26,578	1,59,818	2,66,760
Hassan	**Rural**	3,39,911	90,891	2,49,020
	Urban	89,381	80,321	9,060
	Total	4,29,292	1,71,212	2,58,080
D. Kannada	**Rural**	2,20,806	1,94,578	26,228
	Urban	2,04,485	1,99,491	4,994
	Total	4,25,291	3,94,069	31,222
Mysore	**Rural**	4,01,655	1,08,475	2,93,183
	Urban	2,86,767	2,70,028	16,739
	Total	6,88,422	3,78,503	3,09,919
Kodagu	**Rural**	1,18,509	93,421	25,088
	Urban	19,794	19,205	589
	Total	1,38,303	1,12,626	25,677
Chamarajnagar	**Rural**	2,03,748	31,279	1,72,469
	Urban	40,450	26,016	14,434
	Total	2,44,198	57,295	1,86,903
Mysore Division	**TOTAL**	28,70370 (100.0)	16,55,700 (57.57%)	12,14,870 (42.32%)

Source: HH-Series Tables, Census of India 2011.

It is evident from the tables that availability of toilet facility is very poor in Gulbarga division. Only 23.68 per cent of the households possess toilet facility within their premises. More than 90 per cent of the rural parts of this region lack this basic facility. Some districts like Bangalore (94.84 per cent), Dakshina Kannada (92.65 per cent) households have better access to toilet facility in their premises, whereas Kodagu and Udupi have about 80 per cent access to toilet facilities.

Missing Toilets in Karnataka

One of the major problems of unsanitary conditions in Karnataka is the increasing number of missing toilets at the time of physical verification.

It was seen from the reliable sources that many toilets have been sanctioned to the people of BPL families with the provision of subsidies from the government. But at the time of actual physical verification, most of the sanctioned toilets were found only on official records without any construction or structure. This was also raised by the Central government. The Union Ministry of Drinking Water and Sanitation (MDWS) has asked Government of Karnataka as well as some other states to find out the reasons behind the enormous disparity in the claims of Karnataka government on rural sanitation coverage and recent data published by the Census 2011. Though the Government of Karnataka claimed to have covered 63.87 per cent rural households under the Total Sanitation Coverage till 2011-12, the Census figures showed that it reached only 31.90 per cent in the villages across the State.

Why don't People use Toilets?

Arghyam, a public charitable trust conducted ASHWAS participatory survey to ascertain the status of household water and sanitation in rural Karnataka in the year 2008-09. This Trust was set up with an endowment from Rohini Nilekani. Since 2005, Arghyam has been supporting efforts to address equity and sustainability in access to water and sanitation for all citizens. This Survey also reported that 72 per cent people of Karnataka do not have access to toilets, 21 per cent have toilets outside their house and only seven per cent have inside their house. ASHWAS listed some of the reasons for not constructing toilets in Karnataka. They are given in Table 10. Two-thirds of the people stated financial problem and about one-third per cent them not in position to construct the toilet for want of space in their house.

Table 8.10: Reasons for not Constructing Toilets

Sl. No.	*Reasons*	*Percentage*
1.	Financial Problem	59.00
2.	No Space	29.00
3.	Don't want/not a priority	06.00
4.	Cultural and Religious Reasons	03.00
5.	Psychological Reasons	03.00

Source: ASHWAS 2008-09.

ASHWAS report also examined the problems people face during open defecation. 26 per cent people remarked that due to open defecation they can defecate only during late evenings or night. 21 per cent of them opined that it is unsafe to defecate openly and also they feel embarrassed during defecation.

Table 8.11: Problems of Open Defecation

Sl. No,	*Problems of Open Defecation*	*Percentage*
1.	Possible to go only in dawn/dark	26.00
2.	Embarrassment	21.00
3.	Unsafe	21.00
4.	Uncomfortable	16.00
5.	Unhealthy	12.00
6.	Water Problem	04.00

Source: ASHWAS 2008-09.

Reasons for Backwardness in Sanitation

According to Human Development Report 2006, six interlocking barriers come in the way of providing sanitation. These could be aptly applied to India and Karnataka. They are: National policy, behaviour, Poverty, gender and supply barriers.

The National Policy Barrier: Effective national policies are conspicuously absent for sanitation than for water. The state of a country's sanitation may shape its prospects for human development. And yet sanitation seldom figures prominently on the national political agenda (HDR, 2006). Karnataka state evolved various water and sanitation programmes. Prominent among them are: Swachcha Gram Yojana; Nirmal Gram Puraskar; Total Sanitation Campaign (TSC); Sachetena; Suvarna Jala; Swajaldhara; Jal Nirmal; ARWSP/National Rural water supply programme. Even with these national level and state level sanitation programmes and policies, it has not possible to achieve at least half of rural sanitation facilities in the state.

The Behaviour Barrier: Attitude of the people matters most in the utilisation and provision of sanitary facilities. Toilet facility is not at all a priority to most of the villagers. Often we find people are resorting to using/misusing only public roads instead of their own personal spheres. Further, participatory research exercises show that people tend to attach a higher priority to water than to sanitation and lack of clean water is a more immediate threat of life than the absence of a toilet (HDR, 2006). It is not enough if one or two households construct the toilet. Entire villagers should come forward to change their attitude towards age-old behaviour.

The Poverty Barrier: Use of toilets is relatively less among poor than rich. Poverty remains a major constraint in gaining access to health and hygiene. Nearly 1.4 billion people without access to sanitation live on less than two dollar a day. For most of them, even low-cost improved technology may be beyond financial reach (HDR).

The Gender Barrier: Women are scarcely consulted before evolving policies and programmes. In fact satisfactory sanitation facilities are more required for women than men. Toilet is a topmost priority to women and girls than men and boys. But people attach least priority in involving women in decision-making process.

The Supply Barrier: Turning from demand to supply shows that progress is impeded not just by the absence of affordable sanitation technology, but also by the oversupply of inappropriate technologies, leading to mismatch between what people want and what governments have offered (HDR, *ibid*).

On the whole, progress made in hygiene and cleanliness is far from satisfactory in Karnataka. Poor implementation of sanitation programme, attitude of the public and public servants come in the way of Total sanitation programme. There is an urgent need for social marketing and sustainable sanitation approach especially rural parts of the state. Social marketing focuses on influencing human behaviour to accept healthy behaviour. Sustainable sanitation highlights that in order to be sustainable, a sanitation approach required to be socially suitable and economically feasible. Sustainable sanitation is participatory-based approach. It differs primarily from the current conventional approach of wastewater management. The new approach not only recognises technology, but also social, environmental and economic aspects. It adopts holistic rather than top-down approach.

Note: *I am grateful to Prof Shaukath Azim for making available his paper, An Analysis of Sanitation Deprivation in Karnataka, presented in the National Conference on Sociology of Sanitation, organised by Sulabh International Centre for Action Sociology in collaboration with Sulabh International Social Service Organisation, held on January 28 and 29, 2013 at Mavalankar Auditorium, New Delhi.*

8.4 Solid Waste Management: A Study of Mangalore City Corporation

Introduction

India is urbanising very fast. India's urban population which was 10 per cent in 1900 rose to 17 per cent in the next fifty years. By 2001, it went upto 28 per cent and in 2011 the urban population stood at 31 per cent which indicates that India is facing rapid urbanisation. The problem of sanitation is a serious problem confronting not only rural society but more so urban population. With increasing population and rising income, the lifestyle of urban residents is also changing. There exists a direct link between affluence and municipal waste. Urban India is adopting a 'throw-away culture'. The residents generate various kinds of wastes of biodegradable and non-biodegradable categories. If proper disposal and management of the waste is not taken up, it could lead to disastrous effects. On the other hand, the waste could become a resource and the society can benefit from these wastes with proper collection and disposal technologies. Majority of wastes can be recycled and the recycling technologies have a promising employment and energy generating options.

This chapter examines the methods of waste disposal undertaken in Mangalore city. It also examines both the causes and effects of inefficient method of waste disposal. In 2008, I had a visitor from New Delhi, visiting Mangalore for the first time. So, I decided take him around Mangalore. First, I took him to Kadri Park and he commented that the place is very clean. After showing him two to three places, I took him to Gokarnatheshwara Temple and he again commented that the place is really clean. I really felt proud of my Mangalore and started observing the places in terms of cleanliness and I found that Mangalore was much cleaner compared to the many towns and cities of India I had visited. It is partly because the city can boast of being the headquarters of Buddivantara Jelle (the district of wise people), as it is known in Karnataka. The district is also cent per cent literate. In fact, Mangalore City Corporation was presented with an excellence award for the first position, in the category of tier II cities, in solid waste management in the second international conference on "solid waste management and exhibition on municipal services, urban development, public works, and clean technology" held from November 9 to 11, 2011 in Kolkata organised by Jadavpur University, Kolkata.

In spite of the first impression a visitor gets and the award it has won in solid waste management, the city is experiencing the rising social costs of development in the form of negative externalities. Increasing levels of pollution, congestion, environmental degradation and depletion of natural resources, displacement of people from their local habitats and also the menace of urban wastes and associated health hazards. The city woefully lacks the most modern and forward looking infrastructure – and is not well-managed in terms of environment in general and waste disposal in particular. Mosquitoes and malaria have been the perennial threats to our health here. Growing garbage has been an eye sore, a challenge to aesthetic sense and health consciousness. In spite of the negative externalities, there is a call and a drive for a clean and green city.

Mangalore

Mangalore (now known as Mangaluru) is the coastal city situated in the west coast of India in the state of Karnataka. It is a small city having a population of nearly five lakhs. Because of the large sea port it is considered as the 'Gateway of Karnataka'. Since Mangalore is close to Western Ghats the terrain is hilly. For the last 2000 years, Mangalore had connection with the outside world, specially the Arab world. In the sixteenth century, Mangalore came under the Portuguese rule and with the fall of Tippu Sultan in 1799 it came under the British. In 1860, the district of Canara was divided into South Canara and North Canara and Mangalore became the headquarters of South Canara district. In 1866, Mangalore Municipality was established under Madras Town Municipal Act. After independence, with the establishment of Karnataka Regional Engineering College, (now National Institute of Technology, Karnataka), Kasturba Medical College, Mangalore Hassan Railway link, establishment of National Highways, Konkan Railway, Mangalore University and many industries, Mangalore further developed.

Following the re-organisation of States, the Mysore Municipalities Act 1964 came into force as a uniform act throughout the state on 1st April, 1965, replacing the Madras District Municipalities Act of 1920.

The provisions of this act gave a new phase to the municipality and it became a city Municipality. Mangalore City Corporation came in to existence on 3rd July, 1980, which was formerly a Municipality and was expanded during 1996-97 by including Surathkal Town Municipality, Katipalla Notified area, Panamboor, Baikampady, Kulai, Hosabettu villages.

The headquarters of MCC is at Lalbagh. Its sub-offices are at Surathkal and Bikarnakatta. As of 2001, the Mangalore municipality covered an area of 73.71 km^2 (28.46 sq. mi.). The city of Mangalore - as corporation unit - is having an area of about 132.45 sq.kms and as per 2011 census, a population of 4,84,785 of which 2,40,651 are males and 2,44,134 are females. Mangalore has a sex ratio of 1014 and literacy rate of 94 per cent. The city is divided into 60 corporation wards. The Mangalore urban area had 32 recognised slums, and nearly 22,000 migrant labourers live in slums within the city limits. Further during April 2002, it was further extended to include Bajal, Kannuru, Kudupu and Thiruvail Panchayath limits into Mangalore City Corporation. There is a proposal to increase the area of MCC to 304 km^2 by including Mulky in the north and Ullal in the south. Mangalore is now famous for banking, education and health facilities.

One of the serious problems faced by the city – its people and its management is waste management, particularly the solid waste management. The city seems to be generating more waste than it can collect and dispose off.

Sanitation in Historical Perspective

Till the beginning of twentieth century, Mangalore was a small place having a trading community living around the old port. The mode of transport was bullock cart. People used to live in traditional tile roofed houses and each house had a big compound. In the end of the compound there were dry latrines. These latrines were cleaned by Thotis (lowest among Scheduled Castes) and they used to take the waste in buckets and wheelbarrows. Around 1940s wet latrines became common where the human waste was directed to a leech pit dug near the latrines. Kitchen waste and other waste was dumped in the drains nearby which was washed away during the monsoon. At this time elephantiasis and malaria were common. It was very common to see in each house one or two persons suffering from elephantiasis. In this last two to three decades due to constant spaying by the Corporation health authorities both elephantiasis and malaria have reduced considerably.

Waste Management

From 1960s Mangalore Municipality started the work of drainage and the latrines and the waste water were connected to the drains and the waste was recycled at Mullakad. However, because of the topography of Mangalore which consists of hills and valleys latrines at the lower levels could not be connected to the drains. Still latrines at the low levels are connected to the leech pits. As a result, water from the surrounding wells could not be used for drinking and the people have to wait for water connection from the City Corporation.

Solid Waste Management

Solid waste management and its disposal is better in Mangalore compared to that in Bangalore and in other places. In fact, last year Mangalore stood second, after Mysore in Karnataka, in cleanliness. It is attributed to the good literacy rate of the city and the district.

For the sake of waste management 47 wards are out sourced and 13 are being maintained by the MCC. In 2003, under the Karnataka Urban Development and Coastal Environment Management Project, a plan was drawn up to upgrade the city's solid waste management capability to 120 tonnes a day by 2020. However, the city is already producing 200 tonnes waste per day. In 2009, the MCC spent Rs 9.88 crores for garbage management (or Rs 1,350 a tonne) with more than one-third of it going to staff salary, according to the draft estimates by the Administrative Staff College of India, Hyderabad. The college, which has prepared a draft sanitation plan for Mangalore, found the following: staff requires proper training on solid waste handling and collection, waste is not being segregated at source, vehicles collecting waste do not have segregated compartments, sanitary workers are not provided with any protective equipment posing health hazards, bio-medical waste from smaller hospitals finds its way into municipal waste, and that there is illegal disposal of waste into the sea which will cause "serious public health and environmental issues".

Solid Waste Management is one of the most important service which is handled by the Health Department. The most pressing problem faced is rapid urbanisation and changing lifestyles have led to the generation of huge amount of garbage and wastes in the urban areas, so much so, over the past few years; just handling this Municipal Solid Waste has assumed the proportion of major organisational, financial and environmental challenge. Despite Municipal solid waste management, being major task of the local government, typical accounting for a sizeable portion of the municipal budget, yet the Urban Local Body is unable to provide effective services. Previously the waste was disposed in an unscientific manner, with crude open dumping in low lying areas being the prevalent practice followed by most Urban Local Bodies. The results of these are foul smell, breeding of flies and other pests and generation of liquid runoffs (Leacheate), which pose a serious threat to the underground water reserves. The area coming under the jurisdiction of Mangalore City Corporation produces an average of 220 tonnes per day of wastes, with a daily collection frequency of 200 tonnes per day. The waste collected has a composition of 60 per cent of organic, 25 per cent of inorganic, five per cent of combustible and 10 per cent of recyclable wastes.

As per Municipal Solid Waste Management and Handling rules 2000, including all administrative, financial, legal planning and engineering functions involved in the whole spectrum of solutions to problems of solid wastes thrust upon the community by its inhabitants. The major components of solid waste management are: Segregation at source, Primary (door to door) collection, Secondary storage, transportation, treatment or processing and disposal.

Source Segregation

This involves separation of wastes into wet, dry/recyclables and household hazardous waste; familiarising people about the solid waste management, system adopted; training programme for retrievers regarding importance of segregation, proper handling of waste and its hazards due to improper handling, and littering of waste to be banned. So far Mangalore has no method of source segregation.

Primary Collection

In December 2012 the MCC launched door-to-door collection of solid waste in some wards by entrusting the job to eight contractors in eight packages. As per the terms of the contract, it was mandatory on their part to collect waste from doorsteps. The contractor could collect a monthly user fee of Rs 30 for collecting waste from residential houses. The monthly user fee for commercial establishments ranged between Rs 100 and Rs 1,000. For hotels and marriage halls, it was between

Rs 300 and Rs 1,000, and for traders in vegetables markets it ranged from Rs 100 to Rs 500. But, the odd collection time in some wards has made the efforts go waste. For instance, workers reach some places at around noon to pick waste when none of the inmates are at home. Now the MCC has decided to collect the waste either before 10 a.m. or late in the evenings. MCC has given a mobile number where the residents can SMS their complaints to this number if solid waste is not picked from their doorsteps. Since two months MCC has banned the use of plastic bags and awareness is created in people's involvement in maintaining the city clean. Similarly efforts are afoot in the segregation of dry and wet waste. Pushcarts and tri-cycles are being used by the contractors for the same. Household wastes bulk generator wastes and street wastes are deposited into secondary collection points.

On 23rd January, 2015 Minister for Urban Development, Karnataka, Vinay Kumar Sorake launched the two package garbage collection system, the first of its kind in Karnataka. M/s Antony Waste Handling Cell Private Ltd. which handles similar projects in Mumbai, Jaipur and New Delhi, has been entrusted with the job in 60 wards of MCC for seven years at an annual cost of Rs 16.62 crores. The contract also involves cleaning of four beaches and mechanical sweeping of 25 km of roads. The company has 55 Mini Tippers, 16 Compactors and 700 employees.

Secondary Storage

Closed metal secondary storage containers are provided. Closed bins systems for secondary storage are provided. Manual handling of waste is minimised by reducing the secondary storage location by transferring garbage directly from door to door collection system to the transportation vehicle. There are approximately 600 RCC bins of 0.8 CC, 24 bricks masonry dustbins, 30 fibre containers and more than 130 other containers.

Secondary Transportation

Covered transportation vehicles are provided. The authorities want to avoiding multiple handling of waste. Regular day-wise clearance frequency is maintained. Twin container dumper placers, Compactors (Back Loaders) and Side Loaders are being used for transportation of waste to the processing site. Rs 214.00 lakh was the capital investments made on the procurement of the transportation vehicles and containers for MSW transportation and reduce manual handling under Karnataka Urban Development and Coastal Environmental Management Projects

(KUDCEMP). Presently there are two trucks, two tippers, one mini lorry, three single container dumper placers and eight twin container dumper placers owned by MCC and one compactor and two side packers and 19 contract trucks operating. These are used to carry wastes to the landfill site at Vamanjur which is 15 kms from the heart of the city.

Disposal Site

Mangalore City Corporation processing a disposal site is having an extent of 37.32 acres of land for the disposal of solid waste located on top of a hill. The site is divided into two portions by a road passing through with 26.69 acres on the north side and 10.63 acres on the south side. To the south side of the existing landfill 25.4 acres of land have been acquired for the construction of new sanitary landfill site. The landfill area is adequate for about 25 years of life. The landfill is constructed in phases to enable progressive development. The development of the landfill over the life would be done in four phases: phase I for six years time frame, phase II, III and IV for three years, six years and for 10 years time frame. To the north side, compost yard for a capacity of 120 tonnes per day of waste is being treated and 68 vermin-composting pits for a capacity of 25 tonnes per day are constructed. The construction of the Municipal solid waste processing and sanitary landfill site was done under KUDCEMP funded through Asian Development Bank loans at a cost of Rs 6.48 crores and Rs 9.39 crores respectively. The compost plant is partially operational with the outsourced 12 personnel, one JCB and one tipper. It generates an average of six tonnes of compost/day taking a feed of 55 tonnes per day.

Landfilling

Sanitary Landfill Site is provided in a six acre land as I phase. Rejects from the compost plant will be land filled. Daily soil top cover of 10 cm will be provided. Presently the sanitary landfill site constructed is not being used. Previous dumped landform will be covered with soil and will be provided with green cover.

Treatment

Aerobic composting and Vermin-composting is provided. There is provision of 120 tonnes per day of waste is aerobically composted and 25 tonnes per day of waste is vermin-composted. Rejects from Compost plant will be transported to sanitary landfill site. Presently MCC is handling the operation and maintenance of aerobic compost plant. Compost plant is generating four to five tonnes of compost/manure through windrow method of aerobic composting. Operation of Vermin- composting is not yet started. Provision is made for running the aerobic compost plant in two shifts. Arrangements have been made for outsourcing the entire treatment and processing unit.

Biomedical Waste Management

The Bio-medical Waste (Management & Handling) Rules notified in July 1998 under the Environment (Protection) Act, 1986, make mandatory for all healthcare facilities irrespective of their size to treat Bio-Medical Waste (BMW) generated by them. In order to comply with the provisions of the Rules, some of the healthcare facilities have installed their own treatment facilities and others are availing services of Common Bio-medical Waste Treatment Facilities (CBWTF). CBWTF has been set by M/s. Medicare Incin Private Limited, No. 47-B, Karnad Industrial Area, Mulky, Dakshina Kannada. MCC has issued notices to all the Hospitals/ Clinics/ Nursing homes to treat the BMW as per the BMW rules 1998 and keep informing regularly to Hospitals/ Clinics/ Nursing homes not to mix the BMW with regular waste. M/s. Medicare Incin Private Limited has installed 7500 kg/day capacity incineration plant but Karnataka state pollution control board has given authorisation for a capacity of 2500 Kg/day. M/s. Medicare Incin Private Limited has provided their own vehicles for collection of biomedical waste from the Hospitals/ Clinics/ Nursing homes/ Laboratories of total 6200 beds throughout DK. Father Muller's Hospital and Yenepoya Medical College have installed their own treatment facilities.

Information, Education and Communication

There is door to door campaigning for educating the public on segregation and door to door garbage collection. Educating school and college students through various activities on solid waste management is being done. School and college level competitions are conducted for students with cash prizes. Also ward level meetings are held to educate the public on Municipal solid waste rules 2000. Street *jathas* are also organised to create awareness among public. Children and students have become messengers of solid waste management. Some of the colleges in association with MCC have started creating awareness on solid waste management, among the school children and public. St Agnes College of

Mangalore has constituted a 'green army' to create awareness in various parts of the city limits on waste management through skits and mime shows. Another NGO called Round Table has expressed its desire to create awareness on solid waste management, segregation of waste from the source in schools. Taking cue from vermi-technology unit at the Department of Zoology in St Aloysius College, the MCC has also started vermi compost units in two wards namely – Court and Padav – in the city on a pilot project basis.

For any study on waste management, the study of people involved is essential. This study also takes into account the people involved specially the sanitary workers.

Caste Structure

MCC employs around 400 people to clean the streets and transport the waste to the dumping yard. These Sanitary Workers are known as Paura Karmikas. During the times of dry latrines, Thotis used to collect the night soil and carry it to the dumping yard. After, the starting of wet latrines these Thotis have been absorbed into MCC. Due to their occupation of carrying night soil, the Thotis have the lowest status among the Untouchables or the Scheduled Castes (SCs). Adi-Dravida is the new name acquired by some Scheduled Caste groups to obliterate the stigma of untouchability (Pais 2004: 60). According to Kakade the idea that change of name would obliterate the stigma of centuries perhaps led the depressed classes to give up their old names and adopt new inoffensive and generic names like Panchamas, Adi-Dravida, Adi-Karnataka, Harijan etc (1949: 5). Probably the process of sanskritization in caste name is complete because in the socio-economic survey of 1993 conducted by MCC not a single Scheduled Caste householder has given his caste name as Thoti.

These Paura Karmikas together with other SCs live in colonies. Valencia (Souterpete) Kodikal, Urwa Market (Welspete), Bejai (Kapikad), Kodialbail (Ballalbagh), Kankanady (Narigudde) and Attavara (Babugudde) are the colonies of SCs in Mangalore. At the turn of the last century these areas were outside Mangalore but due to urbanisation, the city has grown around these colonies. The important groups working as Paura Karmikas are: Adi-Dravida, Adi-Karnataka and Koragas. While Adi-Dravida and Adi-Karnataka are SCs Koragas are Scheduled Tribes (STs). Koragas is a unique group. While they have all the tribal features such as separate dialect, occupation etc. untouchability is also found among them. In fact, they rank lower than SCs. A deeper study how the Koragas entered this profession is required.

Conditions of Paura Karmikas

Unemployment, inadequate housing and poor health may be considered as the major problems faced by the SCs in Mangalore. In spite of the efforts of the govt. there is large-scale unemployment among them. Their housing condition is poor in many colonies where they live. It is a common place to find three to four household living under one roof, with separate kitchens. Often these households are forced to depend upon a single ration card to avail the facilities of public distribution system. Abject poverty, unhealthy living conditions, lack nutritious food, lack of entertainment and the nature of work give rise to various diseases and early death. The worst affected are the Paura Karmikas. As most of them are engaged in cleaning the drains, roads and disposing of the waste, they are exposed to a variety of infectious diseases. Besides, they also have the habit of heavy drinking and smoking. As a result they succumb to various diseases and die early. The survey of MCC has traced 282 widows and 29 widowers out of 3693 married persons. An officer in Wenlock Hospital in Mangalore told the researcher that he has seen three generations of workers in the hospital during his 30 years of service.

Recent Initiatives

Mangalore became the first city in Karnataka to implement an advanced solid waste management system from February 1st, 2015. On January 23, 2015, Mr Vinay Kumar Sorake, Minister for Urban Development, Karnataka launched the two package garbage collection system, the first of its kind in Karnataka. M/s Antony Waste Handling Cell Private Ltd. which handles similar projects in Mumbai, Jaipur and New Delhi, has been entrusted with the job in 60 wards of MCC for seven years at an annual cost of Rs 16.62 crores. The contract also involves cleaning of four beaches and mechanical sweeping of 25 km of roads.

Under the new system, the contractor will deploy 16 specially designed trucks called compactors that will carry 10 tonnes of compacted waste each and 65 tippers that will collect waste from households going into lanes and by-lanes and bring them for onward transport by the compactors. The contractor, who has appointed 700 persons for the job, will be paid on the basis of quantity of waste dumped as landfill site in Vamanjoor at the rate of Rs 3,201 per tonne for waste collected from areas in the north (Surathkal to Mannagudda) and Rs 2,051 for the South (Derebail to Jeppinamogaru).

Highlights of the New Project include:

1. Antony Waste Handling Cell Private Limited will invest approx. Rs 7 Crore on Vehicles for this Project in Mangalore and will submit a Performance Bank Guarantee of approx. Rs 5 Crore.
2. The agreement is for a period of seven years with current estimate of approximately 200 tonnes of waste per day with an approx, value of Rs 18 Crore billing per year.
3. 100 per cent door to door collection from entire 60 wards covering 90 per cent of the properties using hydraulic vehicles of the types of Auto-tipper/refuse collectors etc.
4. 100 per cent Deployment of Hydraulic operated secondary collection vehicles to abolish the current system of open trucks.
5. The agreement also covers sanitation works namely, street sweeping, vegetation cutting, de-siltation of storm water drains (<1.0 m width), foot path/divider cleaning, maintaining sanitation of open space /building maintained by MCC.
6. Mechanised sweeping in of roads for a stretch of 25 km/day and cleaning of four beaches.
7. Adoption of GPS technology to all the secondary collection vehicles, recording the real time fuel level and vehicle location.
8. All the vehicles/equipments to be deployed operated and maintained at the cost of the contractor.

Problems and Challenges

The main problems of Mangalore's waste management are as follows:

1. Increasing quantity of solid waste generation and improper management.
2. Inadequate availability of public/community storage bins and their haphazard use.
3. Objectionable open-space throwing of solid waste.
4. Unsatisfactory and unhealthy practice of Municipal solid waste collection and transportation.

5. Irregular sweeping of streets and public places.
6. Crude methods of (open) dumping – health hazards and deterioration of environment.
7. Unscientific burning of wastes in some places.
8. Not a high level of civic consciousness.
9. Inadequate machinery and equipment.
10. Lack of sufficient and efficient manpower – In MCC today there are 18 A Group employees allotted posts but only 11 are filled, B Group 12 out of 20 filled, C Group 229 out of 352 and D Group 643 out of 788 are filled.
11. The poor socio-economic condition of sanitary workers.

Needs and Plans for the Future

With increasing funding becoming available and keen interest shown by educational institutions and NGOs, MCC has been drawing good plans for the future. Some highlights of these plans:

- A new System would be in place: Waste will be collected from the household and business establishments during fixed time every day. The waste are likely to be collected twice every day. For this purpose Mangalore city would be divided into two zones – North and South, sanitation in 47 wards would be carried out by contractors and in 13 wards by the MCC, for a period of seven years. Compost plant operation would be outsourced for six years. Private security checks for littering with wide use of media and educational institutions. Hydraulically operated vehicles would be used for collection. Sweeping machines would be used to sweep concrete roads.
- Waste being dumped on the roadside between Balmatta and Hampankatta in Mangalore will soon become a thing of the past. Mangalore City Corporation is planning to declare Balmatta-Hampankatta as litter free zone. 'dustbin- free' garbage collection will be introduced from Balmatta-Hampankatta and garbage collected at the doorstep of residents. This will be a pilot project.
- Dustbin-free garbage collection is a part of three package scheme on the solid waste management proposal which is pending before the government for approval. This will be a good step in segregation. Three contract agencies will handle the solid waste

management in the jurisdiction of Mangalore City Corporation in three packages.

Some Recommendations

Under present circumstances, solid-waste management is a challenge as people have started opposing areas being earmarked for waste management as they cause damage to the environment. A community-centred scheme involving all would help to tackle the problem. We understand that health and prosperity in our city can be threatened by ignorance, indifference and unhygienic conditions too. The present study would offer the following suggestions regarding solid waste management to the city authorities as well as waste generators and the general public.

1. Beware of the worsening problem of solid wastes in the city: sustained involving of citizens, NGOs etc.
2. Make compulsory the rules of waste management by households and establishments.
3. Increase and handle community storage bins healthily.
4. Give recyclable waste if possible to trained ragpickers.
5. Debris to be disposed at specific areas in a utilitarian way e.g., landscaping.
6. Treat organic waste via vermiculture at the community level itself.
7. Medical waste to be autoclaved and disposed in a particular way.
8. Implement source segregation at the earliest.
9. Improve means of carrying the wastes.
10. Increase staff involved and improve safety with required devices and healthcare.
11. Enhance professionalism in waste management.
12. Decentralise waste management.
13. Improving the socio-economic condition of sanitary workers.

Conclusion

MCC is making sincere efforts in the direction of better waste management. In April 2011 MCC has embarked on a mission to dispose of the electronic waste systematically. The then Corporation Commissioner K.N. Vijayaprakash said that the Sarvodaya Jagruti Trust, a non-governmental organisation, would collect e-waste from people. Initially e-waste would be collected on a trial basis on a 7-km stretch from Infosys in Kottara to Mphasis in Morgan's Gate. The trust would send the waste to "e-parisara", a government authorised e-waste recycler in Bangalore. On March 16, 2013 MCC launched a new project for solid waste management in the city. The endeavour which has two schemes under it was flagged off. Deputy Commissioner N Prakash inaugurated the Street sweeping machine and symbolically distributed the waste bins to the residents of the pilot wards, Mannagudda and Court ward here in front of the City Corporation.

Waste management should be viewed in the larger context of environmental management. China is facing enormous challenge in this regard. But they see it as an opportunity to improve environmental quality and are introducing new strategies to improve solid waste management in China. Mangalore needs "growth with a future". We need to restore the ecological balance. Curtail consumerism. Revert to good old practices of gardening, composting etc. We need to go from waste creation to waste utilisation with strong economic, environmental, resource conservation, employment generation, quality of life reasons. We need a whole city not a city with holes: potholes and loopholes. We the people of Mangalore City must have positive environmental ethos. Fiscal and financial incentives/disincentives along with environment-friendly technologies would be the plus points.

Note: The above paper was presented in the National Conference on Sociology of Sanitation, organised by Sulabh International Centre for Action Sociology in collaboration with Sulabh International Social Service Organisation, held on January 28 and 29, 2013 at Mavalankar Auditorium, New Delhi.

References

ASHWAS: A Survey of Household Water and Sanitation Karnataka-2008-09, Bangalore: Arghyam.

Chandramouli, C. 2011. Houses, Household Amenities and Assets among Female Headed Households, Highlights from census 2011, Registrar General & Census Commissioner, India, Census of India, 2011.

Censusindia.gov.in. 2011.

District Level Household and Facility Survey (2007-08).

Karnataka. 2010. Mumbai: International Institute of Populations Sciences.

Human Development Report. 2006. Beyond Scarcity: Power, Poverty and the Global Water Crisis. New York: United Nations Development Programme.

India's Sanitation for All: How to Make it Happen: Water for All. Series 18, 2009. Philippines: Asian Development Bank.

Karnataka: Human Development Report 2005. 2006. Planning and Statistics Department. Bangalore: Government of Karnataka.

National Family Health Survey (NFHS-3)-Karnataka 2005-06, 2008. Mumbai: United Nations Development Programme.

UN-HABITAT. 2008. Sanitation: A Human Rights Imperative. Geneva.

http://www.mdws.gov.in/hindi/sites/upload_files/ddwshindi/file s/pdf/

CENTRALLY_SPONSORED_RURAL_SANITATION_1993.p df

http://rural.nic.in/sites/downloads/our-schemes- glance/SalientFeatures TSC.pdf

http://www.mid-day.com/articles/nirmal-bharat-abhiyan-to-be-swachh-bharat-mission/15633186

http://nirmalgrampuraskar.nic.in/NgpRelated.aspx

http://www.tnrd.gov.in/schemes/cen_nba_13.html

http://indiasanitationportal.org/78

http://www.sulabhinternational.org/content/what-manual- scavenging-0

http://www.copasah.net/uploads/1/2/6/4/12642634/an_overview_of_karnatakas_ manual_scavengers_living_condition__obalesha. pdf

CHAPTER - 9

Globalisation and Sanitation

Introduction

Sanitation is a global challenge which is faced by all the under-developed, developing and the developed countries. The requirement of solution for better sanitation in the society is demanded by all the sections of people without any discrimination throughout the world. Sanitation is a challenge which is extremely related to human health. For this reason all the countries are much concerned about the sanitational issues without any political bias. They believe that better sanitation can contribute to better socio-economic life. Hence, this has brought the nations together to work for better sanitation. Thus, sanitation as challenge has now been accepted by all sectors of the society from bottom to top level.

We can observe some international organisations are working very hard to face the sanitation challenge. In fact, sanitation as an issue can be a reason for socio-economic development of a nation and also it can be a hindrance towards socio-economic development of nation. Due to this fact, it has made people to work for better sanitation in the world together. There are different organisations which are working for the sanitation challenge throughout the world. Among them, we can identify World Health Organisation (WHO) and United Nations International Children's Education Fund (UNICEF) as major organisations which are working for sanitation throughout the world. Under WHO, there are thousands of non-governmental organisations which are working for the betterment of sanitation conditions in different nations throughout the world with aid provided by WHO. Following are some of the important contributions of different organisations towards sanitation.

9.1 WHO and Sanitation

WHO is the directing and coordinating authority for health within the United Nations system. It is responsible for providing leadership on global health matters, shaping the health research agenda, setting norms and standards, articulating evidence-based policy options, providing technical support to countries and monitoring and assessing health trends. In the twenty first century, health is a shared responsibility, involving equitable access to essential care and collective defence against transnational threats.

Governance of WHO

The World Health Assembly is the supreme decision-making body for WHO. It generally meets in Geneva in May each year, and is attended by delegations from all 194 member States. Its main function is to determine the policies of the Organisation. The Health Assembly appoints the Director-General, supervises the financial policies of the Organisation, and reviews and approves the proposed programme budget. It similarly considers reports of the Executive Board, which it instructs in regard to matters upon which further action, study, investigation or report may be required.

The Executive Board is composed of 34 members technically qualified in the field of health. Members are elected for three-year terms. The main Board meeting, at which the agenda for the forthcoming Health Assembly is agreed upon and resolutions for forwarding to the Health Assembly are adopted, is held in January, with a second shorter meeting in May, immediately after the Health Assembly, for more administrative matters. The main functions of the Board are to give effect to the decisions and policies of the Health Assembly, to advise it and generally to facilitate its work.

Secretariat of WHO is staffed by some 8000 health and other experts and support staff on fixed-term appointments, working at headquarters, in the six regional offices. The Organisation is headed by the Director-General, who is appointed by the Health Assembly on the nomination of the Executive Board.

Health Policy

Health policy refers to decisions, plans, and actions that are undertaken to achieve specific healthcare goals within a society.

An explicit health policy can achieve several things: it defines a vision for the future which in turn helps to establish targets and points of reference for the short and medium term. It outlines priorities and the expected roles of different groups; and it builds consensus and informs people.

Water Supply, Sanitation and Hygiene Development

Around 1.1 billion people globally do not have access to improved water supply sources whereas 2.4 billion people do not have access to any type of improved sanitation facility. About two million people die every year due to diarrhoeal diseases; most of them are children less than five years of age. The most affected are the populations in developing countries, living in extreme conditions of poverty, normally peri-urban dwellers or rural inhabitants.

Among the main problems which are responsible for this situation are: lack of priority given to the sector, lack of financial resources, lack of sustainability of water supply and sanitation services, poor hygiene behaviours, and inadequate sanitation in public plaçes including hospitals, health centres and schools. Providing access to sufficient quantities of safe water, the provision of facilities for a sanitary disposal of excreta, and introducing sound hygiene behaviours are of capital importance to reduce the burden of disease caused by these risk factors.

International Year of Sanitation 2008

The United Nations General Assembly through its Resolution A/C.2/61/L.16/Rev.1 dated 4th December, 2006 declared 2008 as the International Year of Sanitation (IYS). The resolution expressed concern on thc slow and insufficient progress in providing access to basic sanitation services at the global level and recognised that progress can be attained through active commitment and action by all States, as well as Unitcd Nations agencies, regional and international organisations, civil society organisations and other relevant stakeholders.

At WHO, cver since its establishment, environmental sanitation has been recognised as a foundation of a sound public health structure. Article 2(l) of its 1948 Constitution calls for the improvement of sanitation and other aspccts of environmental hygiene. Over the last 50 years, WHO has generated, evaluated and shared new knowledge on safe disposal of excreta, sewage and community waste, and has been at the forefront of exploring linkages between water, sanitation and health.

WHO has collaborated with key partners on international development efforts to raise the profile of sanitation, such as the International Drinking Water and Sanitation Decade (IDWSSD) (1980-1990) and the Johannesburg World Summit for Sustainable Development (2002). In Johannesburg, the Millennium Development Goals (MDG) target on sanitation was set to halve the proportion of people who do not have access to basic sanitation by 2015.

WHO's Director-General stated that 'lack of sanitation kills'. It degrades health, especially that of children, and undermines education. It affects whole communities but consistently those most severely affected are the poor and disadvantaged. 2.6 billion people lack better sanitation worldwide. They are badly off track in meeting the MDG target. Even meeting the target would leave a truly huge population without one of the basic underpinnings of a healthy community. That is the classic approach. It is what many here would expect WHO to say. And it is true. Improving sanitation represents one of their best options to really accelerate health, social and even economic development.

The work of WHO has shown that sanitation does improve health—simple achievable interventions reduce, for example, diarrhoeal disease by 391 million cases per year. Simple solutions exist that work in the poor urban and rural communities which are most affected. In terms of economics it is for every rupee invested, there are benefits that can, on average, be valued at nine times as much. Those benefits stack up to children, households and communities in the poor urban and rural communities that need them most.

WHO has recognised the importance of sanitation since its inception, the first ever World Health Assembly defined sanitation as a priority, and to this day WHO continue to recognise its importance. WHO will continue to ensure that objective, balanced information is available to support policy-making and decision-taking, advocate investment in sanitation as a cost-effective health intervention, increase their impact by enhancing existing and new partnerships, and assist key partners at all levels by sharing the tools and guidelines we develop. Lack of sanitation is an affront to human dignity. twenty one works have been published related to sanitation in between 1990 to 2007 by the WHO.

The Challenge for Better Sanitation

Official statistics from WHO and UNICEF suggest that about 3.8 billion people (60 per cent) in 2004 have access to "improved" sanitation globally. The regions with the lowest coverage are sub-Saharan Africa (37 per cent), Southern Asia (38 per cent) and Eastern Asia (45 per cent). Underlying issues that contribute to the challenging situation include lack of political will, inadequate financial resources, weak institutional frameworks, neglect of consumer preferences, and cultural beliefs. To reach the MDG target on sanitation, the global coverage should be at least 75 per cent by 2015. This would mean an additional 1.6 billion people would have to be provided with sanitation systems. Meeting the MDG target would avert 391 million cases of diarrhoea per year. Health gains from sanitation are incorporated in existing which shows that every US dollar invested in sanitation would give a return of about US$9.

Initiatives by the WHO

In response to the call for action of the UN General Assembly, WHO will provide support to the objectives of the IYS 2008 to accelerate progress on sanitation and hygiene and ensure that related health concerns are addressed. Strategically, WHO is best placed to:

- Advocate for policy changes to improve coverage;
- Improve stakeholders' access to sanitation and health information;
- Enhance partnership and linkages with key stakeholders and programmes.

Advocate for Policy Changes to Improve Coverage: It refers that WHO to participate as a health voice in international, regional and national events, providing policy-makers of donors and countries with information on the health and economic benefits of investing in sanitation and hygiene, and encouraging them to modify their policies and programmes, as necessary. Such events are as follows:

- IYS Global launch, New York - 21 November 2007
- East Asia Sanitation Conference, Japan - 30 November - 1 December 2007
- South Asia Sanitation Conference (SACOSAN) - 2008
- Africa Sanitation Conference (AFRICASAN) - February 2008

- National Sanitation and Hygiene Weeks (March 2008)
- World Water Day (22 March 2008)
- World Environment Day (5 June 2008)
- Stockholm World Water Week (August 2008)
- Environment and Health African Ministerial Conference (Gabon) - August 2008
- World Habitat Day (6 October 2008)
- IYS launches at country level (dates to be determined by countries)
- World Water Forum - 2009

These resulted in commitment by donors and countries to develop policies on improving access on sanitation and hygiene as an intervention for addressing related health issues.

Improve Stakeholders' Access to Sanitation and Health Information: It is to promote and disseminate available information on sanitation, hygiene and health from WHO-led websites and other initiatives. As appropriate, existing databases will be improved and assistance will be provided in their revitalisation. Existing information sources include:

- *Sanitation Connection:* a web-based network of information on sanitation and hygiene. This is being revitalised by IWA and will be launched in time for IYS.
- *HIA database:* a web-based repository of tools and studies on Health Impact Assessment (HIA).
- *Health and Environment Lexicon:* a web-based lexicon for health and environment terminologies including sanitation and hygiene.
- *JMP:* a joint WHO/UNICEF activity on monitoring progress on water and sanitation coverage.
- *Global report on sanitation:* an activity of analysing performance of donors and countries on sanitation and hygiene.
- *WHO's Water, Sanitation and Health (WSH) web site:* a web-based repository of WSH publications.
- *WSH lists:* with more than 3000 email addresses that can receive information on water, sanitation and hygiene.

Enhance Partnership and Linkages with Key Stakeholders and Programmes: Participate in key activities of the UN-Water Task Force on Sanitation for the IYS, including the development of: an action plan; a communication strategy plan; a joint publication on sanitation; a website; and global launch.

It also tries to explore possible cooperation with other stake-holders, such as:

(a) Sustainable Sanitation Alliance: An alliance of agencies on sustainable sanitation with working groups on sanitation in cities, sanitation and health, sanitation and climate change, sanitation and emergencies, community sanitation, sanitation and joint monitoring, and knowledge management.

(b) World Toilet Association: A Democratic People's Republic of Korea-based international NGO promoting and advocating improved and sustainable sanitation condition worldwide.

(c) World Toilet Organisation: A Singapore-based NGO promoting improved sanitation standards for public toilets.

(d) World Business Council for Sustainable Development: A global association of about 200 members dealing exclusively on business and sustainable development with activities being started on sanitation.

(e) Sulabh International: A India-based international NGO promoting and advocating improved and sustainable sanitation condition world-wide by means of Sulabh toilets and bathrooms.

9.2 UNICEF and Sanitation

United Nations International Children's Emergency Fund (UNICEF) was created by the United Nations General Assembly on December 11, 1946, to provide emergency food and healthcare to children in countries that had been devastated by World War II. In 1953, UNICEF became a permanent part of the United Nations System and its name was shortened from the original United Nations International Children's Emergency Fund to United Nations Children's Fund. However, it has continued to be known as UNICEF, the popular acronym based on previous title.

UNICEF relies on contributions from governments and private donors. Governments contribute two-thirds of the organisation's resources; private groups and some six million individuals contribute the rest through the National Committees. It is estimated that 91.8 per cent of their revenue is distributed to programme services. UNICEF's programmes emphasise developing community-level services to promote the health and well-being of children. UNICEF was awarded the Nobel Peace Prize in 1965 and the Prince of Asturias Award of Concord in 2006.

Most of UNICEF's work is in the field, with staff in over 190 countries and territories. More than 200 country offices carry out UNICEF's mission through a programme developed with host governments. Seventeen regional offices provide technical assistance to country offices as needed.

Water, Sanitation and Hygiene

According to the latest estimates of the WHO/UNICEF Joint Monitoring Programme for Water Supply and Sanitation (JMP), released in early 2013 (collected in 2011), 36 per cent of the world's population – 2.5 billion people – lack improved sanitation facilities, and 768 million people still use unsafe drinking water sources. Inadequate access to safe water and sanitation services, coupled with poor hygiene practices, kills and sickens thousands of children every day, and leads to impoverishment and diminished opportunities for thousands more.

Poor sanitation, water and hygiene have many other serious repercussions. Children, particularly girls, are denied their right to education because their schools lack private and decent sanitation facilities. Women are forced to spend large parts of their day fetching water. Poor farmers and wage earners are less productive due to illness, health systems are overwhelmed and national economies suffer. Without water, sanitation and hygiene, sustainable development is impossible.

UNICEF works in more than 100 countries around the world to improve water supplies and sanitation facilities in schools and communities, and to promote safe hygiene practices. UNICEF sponsors a wide range of activities and work with many partners, including families, communities, governments and like-minded organisations. In emergencies UNICEF provides urgent relief to communities and nations threatened by disrupted water supplies and disease. All UNICEF water supplies and sanitation programmes were designed to contribute to the Millennium Development Goal for water and sanitation. The goal - to halve, by 2015, the proportion of people without sustainable access to safe water - has been achieved globally, but the same target for sanitation is so far off track that it is unlikely to be met by 2015.

Progress on Drinking Water and Sanitation

The WHO/UNICEF Joint Monitoring Programme for Water Supply and Sanitation reports every two years on progress towards the drinking water and sanitation target under Millennium Development Goal 7. This target calls for halving the proportion of the population without sustainable access to safe drinking water and basic sanitation between 1990 and 2015. Estimates presented in its 2012 update report describe the situation at the end 2010 and supersede those of the Joint Monitoring Programme for Water Supply and Sanitation update published in March 2010.

The report brings welcome news: measured by the proxy-indicator consistently used by the joint Monitoring Programme for Water Supply and Sanitation since 2000, the MDG drinking- water target was met in 2010, five years ahead of schedule. However, the job is far from done. An estimated 780 million still lacked safe drinking water in 2010, and the world is unlikely to meet the MDG sanitation target. A reduction in urban-rural disparities and inequities associated with poverty; drinking-water coverage in countries in sub-Saharan Africa and Oceania; putting sanitation 'on track'; and universal coverage beyond 2015, all remain high on the development and public health agenda. UNICEF knows that key to addressing these challenges are its partnerships with sister UN agencies, voluntary organisations active at the community level, women's groups and donors. The organisation also works with an array of celebrities, including members of the Indian cricket team and leading actors from the Indian film industry, as well as hundreds of thousands of unnamed volunteers who tirelessly give their time and influence to ensure that, together, they are able to help every child realise his or her full potential.

UNICEF in India

UNICEF has been working in India since 1949; it is the largest UN organisation in the country. UNICEF is fully committed to working with the Government of India to ensure that each child born in this vast and complex country gets the best start in life, thrives and develops to his or her full potential. The challenge is enormous but UNICEF is well placed to meet it. The organisation uses quality research and data to understand issues, implements new and innovative interventions that address the situation of children, and works with partners to bring those innovations to fruition.

UNICEF uses its community-level knowledge to develop innovative interventions to ensure that women and children are able to access basic services such as clean water, health visitors and educational facilities, and that these services are of high quality. At the same time, UNICEF reaches out directly to families to help them to understand what they must do to ensure their children thrive.

What makes UNICEF unique in India is its network of 13 state offices. These enable the organisation to focus attention on the poorest and most disadvantaged communities, alongside its work at the national level.

UNICEF in India is essentially connected with water, environment and sanitation. UNICEF's long standing support for improving water supply, sanitation and hygiene stems from a firm conviction and based on sound evidence that these are central to ensuring the rights of children. In fact, it is essential for children to survive, grow and develop into healthy and fulfilled citizens of the world. In the broader context, UNICEF's activities in water, sanitation and hygiene contribute to the achievement of the Millennium Development Goals.

Fast Facts of better Sanitation

UNICEF has given certain facts about sanitation among children. They are as follows:

- Hand washing with soap, particularly after contact with excreta, can reduce diarrhoeal diseases by over 40 per cent and respiratory infections by 30 per cent. Diarrhoea and respiratory infections are the number one cause for child deaths in India.
- Hand washing with soap is among the most effective and inexpensive ways to prevent diarrhoeal diseases and pneumonia.
- With 594 million people defecating in the open and 44 per cent mothers disposing their children's faeces in the open, there is a very high risk of microbial contamination (bacteria, viruses, amoeba) of water which causes diarrhoea in children.
- Children weakened by frequent diarrhoea episodes are more vulnerable to malnutrition and opportunistic infections such as pneumonia. About 48 per cent of children in India are suffering from some degree of malnutrition. Diarrhoea and worm infection are two major health conditions that affect school age children impacting their learning abilities.

- Adequate, well-maintained water supply and sanitation facilities in schools encourage children to attend school regularly and help them achieve their educational goals. Inadequate water supply and sanitation in schools are health hazards and affect school attendance, retention and educational performance.
- Adolescent girls are especially vulnerable to dropping out, as many are reluctant to continue their schooling because toilet facilities are not private, not safe or simply not available.
- Women and girls face shame and a loss of personal dignity and safety risk if there is no toilet at home. They have to wait for the night to relieve themselves to avoid being seen by others.

Estimated Sanitation in India

- Only 31 per cent of India's population use improved sanitation (2008);
- In rural India 21 per cent use improved sanitation facilities (2008);
- One hundred and forty-five million people in rural India gained access to improved sanitation between 1990 and 2008;
- Two hundred and eleven million people gained access to improved sanitation in whole of India between 1990 and 2008;
- India is home to 594 million people defecating in the open; over 50 per cent of the population;
- In Bangladesh and Brazil, only seven per cent of the populations defecate in the open. In China, only four per cent of the population defecates in the open.

According to UNICEF, 88 per cent of the population of 1.2 billion has access to drinking water from improved sources in 2008, as compared to 68 per cent in 1990. Only a quarter the total population in India has drinking water on their premise. Women, who have to collect the drinking water, are vulnerable to a number of unsafe practices. Only 13 per cent of adult males collect water. Sixtyseven per cent of Indian households do not treat their drinking water, even though it could be chemically or bacterially contaminated.

According to the Public Health Association, only 53 per cent of the population wash hands with soap after defecation, 38 per cent wash hands with soap before eating and only 30 per cent wash hands with soap before preparing food. Only 11 per cent of the Indian rural families dispose child stools safely. 80 per cent children's stools are left in the open or thrown into the garbage. Only six per cent of rural children less than five years of age use toilets. WASH Interventions significantly reduce diarrhoeal morbidity by 36 per cent from better sanitation.

UNICEF supports the national and state governments in developing and implementing a range of replicable intervention models for sanitation, hygiene and water supply. UNICEF's Childs Environment Programme in India supports the government's flagship programmes of Total Sanitation Campaign to improve access to and use of sanitation facilities and the National Rural Drinking Water Programme to provide adequate safe water to every rural household in India. The Childs Environment Programme also works with Sarva Siksha Abhiyan and Integrated Child Development Services, to promote hygiene water and sanitation services in schools, Anganwadi centres and health centres with lasting outcomes.

9.3 World Toilet Organisation (WTO)

Founded on 19 November, 2001, World Toilet Organisation (WTO) is a global non-profit committed to improving toilet and sanitation conditions worldwide. It was founded by Jack Sim with the stated aim of being a global network and service platform wherein all toilet and sanitation organisations can learn from one another and leverage media and global support to influence governments to promote sound sanitation and public health policies. WTO empowers individuals through education, training and building local marketplace opportunities to advocate for clean and safe sanitation facilities in their communities. The World Toilet Organisation was established with the aim to break the taboo around toilets and the sanitation crisis. Since 2001, WTO has lobbied governments, public and private sector stakeholders and the international community to prioritise sanitation in the development agenda.

Breaking the silence on the sanitation crisis is at the heart of WTO's efforts. WTO established World Toilet Day and the World Toilet Summit in 2001; this was followed by the World Toilet College in 2005. Through its various initiatives, WTO continues to provide an international platform for toilet associations, governments, academic institutions, foundations, UN agencies and corporate stakeholders to exchange knowledge and leverage media and corporate support in an effort to promote clean sanitation and public health policies.

On 24th July, 2013, WTO achieved a key milestone for the global sanitation movement when 122 countries co-sponsored a UN resolution tabled by the Singapore government to designate 19 November, World Toilet Day as an official UN day. World Toilet Organisation was granted consultative status with the United Nations Economic and Social Council in 2013.

World Toilet Summit

World Toilet Summit is a unique global event established by the World Toilet Organisation to bring together various sanitation stakeholders under one roof to connect and collaborate on innovative inventions, projects and products in the sanitation sector. This annual event is jointly organised by a host government and the World Toilet Organisation. World Toilet Summit aims to empower delegates, exhibitors and sponsors to exchange knowledge, expertise and resources in scaling up impact and innovation in the sanitation marketplace.

The World Toilet Organisation has successfully held 13 World Toilet Summits since 2001. The 12 summits were held in major cities worldwide including Singapore, Seoul, Taipei, Beijing, Belfast, Moscow, New Delhi, Macau, Hainan, Philadelphia and Solo, Indonesia. WTO and World Education Foundation organised the 14th annual World Toilet Summit on 19–20 January, 2015 under the aegis of Ministry of Urban Development, Government of India. Mr Venkaiah Naidu, Minister for Urban Development, stressed the importance of urbanisation and how toilets and sanitation plays a major role for development. He also stressed 80 per cent of the diseases in India are water borne or through water contamination, hence it is imperative to adopt sanitation programmes to keep these diseases in check. Lack of access to clean water and sanitation contributes to 1.8 million deaths from diarrhoeal disease globally per year. Therefore, a massive construction of toilet is required with the cooperation of state and centre. Organised at Vigyan Bhawan, New Delhi, the two-day summit witnessed participation from various stakeholders including governmental, Municipal Corporation, corporate and non-government organisations among others. The event deliberated on various aspects related to sanitation including the way forward, the experiences in other countries and evolving technologies which can play a pivotal role in the area of sanitation and can help overcome the issue of open defecation, which is rampant in India.

The World Toilet College (WTC)

The World Toilet College (WTC) started as a social enterprise in 2005, with the belief that there is need for an independent world body to ensure the best practices and standards in toilet design, cleanliness, and sanitation technologies are adopted and disseminated through training and capacity-building courses, in both rural and urban contexts.

The lack of toilets is an endemic problem. However, where there are toilets, the absence of poor management and hygienic maintenance are equally serious issues. A well-kept toilet will encourage proper usage and prevent deadly diseases. The ultimate goal of WTC's programmes is to ensure the dignity of sanitation workers and elevate the otherwise poor image (and consequent low pay) reserved to this employment category in many places around the world.

It is done by training and providing toilet caretakers with professional skills in both cleaning and performance of small repairs, thereby boosting their self-confidence by providing them with the opportunity to master a profession while at the same time enhancing their productivity.

WTC's training courses are professionally delivered by EcoSan experts and by certified trainers who have earned their certification and skills at WTC. WTC continues to empower individuals to invest in their professional and personal development by being part of a supportive network of sanitation stakeholders. Over the years, WTC has partnered with prestigious institutions including the Singapore Polytechnic. WTC has also obtained the Approved Training Organisation accreditation for three consecutive years till 2012. Since 2005, WTC has trained more than 4,000 people across its various courses.

World Toilet Organisation in India

In late 2011, World Toilet Organisation established its centre in India to increase access of rural households to safe and affordable sanitation. On the ground, WTO works closely with local implementing partners' eKutir, a social business, based out of Odisha, and Sattva, a media and social business consulting firm based out of Bangalore.

The pilot project was set up in Odisha where eKutir had established its strong rural base. By deploying eKutir's micro- entrepreneurs to further centre's mission in providing safe and affordable sanitation to the rural population, this partnership allows the WTO and eKutir to create more livelihoods, boost health and dignity among the farming households. eKutir has been able to establish 25 micro-entrepreneurs working for the sanitation cause in three different states of India.

With the establishment of the centre, farmers have access to low-cost and affordable toilets. As a result, households reduce their medical expenses as they do not fall sick as often and this increases their savings. With a proven track-record of impact in the pilot villages of Odisha, WTO and eKutir are collaborating on broadening this impact to other states in India. Currently, the partnership between World Toilet Organisation and eKutir aims to reach out to over 20,000 households by 2014.

9.4 Non-Governmental Organisations (NGOs) and Sanitation

A non-governmental organisation (NGO) is a citizen-based association that operates independently of government, usually to deliver resources or serve some social or political purpose. The World Bank classifies NGOs as either operational NGOs, which are primarily concerned with development projects, or advocacy NGOs, which are primarily concerned with promoting a cause. NGO is any non-profit, voluntary citizens' group which is organised on a local, national or international level. Task-oriented and driven by people with a common interest, NGOs perform a variety of service and humanitarian functions, bring citizen concerns to governments, advocate and monitor policies and encourage political participation through provision of information. Some are organised around specific issues, such as human rights, environment or health. They provide analysis and expertise, serve as early warning mechanisms and help monitor and implement international agreements.

NGOs in Sanitation

The majorities of NGOs have considerable strengths and play important and varied roles in the sanitation sector. NGOs have assisted in facilitating better access for the poor to sanitation services and typically offer on-the-ground impact in increasing access to services within relatively short timeframes through established community relationships. They often have the ability to reach remote places or illegal settlements where service provision is challenging and have been shown to be adept at setting sanitation within a holistic development frame, commonly taking an integrated and longer-term programmatic approach to meeting community needs. They are adaptable to circumstance and taking on different roles in response to the local community and policy contexts. At the same time, NGOs are able to draw on national and also international experience through their networks of practitioners, facilitating the exchange of new ideas from one area to the next.

The various roles played by NGOs in the sanitation sector can be broadly grouped into six categories:

- Facilitation of service delivery including direct service provision (particularly in emergency and humanitarian relief contexts or in areas characterised by extreme poverty or geographical remoteness) or playing an intermediary or broker role between communities and service providers.
- Community education, awareness-raising, sanitation and hygiene promotion and marketing including stimulating demand, gender sensitive approaches, supply chain strengthening and implementing behaviour change programmes.
- Building partnerships and promoting networking between different sector actors including representing community views to governments and service providers and translating and communicating national policies and regulations to the local level.
- Capacity building for local governments, service providers, in-country civil society groups and end users (households and communities).
- Research and innovation including demonstration and piloting of innovative and locally adapted approaches and technologies.
- Engaging in policy dialogue including promoting proven approaches and technologies, communicating lessons learnt, communicating community needs, advocating gender equity and monitoring the effectiveness of programmes and government initiatives.

The broad strengths NGOs bring to these roles need to be considered with reference to limitations of NGO roles and activities. Whilst there are many examples of success, it is also true that NGOs have at times played potentially detrimental roles (though through good intentions). NGOs are taking funds from various donor agencies. Though they operate within the legal framework of the country, in most cases they are accountable to the donor agencies.

References

http://www.unicef.org/india/wes.html

http://en.wikipedia.org/wiki/World_Toilet_Organization

http://www.investopedia.com/ask/answers/13/what-is-non- government-organization.asp

Chapter - 10

Sulabh Sanitation Movement in India

Introduction

Sulabh International Social Service Organisation, a non-profit voluntary social organisation founded in 1970 by Dr Bindeshwar Pathak, is dedicated to Gandhian ideology of emancipation of scavengers. Sulabh has been working for the removal of untouchability and social discrimination against human scavengers, a section of Indian society condemned to clean and carry human excreta manually. Sulabh is noted for achieving success in the field of cost-effective sanitation, liberation of scavengers, social transformation of society, prevention of environmental pollution and development of non-conventional sources of energy.

Sulabh is not about community toilets only, it's a social revolution, freedom from detestable social customs of discrimination based on caste and creed, end of shameful practice of defecation in open places, eradication of the inhuman practice of manual scavenging and liberation of scavengers engaged in this occupation end of spread of contagious diseases and epidemics, boost to non-conventional energy sources, enormous employment opportunities, educational institutions – including multiple schools and vocational training centres, a toilet museum in the heart of national capital of India, mention in United Nation's World Development Reports, multiple national and international awards, presence in thousands of cities, and invitations from various countries to design and develop the sanitation system for respective nations.

10.1 Dr Bindeshwar Pathak - The Founder

Dr Bindeshwar Pathak is a great humanist and social reformer of contemporary India. To the weaker sections of society especially, his is the compassionate face of a paternal redeemer. He has the vision of a philosopher and the undying zeal of a missionary. He is the icon of sanitation and social reform who has made a difference in the lives of millions of people. In fact, he has turned the pages of history where with his efforts the erstwhile untouchables have been allowed by the society to intermingle with them, to live on par with them, dine with them and offer prayers in the temples. He has created a new culture which embraces the poor and extols the dignity of labour. His boundless love for the downtrodden finds expression in myriad and tangible ways. No wonder those who know him intimately swear that Dr Pathak is born to help the helpless. He is the leader of an international crusade for restoration of human rights and dignity to millions of scavengers (cleaners and carriers of human excreta), traditionally known as untouchables; and for providing safe and hygienic human waste disposal system which can benefit 700 million Indians who go for open defecation. It is a far grimmer scenario when womenfolk have to go out for defecation in the open exposing human dignity and risking criminal assaults. He has identified himself with the problems of the untouchables. Dr Pathak's multi-pronged efforts in bringing scavengers, worst victims of institutionalised caste discrimination and engaged in sub-human occupation, in the mainstream of national life, have taken the shape of a movement for social justice.

Dr Pathak is an internationally acclaimed expert on sanitation and has developed and implemented on pan-Indian scale a low-cost and appropriate toilet technology (popularly known as the Sulabh Shauchalaya system) recommended as a Global Best Practice. To him goes the credit of sensitising towards sanitation, Indians and those engaged in the sanitation work. Apart from low cost sanitation, his contributions are widely known in the areas of bio-energy and bio-fertiliser, liquid and solid waste management, poverty alleviation and integrated rehabilitation programme for the liberated scavengers. In fact, he is a Renaissance Man and combines in himself the traits of a social scientist, an engineer, an administrator and an institution-builder. What is remarkable is that he has ingeniously utilised all these expertise to enrich and empower the depressed classes, improve community health, hygiene and environment. Thus, he is fulfilling the dreams of Mahatma Gandhi and Dr Bhimrao Ambedkar.

Radical Beginning

- Dr Bindeshwar Pathak was born in 1943 in village Rampur-Baghel in the Vaishali District of Bihar, into a Maithil Brahmin family, a community which has over generations, provided India with some of its most eminent thinkers, academicians, and civil servants.
- Dr Pathak took up sociology in 1961 as one of the subjects in Bachelor of Arts, Part-I in Patna University and later opted for sociology as a subject in the Honours class. He wanted to be a lecturer in the Department of Sociology in Patna University but that dream remained unfulfilled due to vicissitudes of fortune. However, after passing secondary school examination he did become a school teacher, did small jobs and finally he wanted to do M.Sc. in Criminology from Sagar University, Madhya Pradesh, but that too did not happen.
- With marriage in 1965 came new responsibilities. With the help of an old family in the Bihar Electricity Board, he joined the Patratu Thermal Power Station as a daily wage earner on Rs five per day. After a year, deep frustration followed as the thought slowly began to emerge that why not do something, to justify birth in a high caste family, and also work to benefit society and thus, carve one's own place and identity. "I am going to turn the pages of history". In 1968, he said this to his father-in-law. Later he proved this.

  He next joined his father's business in promoting the sale of Ayurvedic and other indigenous medicines to sugarcane co-operatives. This required carrying heavy packs on the back and shoulders over long distances into the heart of the old indigo plantation areas of Champaran and Darbhanga. But, through the travails grew the realisation that in our Eastern values, knowledge is superior to trade.
- With his father's consent, and a fateful loan, he set off on a long journey; this time for completing a Masters in Criminology at the University of Sagar in Madhya Pradesh. However, whilst sipping tea at Hazipur railway station, two elder relatives, in a chance meeting, persuaded him to drop his study plans and proceed to Patna for a job in the Bihar Gandhi Centenary Celebrations Committee in 1969. Later the 'very famous' in the Committee were contacted but no job! Also by this time his seat

at Sagar for the Master's study, had been filled; so, back to square one.

- For four months, he worked as an unpaid translator from English/Hindi/English, and then his luck turned and he got a job for Rs 200 per month in the Centenary Celebration Committee on Restoration of Human Rights. This committee was formed with the object of restoring human right and some dignity to the lowest class of people whose sad lot in life, in perpetuity, was collecting human faeces manually - now called 'scavengers' from 'untouchables' before Independence. His job was to explore and find alternative scavenging system, and more daunting, how these scavengers could be brought into the mainstream of Indian society.
- It was Mahatma Gandhi's most ardent wish, "I may not be born again, but if it happens I will like to be born in a family of scavengers, so that I may relieve them of the inhuman, unhealthy and hateful practice of carrying head-loads of night soil". But young Bindeshwar was brought up as a Brahmin. Right from childhood it had been drilled into him, not to touch an untouchable, or take water from their head, or eat cooked food at anyone's house. Once shrieking and protesting, he was forced by his grandmother to publicly swallow cow dung, sand, and Ganges water as he touched an untouchable!
- These deep-rooted prejudices evoked no sympathy for his superior, Mr Sarju Prasad, who said it all in his prophetic wisdom. "I don't care to which caste you belong, I don't know whether you an engineer or not, but without being an astrologer I see light in you, and can envision you to be able to rise to the task".
- He was given two books to read. One published by the World Health Organisation on Excreta Disposal for Rural Areas and Small Communities by two sanitation engineers, Edmund A. Wagner and J.N. Lanoix and another in Hindi by Rajendra Lal Das. The WHO publication was subject to very close study, and many passages of it, left a lasting lifetime's impression in young Pathak's mind. "Suffice it to say here that out of the heterogeneous mass of latrine designs produced all over the world, the sanitary pit privy emerges as the most practical and universally applicable type".

- The WHO publication laid out the following seven conditions to meet the criteria for a sanitary latrine.
  1. The surface soil should not be contaminated.
  2. There should be no contamination of the ground water that may enter by way of springs or wells.
  3. There should be no contamination of the surface water.
  4. Excreta should not be accessible to flies or animals.
  5. There should be no handling of fresh excreta. Or when this was indispensable, it should be restricted to the barest minimum.
  6. There should be freedom from odours or unsightly conditions.
  7. The method used should be simple and inexpensive in construction and operation.

  However, the suggestions in these books were for the application of this technology only in rural areas. Applying his mind, Pathak thought the soil conditions of rural and urban areas in the same. So, the same technology can also be used in urban areas. Therefore, he concluded that this technology, after some improvement could be a viable alternative to scavenging. Accordingly, he innovated modified and developed alternatives to suit the urban conditions, at the same time, making four to five new designs for different site conditions such as, congested areas, restricted spaces etc.

- Perusal of WHO's books helped Dr Pathak develop a technology which has proved to be revolutionary. The two-pit pour-flush technology is remarkable for its many advantages; it is hygienically appropriate, cost-effective and easy to construct and maintain with locally available materials. The design and specifications can be modified to suit the needs and the paying capacity of the user. The toilet can be located inside the house or outside. It can be constructed in different physical, geological and hydrological conditions and does not pollute surface or ground water. Its maintenance is simple and does not require the services of a scavenger or large volumes of water. There is a potential for up gradation as it can later be connected to sewers, once sewage is introduced in the area. A low volume-flushing cistern can be attached and the whole set-up needs very little space. Additionally fertiliser is generated. Earlier the world had only two technologies –sewer system and septic tanks. Both require excessive water for flushing, unlike the Sulabh technology.

- Thus, began Dr Pathak's lifetime's involvement in this programme of the highest social importance, and dearest to Mahatma Gandhi. He went on to live with scavengers for four months, ate their food, and shared their lives with them. In this simple, but very direct way he set out to "cleanse" himself of caste prejudice, and elevate himself, technologically and socially, to be capable of finding alternates, not only to methods of scavenging but, more importantly to restore some semblance of human right and dignity to scavengers.
- He returned from the scavenger colony totally converted and firm in his resolve that he would thenceforth dedicate his life for the cause of scavengers. However, by the time they could chalk out any programme for training and demonstration, the tenure of the Gandhi Centenary Celebrations Committee came to an end, with the Government of Bihar deciding to wind it up. But the visionary Chief Minister, Daroga Prasad Rai, decided to continue with the programme of abolition of scavenging but through some other organisation. He held the view that government alone could not implement programmes of social importance and that the government and NGOs should closely work together to achieve the desired results. An organisation had to be found to carry out the programmes. Dr Bindeshwar Pathak's date with destiny had arrived! He now did not falter, and on 5th March, 1970 the Sulabh Swachh Shauchalaya was launched. This was first small step in the long journey of many thousand miles towards eradicating untouchability and social discrimination.
- The United Nations Centre for Human Settlements has recognised Sulabh's cost-effective and appropriate sanitation system as a global 'Urban Best Practice' at the Habitat –II conference held at Istanbul (Turkey), in June, 1996. The economic and Social Council of United Nations has granted Special Consultative Status to Sulabh in recognition of its outstanding service to mankind. The United Nation centre for Human settlement and Dubai Municipality award to the Sulabh

design selected from out of 1100 entries from 125 countries have conferred cost-effective best sanitation technology to Sulabh with US$ 30,000 and a Gold Trophy. Government of India conferred 'Padma Bhushan' in 1991 on Dr Pathak for his work in sanitation development and social service. His holiness John Pope Paul II gave audience to Dr Pathak at the time of conferment of the International St Francis Prize for environment (Chanticle of all creatures) in the year 1992.

10.2 Origin and Objectives

Sulabh is the brain-child of Dr Bindeshwar Pathak. During 1968, he was drafted into a committee to design celebration of birth centenary of Mahatma Gandhi, which was due in 1969. Gandhi worked tirelessly to restore the human rights and dignity of scavengers and to eliminate the evil of untouchability from the society. This was a turning point in young Dr Pathak's life.

He started 'Sulabh Svachchh Shauchalaya Prashikshan Sansthaan' (Sulabh Clean Toilet Training Institute) in 1970, which was later registered as 'Sulabh Shauchalya Sansthan' (Sulabh Toilet Institute). It was further renamed as 'Sulabh International' in 1980 before adopting its present name – Sulabh International Social Service Organisation.

His idea of providing sanitation was ridiculed initially and did not get any support from any corner. Clean and hygienic sanitation was not a priority even for the government of the day. Dr Pathak recalls that when he sought government aid for his proposal, he was advised by a Bihar state official to make the scheme commercially viable so that it can become a success without government aid. Finally, in 1973, almost four years after Dr Pathak first became involved in the subject, the commissioner of Arrah municipality in Bhojpur district of Bihar came to his rescue and gave him the job of constructing two toilets. He did this job for a meagre Rs 500. Thereafter, Sulabh saved a similar opportunity in the town of Buxar. The first Sulabh public toilet was constructed in Patna in 1974. After the success of Sulabh experiment in Arrah, Dr Pathak proudly remembers that he never had to ask for work again, as Sulabh has got plenty of invitations thereafter.

Objectives

Sulabh is envisioned as an agent of social and cultural change. Inspired by Gandhian philosophy of truthfulness, non-violence, and altruism, Sulabh believes in the Gandhian principle of trusteeship. Sulabh is based on compassion for and development of fellowmen. Sulabh seeks to develop an egalitarian society, based on equal opportunity for every human being irrespective of their caste, race, and natural of a happy home, free from unhygienic and unhealthy practices. The objectives of Sulabh are as follows:

1. To restore human rights and dignity
   - Liberation of scavenger's from unhealthy and subhuman occupation of manual handling of excreta by converting bucket privies into Sulabh Shauchalya (pour flush latrine with twin pits for on-site disposal of human waste.
   - Rehabilitation of the relieved scavengers and their wards in other jobs after training.
   - Help in social up gradation of scavengers and their promotion as equal in society.
   - Set up information and employment exchange centres to help scavengers getting employment either in the government or non-governmental organisations.
   - Open English-medium schools to provide education to the sons and daughters of scavengers along with others; and
   - Help scavengers build their houses away from slums so that they can be taken out from the unhealthy environment.
2. Prevention of environmental pollution and improvement of health, hygiene and ecology:
   - Educate people not to defecate in the open, lanes, bye-lanes, parks, streets, by the side of roads or railway tracks etc.
   - Motivate people to get bucket privies converted into Sulabh Shauchalaya and to have toilet facility in houses where non-exists.
   - Provide community toilet complexes with bathing, laundry and urinal facilities on the pay and use, basis in slums and for pavement dwellers, rickshaw-pullers, floating population and also for those communities in whose houses latrine cannot be constructed due to space constraint; and
   - Persuade people to plant at least five trees per family and also to plant trees around public toilets for environmental protection.

3. Harness non-conventional energy sources from human waste and other wastes and save fuel and forests.
4. Procure manure from Sulabh Shauchalaya and Sulabh toilet complexes and use it to raise farm productivity.
5. Promote job-oriented education and primary healthcare.
6. Form groups of people from all walks of life throughout the country and abroad to build public opinion against social evils and for the cause of economically poor and neglected sections of the society.
7. Create new job opportunities by training change-agents for integrated rural development.
8. Promote consultancy, research and development in technical and social fields.
9. Diffusion of innovations, education, motivation and awareness through miscommunication.

10.3 Emergence and Growth

Dr Bindeshwar Pathak joined the liberation of scavengers' cell of the Bihar Gandhi Centenary Celebration Committee in 1968 when he was entrusted with the task of finding out an alternative to scavenging. Dr Pathak modified and developed a technology of two-pit pour flush toilet (popularly known as *Sulabh Shauchalya*). He also succeeded in demonstrating the effectiveness of the two-pit pour flush toilet system. Today, engineers not only from India but even from the World Bank have accepted that the on-site defecation and unhygienic, unsafe systems of human waste disposal like trench and borehole latrines in the developing countries of the world.

By the time, Dr Pathak found the alternative to scavenging; the Bihar Gandhi Centenary Celebration Committee was dissolved by the Government. In 1970, Dr Pathak founded a non-profit making voluntary social organisation. *Sulabh Shauchalaya Sansthan* (now known as Sulabh International Social Service Organisation) to carry out the work of liberation of scavengers from the sub-human practice of manual excreta cleaning in India and other related jobs. Thus, the seeds of the Sulabh Sanitation Movement were sown in 1970.

The mass movement by Dr Pathak started spreading all over the country with a cadre of about 50,000 Sulabh volunteers, now working from right atop the mountain at Vaishnav Devi, to deep down in South and in the farthest corners in the east and the west of the country, in 25 States and 987 towns. An organisational set up like this has not been made to spread out so fast and be managed by any other social voluntary organisation so far. Sulabh does not receive any aid, or subsidy from internal or external agencies; it raises its own resources to run its pan-India system and its campaign against social evils and helps the weaker sections of society.

After developing a technology, Dr Pathak evolved a methodology which also spelt out how a non-profit making social organisation could work as a catalytic agent between the governments, local bodies and the beneficiaries. It was felt that the government alone could not liberate scavengers from the sub-human occupation. House-to-house contact and campaigns in local languages for their liberation was suggested as part of the methodology which was adopted by the Bihar Government. Later on, it was adopted by many State Governments.

Further, Dr Pathak tried to bring the scavengers' liberation programme from the micro-level to the macro-level. In 1973, he had put up just two Sulabh Shauchalaya for demonstration in the compound of the Ara municipality, a small town of Bihar. Since then Sulabh has converted about one million bucket latrines into Sulabh Shauchalayas throughout the country; and more than a million scavengers have been liberated and more than 640 towns have been made scavenging-free.

In 1974, the Sulabh Founder gave another concept of maintaining the community toilets and bath on the pay-and-use basis. Before 1974, public latrines in India were regarded as hell holes. Nobody was able to find a solution to this problem. Dr Pathak found one and on that basis, over 6,000 public toilet complexes are being maintained absolutely clean, spick and span in 25 States and four Union Territories, in 1,075 towns, including metropolitan cities of Delhi, Mumbai, Kolkata, and Chennai. These Sulabh toilet complexes are used by over the million people a day.

Seeing the success of the scavengers' liberation movement in Bihar, the Ministry of Works and Housing, Government of India, in collaboration with the WHO and UNICEF, organised a national seminar at Patna in 1978 on conversion of bucket latrines and liberation of scavengers. In this seminar, representatives from the Planning Commission, Ministry of Health, Ministry of Works and Housing, international agencies like WHO, UNICEF, World Bank and the Secretaries and Chief Engineers of all the State Governments participated. They all approved the Sulabh technology and methodology for adoption by individuals as well as institutions. And, thus, the work of liberating scavengers and the maintenance of public latrines and baths started from Bihar to spread throughout the country in due course.

Dr Pathak persuaded the Ministry of Home Affairs, Government of India, to include liberation of scavengers and their rehabilitation programme on the "whole–town approach" basis. Under the scheme, the implementation of Protection of Civil Rights Act 1980-81, was taken up in two towns of Bihar; Biharsharif and Purnia. In 1981-82, three more towns of Bihar, Daltonganj, Chaibasa and–Madhubani now in Jarkhand, were taken up. Later the programme was moved on to other States. The State Governments agreed to provide alternative employment to liberated scavengers and hence, all of them got jobs. No one has become unemployed so far. The Ministry of Welfare, Government of India, later took charge of this programme.

The first Sulabh public toilet linked plant was set up at Adalatgani, Patna in 1984. It produced electricity from biogas which was supplied to the three kms. long Bailey Road, Patna.

With the help of the Ministry of Welfare, Government of India, Welfare Department, Government of Bihar, and the Bihar State Scheduled Castes Development Corporation, Sulabh started a training and rehabilitation programme for the wards of scavengers in different trades like shorthand, typing, motor driving, mechanics, masonry work, carpentry, cane work, etc., in 1985. A large number of children of scavengers have already been trained. This programme is being extended to cover the entire country. The programme was later expanded to include regular education and technical training.

In 1985, the UNDP and the World Bank after evaluation of the Sulabh technology of the pour flush toilet and in the methodology of the maintenance of public toilets and baths on 'pay-and–use' basis passed it on to the countries of South-East Asia, Africa and Latin America for their adoption.

In 1986, Dr Bindeshwar Pathak persuaded the Ministry of Welfare to give stipends to the wards of Muslim and Christian scavengers also for training and rehabilitation. Earlier, these were available only to Hindu scavengers. Without this, the wards of Muslim and Christian scavengers would have been left out and the movement for their liberation and rehabilitation would have suffered a setback.

Dr Pathak solved the problem of entry of Harijans into Nathdwara Temple in Udaipur, Rajasthan for prayers in 1988. The controversy of entering the temple had taken a serious turn and so many attempts, made by others had failed. The situation became so serious that the then President of India, Mr R. Venkataraman, wanted himself to lead Harijans into the temple. Even the political leaders and the State Government officials had to go to the temple with police protection. This attracted Dr Pathak's attention who, with 100 scavengers and orthodox Vedic Maithil Brahmins, entered the Nathdwara Temple, offered prayers and recited bhajans and kirtans. The scavengers had the whole group took their meal together. This programme was performed without police protection. On return from Nathdwara Temple Dr Pathak along with the scavengers and the Vedic Brahmins was given audience by the then president, Mr R. Venkaraman, the then Vice-President, Dr Shankar Dayal Sharma and the late Prime Minister Mr Rajiv Gandhi. This act of Dr Pathak was quite in line with Dr Ambedkar who had led a group of Harijans to draw water from a public tank, Chodo Talen at Mahad in Kolaba district of Maharashtra in 1927 and let another satyagraha to establish the right of the Untouchables to enter the famous temple of Kalaram in Nasik in 1930.

On his return from Nathwara, Dr Pathak launched a campaign to help the Scheduled Castes offer prayers in temple and performing puja at their home by Vedic Brahmins. Also, in 1989, he started common puja and dining programmes where members of the Scheduled Castes do fasting, sit on the puja and prepare Prasad. They also prepared food for lunch or dinner. After the puja was over, the Prasad and food were distributed by Scheduled Castes to all, including Vedic Brahmins, who also ate with them. This programme, which is continuing since then, has got a wide acceptance.

To improve the social status of scavengers in India, Dr Bindeshwar Pathak has launched a movement to socially upgrade them. This is a novel concept. There was a question mark as to whether after liberation, training and education, scavengers and their children will have upgraded status in society to be on par with the so-called upper caste people. To socially upgrade the scavengers' status in society, Sulabh started a social up gradation campaign one high status family in society has to "socially adopt" a scavenger family who will be treated like family members. The association with these high-status people, will raise the status of the scavengers. This programme has taken off very well. So far, 5,000 scavenger families have been "adopted" by high status people, including judges, advocates, journalists, ministers and planners. Among them are the former Union Dy. Commerce Minister, Mr Salman Kurshid; Planning Commission Member Ms. Chitra Naik; Times of India Editor, Mr Dilip Padgaonkar; former Prime Minister , Mr. I. K. Gujral and many others.

In February 1992, Sulabh organised a "National Seminar on Liberation and Rehabilitation of Scavengers" in New Delhi in which Vice-Chancellors, Professors, planners, and administrators passed a resolution to make it a people's movement. The seminar was inaugurated by the former President of India late Gaini Zail Singh. Dr Pathak regularly takes steps to create social awareness against unfounded beliefs and prejudices. He organises conferences, seminars, workshops, play and folk dances on these themes. The attempt is to involve a large number of people for all walks of life in order to speed up the pace of the movement.

On the principle of Baba Saheb Ambedkar, "educate, organise and agitate" Sulabh has set up in 1992 an English medium school in Delhi for the sons and daughters of scavengers wherein education is given in three principal areas: general theoretical education, compulsory vocational education (knowledge of office management, shorthand, typing and computer training), and optional vocational education (intensive training in specific vocations) so that they may not have to wait in long queues for employment. This will also enable them to be self-employed or get jobs. Fifty per cent of the school's enrolment is of scavengers' children and the rest is from other families to visibly obliterate discrimination. This unique experiment is being extended to other states also. The idea is: Education alone can empower the weak and poor.

The first of its kind in the world, the Sulabh International Museum of toilets was set up in Delhi in 1994. The Museum, through artefacts, pictures, posters and other available materials, tells the story of the development of toilets through the ages. This is the star attraction at the Sulabh Service Centre, Palam.

In 1996, Sulabh has demonstrated an eco-friendly low-cost technology for wastewater treatment through duckweed. The technology besides having low operational and maintenance costs, gives economic return in terms of pisciculture.

Further, in 1997, Sulabh developed a new technology for composting of biodegradable wastes. The technology known as Sulabh Thermophilic Aerobic Composting (STAC) requires only 8-10 days to degrade any biodegradable materials without churning.

Sulabh set up a People's Commission on the Abolition of Scavenging in 1998. Prime Minister Mr Atal Bihari Vajpayee inaugurated the Commission at a function organised on November 26, 1998 to honour him with the Honest Man of the Year Award 1997. Justice M. N. Venkatachallaih, former Chief Justice of India, and Chairperson of the National Human Rights Commission is the Chairman of the Advisory Board of the Commission. In 2000, Sulabh started the programme of Sulabh towards Villages, a national campaign to improve rural sanitation. It involved women in sanitation, health and hygiene.

In 2002, Sulabh developed a new and convenient technology to make biogas plant effluents free from colour, odour and pathogen free. The technology known a SET (Sulabh Effluent Treatment) lowers BOD (Biological Oxygen Demand) of effluent to less than 1 mg/1, making it suitable for agriculture, aquaculture or safe discharge into a river or any water body or cleaning of floors of public toilets.

In 2003, Sulabh took steps to establish a Sulabh University of Sanitation. It also undertook compilation of encyclopaedia on sanitation. WASH campaign was launched in collaboration with Water Supply and Sanitation Collaborative Council, Switzerland. Another Sulabh Vocational Training Centre for liberated scavengers (Nai Disha) at Alwar, Rajasthan was also started. It is significant to note that UNDP recognises Sulabh technologies in its Human Development Report 2003. A Sulabh delegation visited Afghanistan to take up sanitation work.

In 2005, Sulabh International Academy of Environmental Sanitation registered under the Societies Registration Act 1860 by the Registrar, Registration, Govt. of Delhi. Sulabh activities find mention in President of India APJ Abdul Kalam's book "Mission India - A Vision for Indian Youth".

In 2006, UNDP re-recognises Sulabh Technologies in its Human Development Report. Further, Stanford University includes article on Sulabh - "That Gandhi may not be born again" in its Curriculum. In the same year five public toilets with biogas plants were set up in Kabul, Afghanistan with the financial support of the Govt. of India.

Sulabh organised the World Toilet Summit 2007 in collaboration with World Toilet Organisation (WTO) in which representatives of 44 countries participated. And after the three-day conference, a Delhi Declaration was issued for a cleaner world.

The United Nations Department of Economic and Social Affairs (DESA) invited Sulabh International Social Service Organisation to host 'Mission Sanitation', a special cultural event in collaboration with UN-NGO-IRENE Network at the United Nations, New York City on July 2, 2008, to seek and raise awareness and accelerate progress towards improved sanitation world wide. The liberated women scavengers also visited the Statue of Liberty at the New York harbour to declare their liberation from the sub-human, demeaning and humiliating profession of cleaning dry privies and physically carrying human excreta (night soil) of others, to make a living for their families. On coming back home, they paid tributes to Mahatma Gandhi at his Rajghat Samadhi, in New Delhi on July 5, 2008.

Former President of India, Smt. Pratibha Devisingh Patil, met Mrs Usha Chaumar and other liberated scavengers at Rashtrapati Bhawan on July 25, 2008 on their return from New York. The President wished them a happy and prosperous new life, after being freed from age-old social prejudices. The President said that only after more scavengers are liberated that Mahatma Gandhi's dream would come true.

A history of sorts was created when people witnessed an unprecedented event of common dining in Hazoori Gate colony of Alwar, where families of erstwhile untouchable scavengers use to live, on 21st December, 2008. That, those who thought even the shadow of a scavenger befalling them will pollute them, have now shared common dining is no less than achieving almost the impossible. Mahatma Gandhi and Dr Bhimrao Ambedkar had dreamt of such a happening. Now the dream comes true. This act will help remove, to a considerable degree, social untouchability and discrimination from the caste ridden Indian society: a shameful practice attached to 5,000 years of social prejudice. It will be beginning of a beginning and lighting of a candle in the darkness; a first step in the journey of miles.

It was a proud moment for liberated untouchable families from remotest parts of India when they were invited to national capital to share dining with families of 'Upper Social Strata (of those in whose houses the scavengers had earlier cleaned toilets)' in presence of Prof Rajmohan Gandhi, the grandson of Mahatma Gandhi on 5th January, 2009. Though some of them have earlier even travelled to New York for a special UN session programme, it was a moment of joy and pride for liberated scavenger families of Alwar in Rajasthan when their 'earlier masters' of ancient caste hierarchy agreed to dine with them in 2009.

In 2012, the Supreme Court of India expressed shock over the manner in which the bodies of deceased Vrindavan widows were disposed by chopping into pieces and packing in gunny bags. It directed the Chief Medical Officer of Civil Hospital of Mathura to ensure last rites of any deceased women in the shelter homes be performed as per their religion. It also pulled up the National Commission for Women and its Uttar Pradesh counterpart for their apathy to the pitiable condition of Vrindavan widows and asked the state government to provide adequate food and hygienic living environment for them.

Further, the Supreme Court directed the National Legal Services Authorities (NALSA) to contact Sulabh International Social Services Organisation to find out whether they could come forward to help the 1,780 odd widows living in four government shelters in Vrindavan. In its social justice litigation plaint filed before Hon'ble Supreme Court of India, the NALSA had sought protection and amelioration of the situations faced by old and destitute "Vrindavan Widows". On getting this request without giving a second thought, within forty-eight hours Dr Bindeshwar Pathak, accompanied by volunteers working for the organisation, visited on August 12, 2012 Vrindavan and was terribly moved by the plight of these widows and conditions that they live in. There and then he gave them the necessary monetary help and within a month, thereafter, each of these widows was getting an honorarium of Rs 1,000 monthly for their needs from Sulabh. Sulabh has also provided five ambulances in each of the five widow shelter homes along with doctors and nurses and regular eye and medical check-ups are also held. Most of all, Sulabh has given them what they required most—love, affection, compassion, respect and dignity.

The National Conference on Sociology of Sanitation, organised by Sulabh International Centre for Action Sociology in Collaboration with Sulabh International Social Service Organisation, was held on January 28 and 29, 2013 at Mavalankar Auditorium, New Delhi. The inaugural session had dignitaries like Honourable Mrs Meira Kumar, former Speaker, Lok Sabha; Honourable Mr Jairam Ramesh, former Minister for Rural Development, Government of India; Honourable Mr Bharatsinh Madhavsinh Solanki, former Minister of State (Indedependent Charge), Department of Drinking Water and Sanitation, Government of India and Professor Yogendra Singh, Emeritus Professor, Jawaharlal Nehru University, New Delhi, as honoured guests and speakers. The function was attended by esteemed sociologists, social scientists and sanitation experts from all over the country, who were kind enough to contribute their scholarly papers for the occasion. The papers presented are now brought up by Dr Bindeshwar Pathak in a book, Sociology of Sanitation.

In July, 2013 eight sociologists were invited by Dr Bindeshwar Pathak to the Headquarters of Sulabh International Social Service Organisation, New Delhi for a two-day workshop and they were also asked to write a book each on Sociology of Sanitation. This book is the result of this workshop.

Present Status

Sulabh has more than 8,000 public toilets in 25 states and three union territories of India. Sulabh public toilets are used by 15 million users everyday at a nominal payment of Rs 1- 2 for a single use, which roughly translates into a revenue of Rs 550 million per annum. Sulabh has already built more than 1.2 million toilets for households at a nominal payment. Sulabh also provides mobile toilet van facility at a nominal payment which is sought by large fares and at occasions of public gatherings. This number of service-users is matched by the Indian Railways in the entire world.

Sulabh has expanded its network internationally. It has branches operating in Bhutan and Afghanistan. In Kabul (Afghanistan) the construction of five public toilet complexes has completed. Besides, many countries have sought guidance, consultancy, and services from Sulabh. Some of these countries are Nepal, Indonesia, Mozambique, Kenya, South Africa, Ethiopia, Uganda, and Burkina Faso.

Sulabh has built world's biggest toilet complex in the town of Shirdi in Nasik District of Maharashtra for pilgrims visiting the shrine of Sai Baba. The complex is equipped with 148 toilets and 108 bathrooms that allow space for dressing, babysitting and breast-feeding. 5000 lockers take care of the belongings of the continuous stream of pilgrims. The complex is lit by the electricity made available through biogas generation from human excreta. Around 30,000 to 50,000 visitors use these facilities every day.

A combined Sulabh action plan on human waste disposal and social reforms has freed over 60,000 scavengers. It has also provided jobs directly to 60,000 people, and has created one crore man-days work, making 240 towns scavenging free. However, indirect employment and socially positive externalities are not accounted here.

Sulabh, however, is no longer about public toilets only. It has adopted a holistic development approach for the under privileged. Other Sulabh initiatives include public schools and vocational training for scavengers, slum welfare programme, empowerment of women through education and employment, toilet museum, research and development in sanitation, training for NGOs, and international consultancy for sanitation.

10.4 Areas of Major Initiative

Sulabah International has its head-office in 'Sulabh Gram' (Sulabh village), near domestic airport in Delhi. This office is spread over a wide area of around 44 acres and is the epicentre of the activities of Sulabh and houses many facilities, including a prayer and conference hall, library and a museum of toilets. The hall has a seating capacity of around 100 persons. Every day at Sulabh begins with prayer in this hall. Major initiatives of Sulabh are as follows:

Sulabh Technologies

Sulabh has a separate and regular facility for Research and Development in sanitation technologies in Sulabh Gram. One of the major achievements of Sulabh Technologies is 'Twin –Pit, Pour Flush Toilet', which provides an on-site human excreta disposal mechanism and is an easy and cheap alternative to the dry toilets. It is not only easy to build and maintain but also requires much smaller space and financial resource commitment.

Each pit has a capacity of three years to sustain, if used by 10 persons everyday; however, the size of pits can be modified for user requirements. One pit is used at a time while the other one remains blocked. When the first pit gets filled up it is blocked and excreta is diverted to the other pit which is put to use. By the time the second pit is filled up with the excreta the first pit dries and becomes free of foul smell and can be used as a rich fertilizer for plants. These pits are completely free from need for engaging the services of scavengers, do not create health hazards, are environmental friendly, and cost-effective.

Sulabh has developed different designs of these pits so that, these can be built in space-constrained places. In addition, in a bid to reduce costs and increase customisation of locally available resources, Sulabh has built pits with bricks, cement rings, stonc, bamboo, and wood logs. The pits are designed and built with consideration to protecting the ground water resources and prevent the microbial spread.

These pits are well-covered and protected to keep them free from insects, flies, and mosquitoes. This system does not require the connectivity to the costly sewage network; however, if desired, can be easily connected to that anytime.

Another major achievement of Sulabh Technologies is the 'Sulabh steep slope toilet pan'. The flush pan has a slope of 25° - 28° that is steeper than the common flush pan, which is nearly flat. This pan has an especially designed trap with 20 mm water-seal requiring only 1.5-2.0 litres of water for flushing as compared to the common flush pan, which require 12-14 litres of water. This pan not only helps conserve water but also ensures easy and quick drying of the toilet pits.

Sulabh Public Toilet Complex

Sulabh built first toilet in 1973 in Arrah, Bihar and first toilet complex in 1974 in Patna, Bihar. Since then, Sulabh has become synonymous with public toilet and bath complexes nationwide. Mostly these complexes are built by Sulabh in slum areas. In addition, municipalities, NGOs and other agencies sometimes ask it for building and maintaining a Sulabh complex. In such cases, the requesting body providing land and bears other infrastructure costs; however Sulabh operates and maintains the complex once it is built, with the revenues earned from the complex. Sulabh has built and operates such complexes for multiple municipalities, NGOs including Rotary club, Lions club etc., and many major corporate houses including ITC and Tata.

A typical Sulabh complex employs two to four persons, who work in shifts; however, there are complexes at Railway stations and other places that need to work for full 24 hours, hence, such complexes employ up to six persons. Most of such employees belong to scavenger class and are freed and trained by Sulabh. These workers are paid approximately Rs 3,000 to Rs 6,000 depending upon their working hours, location of employment and foot-fall.

Some of the complexes are turned into environment-friendly mode and are equipped with biogas plants. Such plants are able to process human excreta and produce energy for their own requirements at least, and in some case, illuminating nearby streets and areas also.

Biogas Plants

Sulabh presently runs 160 bio-gas plants all over the nation. These plants run on human excreta. This is an innovation by Sulabh and provides three-pronged benefits of hygienic sanitation, renewable bio-energy source, and mineral-rich manure. Sulabh has also made the biogas generation option economically feasible after a long research.

Sulabh pioneered the idea of biogas generation from public toilet complexes. Through a detailed and long research, Sulabh has developed a new technological design of the bio-gas plant that is more efficient and is also approved by the Ministry of Non–conventional Energy Sources. This design is known as 'Sulabh Model' of biogas plants. This model does not require manual handling of excreta and ensures complete resource recovery. The biogas, thus, generated can be carried through pipelines and can be used for cooking, lighting, electricity generation, and body-warming. The effluent is treated with sand, activated charcoal and ultra violet rays to make it colourless, odourless and pathogen free and fit for re-use for gardening, agriculture, floor cleaning, toilet usage, and other non-drinking purposes.

Waste Water Treatment

After untiring efforts of 26 years, Sulabh has come up with a technology of waste water treatment that is economically feasible and environmental hazard free. Since, there is no economic incentive to take up the treatment of waste water, resource constrained local bodies dump it into sources of water, like lakes, rivers and sea. This causes severe health hazards, epidemics, pollution of water sources, and problems of sustenance.

However, Sulabh has developed Duckweed based cost-effective and economically viable technology of waste water treatment. Duckweed is a small free-floating water plant of Lemnaceae family, which is a good feed for fish, and is important in the process of bioremediation because it grows rapidly, absorbing excess mineral nutrients, particularly nitrogen and phosphates. However, a cover of duckweeds reduces evaporation of water as compared to a clear surface, thereby hampering the functioning of water body's ecology. Sulabh, however, has come up with an excellent way of keeping the duckweed within a limited area of the water body by growing it in a constrained frame over the water body. Fish can eat it by crossing the frame underwater but the plant grows within thc frame only. Duckweed treats the water by absorbing excess mineral and also fish multiply at two to three times higher growth rate with duckweed feed.

The first pilot project for duckweed-based water treatment was funded by the Ministry of Environment and Forests and successfully completed by Sulabh in collaboration with the Central Pollution Control Board (CPCB). On the basis of this success and findings, CPCB has issued guidelines for duckweed-based waste water treatment as a feasible and desirable technology.

Sulabh International Institute of Technical Research and Training (SIITRAT)

SIITRAT runs refresher and training courses for interested persons for skill building for constructing, operating, and maintenance of various low-cost water supply and sanitation schemes, and human excreta-fed biogas plants. Special training modules are designed with expert advice and experts of different disciplines are invited for lecturers and demonstrations of innovative and update techniques and technology.

SIITRAT has also developed a new technology – Sulabh Thermophilic Aerobic Composter (STAC). This technology requires only 8 to 10 days for making compost from any biodegradable waste, without any manual handling during composting. This technology does not require recurring expenditure. This technology is able to convert organic waste into manure and soil conditioner, to prevent spread of weed and disease. Also, it drastically reduced the cartage costs of waste to disposal sites.

Sulabh International Institute of Health and Hygiene (SIIHH)

SIIHH was set up in 1994 with a purpose of providing total health-care. SIIHH is an outcome of Sulabh's emphasis on development of integrated health-care approach, with an added emphasis on yoga, use of medicinal plants, hygiene and health conscious attitude, and safe and clean food and drinking water. The focus of this integrated health planning is women, children and youth in rural areas and in urban slums.

The modus operandi is to create awareness through education and training programmes for volunteers, school teachers, and school kids. SIIHH has trained over 8,000 women volunteers in Northern India to work for promotion of health and hygiene. SIIHH also publishes manuals in Hindi, English, Telugu and Nepali. SIIHH also works to create awareness about contagious disease, STDs, AIDs, maternal care, and population control through contraceptives and other artificial means.

SIIHH has established health centres in various Sulabh toilet complexes to provide advice and support to individuals for maintaining health and hygiene. SIIHH has also established school sanitation clubs in various schools, including multiple public schools, which promote awareness about general health and hygiene insanitation through discussions, debates, and competitions. In addition, SIIHH had a Run Mass campaign among school children to emphasise the importance of cleanliness in food habits and washing hands before having food.

Many of the SIIHH initiatives are appreciated as well as partnered by national and international development agencies.

Sulabh International Museum of Toilets

Sulabh International Museum of Toilets is said to be only one of its kind in the entire world. The Museum has artefacts and their replica from different civilisations existing at different times. In addition, it has a detailed history of evolution of toilets since earliest available instances from 2500 B.C. and also the details of linguistic evolution of terms related to toilets and sanitation. It showcases several designs used in different countries at various points of time and exhibits a rare and interesting collection of chamber pots, bidets, water closets, toilet furniture and privies.

The purpose of this museum is to educate students and general public about the historical trends in the development of toilets; to provide information to researchers about the design, materials, and techniques adopted in the past and those in use in the contemporary world; to help policy-makers to understand the efforts made by predecessors in this field throughout the world; to help the manufacturers of toilet equipment and accessories in improving their products by functioning as a technology storehouse; and to help sanitation experts learn from the past and solve problems in the sanitation sector.

The Sulabh technologies innovations and methodologies are recognised as sustainable, replicable and affordable and are recommended by the WHO, World Bank, UNDP etc., for adoption in all Third World countries. While giving shape to its dream projects Sulabh has established coordination with various national and international agencics, including British Council, US-AID, BORDA, a German organisation, Commission of European Union, Belgium, GERES, France, CEEIC, HRIEE, China and Haskoning and Euroconsult, both Dutch firms.

10.5 Action Sociology

Sociology is understood as the science of society. It is also described as study of social groups. Sociology is generally divided into Pure and Applied Sociology. Pure sociology refers to a form of sociological practice that is primarily concerned with addressing professionals through the production of academic knowledge, publications, associations, and insights. Specifically, pure sociologists typically conceptualise research as the production of knowledge and empirical insights as an end in themselves. As such, basic or professional sociologists typically advocate sociological practice that builds our existing knowledge base without necessarily engaging with the rest of the world. This approach is often referred to as "basic" or "academic" sociology because it does not require public or practical engagement by or with scholars working in the field, but rather advocates the pursuit of knowledge as a goal in and of itself, which does not necessarily need to find practical use or consumption in the wider world.

Applied Sociology - sometimes referred to as pragmatic or practical sociology - refers to a form of sociological practice that is primarily concerned with using sociological theories and research to intervene in the ongoing activities contained within applied or practical settings, like offices, parks, schools, and other places where daily life takes place. Applied sociologists use sociological theory, methods and skills to collect and analyse data and to communicate their findings and to understand and resolve social problems. Applied sociology meets the needs of persons and groups who want to use the knowledge generated through research to enhance their understanding of an issue and/or to evaluate a social problem.

To that end, applied sociologists work with a variety of organisations, such as: government foundations, businesses, educational institutions, and social service agencies. Individuals who do applied sociology differ from those who do basic sociology in that they use their research findings as well as sociological theory to resolve real-life problems. Rather than simply producing knowledge, applied sociologists seek to use sociological tools and insights to help individuals, groups, organisations, and institutions improve their functions, protocols, and/or interpersonal and structural processes of activity. As such, applied sociologists typically advocate sociological practice that produces insights that may be used immediately to improve the social functioning of individuals and social structures.

Dr Bindeshwar Pathak has studied sociology at the Masters and Doctoral level. Since 1968 when he was drafted into a committee to design celebration of birth centenary of Mahatma Gandhi, which was due in 1969 he has undertaken Mahatma Gandhi's unfinished task to restore human rights and dignity to the 'Untouchables' while providing affordable sanitary facilities to masses throughout the country. Dr Pathak is really an Action Sociologist. To achieve his objectives he established Sulabh International Centre for Action Sociology (SICAS).

Sulabh International Centre for Action Sociology (SICAS)

SICAS was established in 1993 as a means of rehabilitation scavengers, socially and economically. The main idea was to evolve and operationalise a set of innovative, sustainable and replicable activities to ensure social and financial independence of the lowest strata of the society. SICAS has expanded its activities for the development of scavengers at multiple levels. The components of SICAS are as follows:

1. Sulabh Public School

Sulabh Public School was established in Delhi in 1992 with an objective of imparting quality education to children of scavenger community. The school is from primary to class Xth and the present strength of the school is around 400, of which a deliberate 60 per cent belongs to the students from scavenger community and remaining 40 per cent from other social classes. This type of class ratio prevents the social seclusion of children and helps them in mixing up with other communities. In addition, to free education for scavenger community boys and girls, Sulabh provides them with other necessary amenities also like stationary, afterschool assistance for weaker students, fruits and meals, and uniforms. The medium of instruction is English and the school is recognised by Directorate of Education, Government of Delhi.

2. Vocational Training Centre

With the objective of making individual skilled and independent, First Sulabh centre was started in Patna in 1985. Subsequently, another vocational training centre was started in Mumbai, with collaboration of state government of Maharashtra. In Delhi, the Sulabh Vocational Training Centre was started in 1992 in the Sulabh Public School campus, with separate facilities for the training centre. The training is completely free for scavenger community, whereas other willing participants pay a nominal sum for training. The vocational training is provided in the following 10 courses:

1. Audio-visual Repair
2. Electrical Equipment
3. Computer
4. Shorthand
5. Typing
6. Beauty Care
7. Dress designing
8. Embroidery
9. Tailoring
10. Cutting and Sewing

These courses are short-listed on the basis of demand for the services. The curriculum is also in synchrony with the market requirement and is updated periodically. Some of the courses are also certified by Industrial Training Institute (ITI) of India.

Nai Disha Centre set up at Alwar, Rajasthan where 28 women who had been removing and carrying human excreta till March 2003, have been liberated from that filthy and inhuman job and motivated to take up training in various vocations like preparing products such as papads, pickles, and noodles, tailoring, embroidery and beauty care. They were given a stipend of Rs 1,500 a month, which has now been, increased to Rs 1,800 to sustain themselves. This is being funded by Sulabh from its own resources. They have been taught to read and write and to operate their bank accounts. With Sulabh's support, they are selling their products made by them to the local community, thus breaking the myth and stigma of untouchability and oppression. Today, they are treated with respect and as equals in society. Former Prime Minister of India, Dr Manmohan Singh gave audience to erstwhile scavengers and blessed them for starting a new life on 16.05.2006.

3. Social Upgradation Programme

Under this programme, Sulabh asks for volunteers among influential and conscientious citizens to formally and publicly adopt a scavenger family. The adoption is not meant for financial assistance. The adopter and adopted families meet subsequently, visit each other's home on social occasions, and the adopting person tries to help the adopted family in solving their problems.

4. Slum Children Welfare Programme

For children living in slum areas, education, hygiene, social awareness, and self development are mostly unthinkable amenities. Sulabh in a bid to inculcate self-respect in the deprived sections of the society runs a slum children welfare programme for the slum children, who are out of school. The children are brought to the Sulabh School in the afternoon, when the regular school period is over. They are taught and trained in different activities and a variety of skills. The children are also given basic lessons in personal hygiene, functional literacy, and social awareness.

Future Plans

Believing in Gandhian philosophy and willing to work till the last moment of life for holistic social development of deprived, Dr Bindeshwar Pathak is still very enthusiastic about the plans he has for further expanding the work of Sulabh. He terms Sulabh as a movement, not an organisation which has to keep on moving till the last human is served. However, he is worried about the lack of interest of fresh talent in this field of providing healthy and hygienic sanitation.

References

Rasthogi, Siddhartha Kumar. 2014. *A Case Study of Sulabh International Social Service Organisation.* Ahmedabad: Indian Institute of Management.

Pathak, Bindeshwar. 2003. *Sulabh Sanitation Movement.* New Delhi: Sulabh International Social Service Organisation.

——2015. *Sociology of Sanitation.* New Delhi: Sulabh International Social Service Organisation.

Index

Y and Z